CONSERVATION

An American Story of
Conflict and Accomplishment

DAVID CUSHMAN COYLE

RUTGERS UNIVERSITY PRESS

New Brunswick   *New Jersey*
1957

To my wife
Doris Porter Coyle
with deep appreciation
of her encouragement and help
in the writing of this book

FOREWORD

Conservation: An American Story of Conflict and Accomplishment is the suitable and expressive title that David Cushman Coyle has chosen for this book. It is now, in 1957–58, barely fifty years since Gifford Pinchot proposed and President Theodore Roosevelt adopted the term "conservation" to identify the far-reaching public policy they were then launching, the main outlines of which had only just been discerned. Yet today the word has passed into the language not only of the United States but of the entire world, while the doctrine itself is no less widely recognized.

The story in this book tells of a 50-year campaign. A campaign, according to Webster, is "a connected series of operations to bring about some desired result." The nature of the relevant "connected operations," how and by what kinds of people they were conceived and executed, and by whom opposed, are all faithfully and dramatically portrayed in this story. The fifty years of unremitting conflict that has been waged over conservation in all its forms are described here in bold, clear terms. From this prolonged conflict, however, it is shown that the measure of public acceptance that has been achieved upon essentials of conservation policy has indeed been impressive. How the notable accomplishments resulting from this struggle have gone to enrich the peoples of the United States and of other countries throughout the world is vividly portrayed in the closing chapters of this book.

v

One would be hard put to it to find any other single area of United States domestic policy of comparable complexity and affecting so many powerful and diverse interests where so satisfactory a consensus has been achieved in a corresponding space of time. The main lines of policy are drawn, and strongly supported programs are now operative in all the main branches of conservation activity.

This is not to say that the battle is over and the victory won. Basic conflicts are never won in a single campaign. The author has made abundantly clear that although conservationists may draw deep satisfaction from the solid achievements of this 50-year campaign, it is still true, as he says, that "the political battles that are involved in it are as new as the next election."

This book, I believe, provides the first adequate short account of the origins of general conservation policy and practice and of each of its main divisions. It is in effect a short history of conservation and will furnish the general reader with all he needs in order to understand the principles and purposes of conservation, the chief lines of development of each branch, the public policy issues raised, and the motives of the contending forces at work.

This book should also meet an educational need by providing useful reading for college students enrolled in courses in conservation, and in particular those in schools of forestry, engineering, the sciences, and public administration.

That this should be the first book adequately to provide a general survey of the entire field up to now is actually not surprising. For it is only yesterday, so to speak, that we have attained that point of high ground whence it becomes possible to view retrospectively the whole of the controversial past with some detachment. We are indeed fortunate in having as the first overall survey of the subject this lucid, fair, and accurate account from the hand and mind of an expert and articulate observer.

MORRIS LLEWELLYN COOKE

PREFACE

The policy of conserving all the vital natural resources for the best interests of the people, as a unified national program, was first conceived by Gifford Pinchot in 1907, when Theodore Roosevelt was President of the United States and Pinchot was head of the Forest Service. In the half century since then the conservation movement has gained numberless adherents, not only in the United States but throughout the world.

Conservation has never been better defined than by Pinchot's brilliant associate, W J McGee, who described it as "the use of the natural resources for the greatest good of the greatest number for the longest time."

"Conservation" has come to be a good word like "democracy," and, as in the case of democracy, there is a tendency for its enemies to twist the meaning so as to confuse the public. There is also a tendency to recall a long-abandoned forerunner of modern conservation, the nineteenth-century belief that the only way to save the forests was to make the woodman spare the trees. This notion, sometimes called "hair-shirt conservation," is still dragged forth as a bogey by people who do not want any interference with profitable kinds of waste.

But, despite conflicting definitions, conservation has a useful meaning for the people of the United States, and it is more and more clearly understood and embraced by the people of the world. Many books have been published about conservation and about each of its branches, and many more will be published. In this book I shall try to clarify the meaning of the doctrine and practice of conservation, by tracing its history in this country and the kinds of opposition with which it has had to contend. I shall also try to outline how the wise use of resources is related to the development of the United States and to the possibility of a future peaceful development of the world.

In writing this book I have had the help of many friends and acquaintances, to whom I am deeply grateful; I am honored in having their good will and often the benefit of their advice on both technical and literary matters. I am especially indebted to my friend Eric H. Biddle, who first persuaded me to take up this work, and whose patient editing and unswerving determination have been of major influence in bringing it to a conclusion. But on behalf of all those who have helped me I must make clear that the responsibility for the final draft of the manuscript, and the blame for errors of fact and of interpretation, can be laid at no one's door but my own.

My grateful acknowledgments are here offered to: Edward A. Ackerman, Dewey Anderson, J. Leonard Bates, Hugh Bennett, Mrs. Bruce Bliven, Jr., David R. Brower, Louis Brownlow, John Carmody, Oscar Chapman, Earle Clapp, Marion Clawson, Clay Cochran, Morris Llewellyn Cooke, Evelyn Cooper, Gordon Dean, Senator Paul Douglas, Ira Gabrielson, Senator Albert Gore, Ernest Gruening, Nathaniel B. Guyol, James Lawrence Houghteling, Judson King, John Frederick Lewis, Jr., Russell Lord, Walter Lowdermilk, Barrow Lyons, Benton Mackaye, Gordon McCallum, Nelson

McGeary, Wheeler McMillen, W. C. Mendenhall, L. M. Mitchell, Philip Mullenbach, Olaus J. Murie, Fred M. Packard, Mrs. Gifford Pinchot, Orville Poland, Alex Radin, Huston Thompson, Howard Zahniser, and Eugene M. Zuckert.

DAVID CUSHMAN COYLE

CONTENTS

Part One

~~~~~~

THE BEGINNINGS OF
CONSERVATION

Chapter 1

CONSERVATION TAKES FORM

The movement for the conservation of natural resources, as we in the United States think of it today, began to take form in this country in the nineteenth century because of concern about the forests, which were rapidly disappearing. Public-spirited citizens began to demand that the forested parts of the public domain should be reserved to save the timber from devastation. But other people wanted that timber. So from the beginning controversy was an inevitable feature of the conservation movement.

By the year 1900 not only the idea of forest preservation but also the advantages of harvesting timber as a renewable crop had become well established in government practice, but the conservation of all resources as a major national policy had not yet been thought of.

At the present time the public is so familiar with the idea of general conservation that many people may find it hard to believe that Gifford Pinchot was the first to think of it only about fifty years ago. But the use of government powers to promote the wise management of all basic resources for the good of man was regarded as new and astonishing when Gifford Pinchot brought it forward.

Pinchot himself was astonished when the idea suddenly came to him as he was riding his horse in Rock Creek Park near Washington on a dull February afternoon in 1907. He says in his autobiography, *Breaking New Ground,* that it was as if he had been seeing a small light like the end of a tunnel, and then suddenly came out and saw a whole landscape. He had been devoting his adult life to a missionary effort for the promotion of forestry, and if this "whole landscape" had been visible to him all the time he would not have been so surprised. All his associates showed the same signs of standing on a peak and seeing new country ahead. So did Theodore Roosevelt, and he was President and had power to act.

Accordingly, the early chapters of the history of conservation in the United States are in no small degree the biography of Gifford Pinchot, who started his career in the late 1880s and came to a climax of his activity in this field when Theodore Roosevelt was President. The main stem of this history grows in a fairly straight line to the point where the general idea of conservation was established; then it branches out with a particular concern for each of the basic resources. Pinchot and Roosevelt believed that these resources, in either private or public ownership, ought to be used wisely, with the least possible waste, and that where there was danger to the public interest the federal government could properly require good practices by law. They asserted the public interest in conservation along all the main branches that are recognized today, including not only forests but also farm lands, range lands, groundwater, irrigation, and unified river development, not excepting waterpower as an integral part of the public domain.

After Theodore Roosevelt went out of office there followed nearly a quarter century of reaction, war, and "normalcy," during which time conservation made but little growth.

When the second Roosevelt came to power in 1933 all the branches of conservation began to spread far and wide, and each one became a story in itself. But the present-day conservation battles, from attempts of the stockmen to get possession of the public range lands to the struggle over private or public control of hydroelectric power, all represent the continuation of conflicts that were already recognized in the time of Theodore Roosevelt.

Again and again since the beginning of the century the disputes over conservation have caused internal divisions in both the great political parties. In the main they are disputes over who is to control the public domain—the forests, the range lands, the minerals, and the waterpower belonging to all the people and vested by law in the government. There are also secondary battles over appropriations for conservation work, over subsidies to encourage good management of private resources, and sometimes over interagency competition.

Both political parties have always been split into factions on the main question of the proper use of the public domain. In general, the more conservative senators and representatives in both parties tend to oppose conservation policies, though with frequent exceptions because of special interests or local circumstances.

Conservation policies also divide both parties on the perennial question of federal powers. Theodore Roosevelt, as a champion of conservation, was strongly federalist; he believed in using federal powers to the full. This was, in fact, the traditional position of the forerunners of the Republican Party. But the interests that came into power with President William Howard Taft were led by their distaste for conservation into antifederalist positions. The second Roosevelt, also a champion of conservation, was also a federalist, though contrary to the traditions of his party. His opponents on conservation were in general antifederalist, and they were allied with "conservative" forces opposed to other forms of federal control over private business.

This book outlines the story of how conservation came onto the American scene, of how its doctrine took form, of how the conservationists have fought their opponents on many fronts down to the present day, and of what conservation is coming to mean in the underdeveloped parts of the world.

The gospel that Gifford Pinchot and Theodore Roosevelt preached in the first decade of the present century is now fifty years old, but the political battles that are involved in it are as new as the next election. With the increase of the population and the rise in production per worker, the supply of raw materials becomes a more and more crucial matter and governmental policies to maintain resources become vital issues. The remaining national domain becomes more and more valuable, and the effort to protect it against depredation and waste continues to generate fervent heat. Who will control the government programs for conservation of forests, soil, and minerals? Who will get possession of the public range, the national forests and parks, the waterpower, and the multibillion-dollar technology of atomic power? The necessity of deciding those questions gives rise to endless battles over conservation.

Chapter 2

CONQUERED AMERICA

When the Europeans landed in the early 1600s on the shores of North America they came as conquerors. Though the first shiploads of settlers were weak and often hungry, behind them was the pressure of an expanding civilization, with its industry, its organized trade, and its gunpowder. Even though the first invaders might bargain peaceably with the local chiefs for the right to settle on the shore, they were negotiating from strength, as the Indians soon learned when they found themselves faced with a swelling flood of new arrivals. Along the frontier the Indians struggled hopelessly to hold back the tide, and the settlers developed the spirit of conquest by force.

During the first two centuries, however, the European advance was slow. The Indians long held the line of the Appalachians. As the years rolled by, therefore, most of the people of the British colonies ceased to be pioneers. They were settled people living on ancestral acres, in civilized houses that had long since replaced the first log cabins. Their towns were safe from Indian attacks, and the colonial buildings that are standing today show the architecture of people who thought of themselves as dwellers in the land.

At the time of the American Revolution the colonists made it clear to themselves and to the British government that they were no longer Europeans holding a beachhead on a foreign shore, but Americans living in their own country, the land of their fathers. For the time being they had arrived at the goal that had been the dream of the first settlers—a new home where they could be free of the trammels of Europe. This feeling of permanent habitation was not to last, but in the eighteenth century it led the people of the older settlements to think of their fields and forests as property to be cherished and preserved, not as loot to be wantonly turned into money and spent.

Accordingly, we find in the late 1700s some of the same kinds of conservation ideas that have come to the fore in our own times.

For example, Loudoun County, Virginia is now one of the richest counties of that state. Yet in 1780, according to Thomas Jefferson, the soil was "exhausted and wasted by bad husbandry." But John Alexander Binns, of that county, had learned of the use of gypsum and clover for building up the land, by observing the practices of Pennsylvania Dutch farmers near Philadelphia. He started to experiment in 1780, and by 1803 was so successful that he wrote a pamphlet about land improvement, which is now to be found in the Library of Congress among Jefferson's books. Jefferson wrote about Binns to a friend in England, saying that the county of Loudoun "has, from his example, become the most productive one in Virginia, and its lands, from being the lowest, sell at the highest prices." Jefferson also notes that the county "began to depopulate, the people going Southwardly in quest of better lands. Binns' success has stopped that immigration."

Jefferson took a great interest in "horizontal plowing" to prevent soil erosion. He attributes this idea to his son-in-law, Colonel Randolph, who may have heard of terracing as used in other countries and in ancient civilizations. In a letter written March 3, 1817, Jefferson speaks of a reversible plow, contrived by Colonel Randolph, "which throws the furrows downhill both going and coming," thus making it easy for the farmer to plow on the horizontal. He says that the idea is spreading rapidly near Lynchburg, "and will be the salvation of that, as it confessedly has been of this part of the country."

George Washington also was concerned about the erosion of his land on the Mount Vernon estate. When his slaves had no other work in hand, he had them dig mud from the Potomac and wheel it up to fill in the gullies in the fields.

In colonial times there were of course solid forests along the frontier, and westward for hundreds of miles. There the forest was a "resource" only in a minor way. Wood was used for fuel and logs were good for building stout houses and forts, more or less resistant to Indian attacks. But the forest in general was an enemy. It covered the land that the settler needed for crops. It sheltered the savages who often crept up near the frontier settlements to tomahawk and scalp the settlers.

The first job in starting a new farm, then, was to make a clearing. The settler cut down the trees and lopped the branches. When he was ready, his neighbors came together and helped him with the logs for his cabin. Then they had a "logrolling," and piled the surplus logs for burning. After he had laboriously destroyed several acres of virgin forest, the settler had a fair chance to raise a crop of corn without being killed by the savages. This experience was not likely to teach the pioneers that a 40-inch clear-grained white pine was a valuable piece of property to be preserved for some future market. Such a splendid tree was more likely to be thought of as a good hiding place for a marauding Indian looking for a scalp.

One of the first industries to develop in colonial New England was the production of pine masts for naval vessels. The British were building up their navy, and had been dependent on the Baltic forests for the great sticks that were needed in ships of the line. When they found they could get good masts from New England they naturally favored this source, protected by the British flag. Before long, however, it became clear that the best pines were growing scarce in the accessible woods along the rivers. The government therefore started reserving mast trees for the Crown, marking them with the royal broad arrow. In 1691 the new charter of Massachusetts Bay, granted by William and Mary, reserved to the Crown all trees over 24 inches in diameter on lands not already granted to a private owner. The same reservation was soon extended to other colonies.

These early forest reservations had an effect on public opinion in the colonies that was to last for many generations as a source of trouble in the national domain. A century later, in the West, it was still easy for lumbermen to feel that taking timber from government lands was a right of free men; it was striking a blow for liberty against the oppressive bureaucrats in the far-off eastern city of Washington.

When the United States was founded a great outburst toward the west was hardly foreseen, though pioneers were beginning to press toward Kentucky and Illinois in the face of fierce Indian resistance. Yet in the minds of the Americans the exuberance released by political liberty already held the seeds of the wild adventures of the coming century.

In the nineteenth century, as the great West opened up, the people of the United States once more turned to conquest. The frontier moved fast. Not only the hunters and trappers, but lumbermen and railroad builders and cattlemen moved across the country. The spirit of the frontier even influenced the East, where city financiers invested in the new enterprises that were turning the resources of the West into money. For a century the Americans forgot about being dwellers in the land. They were on the move, capturing and despoiling the natural wealth of an empire that seemed to have no end. They had little time to build permanent houses or to improve farms or forests, for as soon as the cream of the land had been skimmed there was always more to the westward. So it happened that toward the end of the nineteenth century the territory of the United States had begun to show distressing signs of devastation. The great empire was not so boundless as the pioneers had thought. It was again time to think of settling down.

But the habits of waste and haste were deeply ingrained in the nineteenth-century traditions of industry, agriculture, and business. When the time came to change these habits to meet new conditions they could not be changed easily.

In the meantime the federal government came into the same landowning position that, in colonial times, had roused the people's resentment against the British broad arrow. When the United States became independent, seven of the original states claimed large stretches of western land that had not yet been settled. The states ceded these claims to the new federal government between 1781 and 1802. This was the beginning of the public domain—land not merely a part of the national territory but also owned outright by the federal government. As the national territory expanded to the Pacific coast and then to Alaska, most of the newly acquired land was wild and came into the Union as government property. There were, to be sure, some privately owned lands where the country was already settled, especially in California and along the Mississippi. Texas joined the United States as a sovereign nation in its own right, so the wild land in Texas came in as the public domain of the state rather than of the federal government.

The new lands were carved up into territories as they became settled, and all those in the "Continental United States" became states of the Union. But the public lands in the western states still belonged to the federal government as sole owner, except those that it had sold or given away. That is, all the states, except the thirteen original ones and

Maine, Vermont, West Virginia, Kentucky, Tennessee, and Texas, were carved out of the public domain, contained much federally owned land, and are still known as the public-land states. The national forests and national parks in the eastern states, however, though now owned by the federal government, are not on the same footing. They were bought by the government from private owners, largely under authority of the Weeks Law of 1911. At their greatest extent the public lands of the United States government amounted to more than 1,800 million acres. It was of course never anyone's intention to hold all this land in public ownership, but to sell most of it to settlers or to give it as subsidies to encourage settlement. The government now owns a total of some 800 million acres, most of it in the eleven western-most states and Alaska.

To encourage settlement and public works the United States has donated more than 300 million acres to the states and to railroad and other corporations. All the public-land states were given a share of the federal land, which they could use or sell to help pay for public schools. In 1862 a special grant was made to finance state agricultural and mechanical colleges, which are therefore known as "land-grant colleges."

In the first years of the Republic the federal government was hard pressed for money to meet the Revolutionary War debt, and it looked to sales of public lands as an important source of cash. There was at first no objection to selling large tracts to a single buyer, who would then do the work of attracting settlers and developing new settlements. The Ordinance of 1785 provided for sales in units of 36 square miles, or in some cases of one square mile, at a dollar an acre.

A committee of the Continental Congress under the chairmanship of Thomas Jefferson devised the system of surveying by which the public lands were divided into plots as settlement spread westward. The land was laid out in one-

mile squares, called "sections," of 640 acres. In the fertile
parts of the country a settler usually got a quarter section,
or 160 acres.

THE ORIGINAL PUBLIC DOMAIN

Acquisition	*Area in million acres*
Ceded by states	233
Louisiana Purchase	523
Red River of the North	29
Ceded by Spain (Florida)	43
Oregon Compromise	181
Ceded by Mexico	334
Purchased from Texas, 1850	79
Gadsden Purchase from Mexico	19
Total in Continental U.S.	1,442
Alaska Purchase	365
Total Original Domain	1,807
Acquired from private owners	48
Grand Total	1,855

SOLD OR GRANTED UNDER PUBLIC LAND LAWS IN U.S. AND ALASKA, TO 1955

Type of disposal	*Area in million acres*	
Grants to states		
For schools, colleges, etc.	98	
For swamp drainage	65	
For building roads, canals, etc.	47	
Miscellaneous	14	
Total to states		224
Grants to railroads		91
Homesteads		286
Veterans' bounties		61
Timber and Stone Act sales		14
Miscellaneous: townsite sales, mineral entries, etc.		355
Grand Total		1,031

LANDS CONTROLLED BY FEDERAL AGENCIES IN CONTINENTAL U.S., 1954

Agency	*Area in million acres owned*
Department of the Interior	
Bureau of Land Management	180
Bureau of Indian Affairs (in trust) (57)	0
National Park Service	15
Fish and Wildlife Service	8
Bureau of Reclamation	9
Total federally owned under Interior	212
Department of Agriculture, Forest Service	168
Department of Defense	21
Other agencies—AEC, TVA, etc.	3
Total federally owned in Continental U.S.	405
Total land area of Continental U.S. plus Alaska	2,300

In 1820 the price of government land was raised to $1.25 an acre. The minimum that the government would sell was gradually reduced to 40 acres by 1834. During the nineteenth century the policy shifted away from trying to sell large tracts to developers and toward making direct sales to individual settlers. Along with this change went a necessary growth of the government sales organization, known as the Land Office. The first district land offices were established in 1800 under the Treasury Department, and in 1812 the General Land Office was set up in the Treasury. In 1849 Congress created the Department of the Interior and transferred the Land Office to it. Today its original job of selling the public lands has almost vanished, though there are a few homesteads still to be found, mainly in Alaska. The remaining public lands are largely divided up into reservations that are held for various purposes, and corresponding agencies have been organized for their management, chiefly in the Departments of the Interior, Agriculture, and Defense. The remaining unreserved land is now handled by the Bureau of Land Management, created in 1946 in the Department of the Interior.

From the start the federal government, though welcoming settlement, had no intention of giving its property away. In 1807 Congress passed a law forbidding anyone to settle on public land without permission. This law could be enforced in the long run, since title to the land depended entirely on the record of sale or grant in the Land Office. That did not mean that it was impossible to steal timber, or to evade some of the legal conditions for getting title. A pioneer could also "squat" temporarily without having title to the land, as long as no one came to enforce the law. In 1841 Congress gave squatters the privilege of getting title to 160 acres by cultivating the land and paying the legal price.

In 1862 came the first Homestead Law, under which the government offered 160 acres of farm land free to settlers if they would live on it and cultivate the land for five years. Various modifications were afterwards adopted for desert lands that the settler could irrigate, and later for lands irrigated by the government.

The principle underlying the homestead laws was that in return for giving the land free the government was entitled to see it occupied by thrifty farmers whose trade would support new market towns and would lead to prosperity and taxpaying ability. The laws were definitely intended to encourage family-sized farms rather than great estates.

The main weakness of the land laws was that in the effort to favor individual settlers Congress neglected to take into account the practical difficulty of working some resources in small units. A sawmill, for instance, with its railroad and other auxiliaries, needed more timber land than could be legally bought from the government. The pioneer spirit met this obstacle by devising ways to get around the law, and the pioneers often went on to develop large monopolistic enterprises that were just what Congress had hoped to prevent.

For example, there was the notorious Timber and Stone Act, passed in 1878. Under this act any citizen could buy 160 acres of nonagricultural land for $2.50 an acre without having to live on it, but he did have to swear that he would use the land himself and was not buying it for someone else. This law resulted in a prodigious amount of false swearing.

Some of the earliest lumber companies in the public-land states got along for a while by simply buying a small tract and then cutting timber from the surrounding government land. When that became too dangerous they invented ingenious ways of getting title to more of the public lands than Congress had intended a single owner to get. One way was to hire dummy settlers.

A professional locator would find a good tract that was salable if put together into one property. Then he would hire a number of city people who would like a trip to the big woods. Sometimes a large group would come out in a special train. Each one was taken to a quarter section that he at once recognized as just what he needed. He was then led to the local land office, where he filed a timber-and-stone claim, paid the fees with money supplied by the locator, and swore that he needed the land for his personal use and benefit. But the only personal use he made of the land was to sell it immediately to the locator for $50 and go happily home on the holiday train. The local attitude was that if those Easterners in Washington insisted on having a foolish law this was an amusing way to get the land just the same.

There came to be a whole literature of classic stories from the federal forest examiners of what they found after 1900 when they began looking into some of the titles to forest lands that seemed too good to be true. One law, for instance, granted all swamp and overflow lands to the states, on the theory that the states might take the trouble to find some use for such lands. In California there was some excellent forest that had been transferred to the state as swamp and overflow land at the instance of a locator who promptly got it from the state. It did not look very wet to the Forest Service man. When he looked up the papers he found that the locator had sworn that he crossed the land in a flatboat. That, as it finally came out, was the truth. He had mounted the flatboat on wheels, had hitched on a yoke of oxen, and had thus succeeded in navigating into possession of a fine stretch of timber land.

Another story often told is about the man who homesteaded a piece of white pine land in Idaho. He swore that he had cleared part of the land and planted potatoes. He had cut timber and made himself a cabin. Later he had dug and eaten potatoes from his hard-won land to nourish him in his labors. It was a touching story of pioneer hardihood, but some of the details were a bit sketchy. The Forest Service man managed to discover some points that put the story in a different light.

The timber locator had hired the homesteader to take up the land for him without too much hard work and without telling any lies. First they hiked in with camping gear, including a small sack of potatoes. They located the survey corner and laid out the homesteader's quarter section. Then the homesteader went to work. He buried the bag of potatoes. He split some strips off a fallen cedar and built a doll house about four feet square, and that was one day. The next day he dug up the potatoes and fried and ate some of them. Then the two men went home and filled out the papers. In this simple fashion the timber locator got title to some three million board feet of the best white pine.

There was also the case of the man who had a "desert" claim that happened to be covered with fine timber. He swore that he had "conducted water upon the land" as required by law to perfect his title, and he had witnesses to swear that they had seen water running in his irrigation ditch. This was all true. He had plowed a single furrow on a dry hillside, and had conducted a barrel of water to the spot, thoughtfully bringing his witnesses along in the same wagon. While the witnesses watched, he poured the water from the barrel and they saw it running in the ditch.

Mining claims also were likely to occur with surprising frequency where the best timber happened to be. William B. Greeley tells in *Forests and Men* how, in 1905, he had the job of checking the landownership along the Western Pacific Railway in northern California. One man had accumulated mining claims carrying 250,000 acres of timber. A block of placer mining claims, Greeley discovered, was advertised for sale with the guarantee that "they will run twenty thousand feet of sugar pine to the acre."

At the end of the nineteenth century the "pioneer spirit" was still vigorous in the West, but growing resistance to haste and waste was beginning to foreshadow a new and more adult attitude. The American people wanted to take more responsibility for protecting their natural resources from needless loss and for protecting their own rights against individuals who were trying to grab the lion's share of the resources.

The public land problems that marked the beginning of the twentieth century have almost entirely disappeared today, largely because most of the remaining national domain is now in reservations or grazing districts where the land is not adapted to distribution under the old land laws. The old-fashioned system of evading the settlement laws is no longer a frequent source of trouble. Today we have to deal with repeated efforts of various interests to get possession of wide stretches of the public lands through Congressional or administrative action. Certain states wanted title to the oil lands in the federal coastal strip, which they finally got in 1953. The Army wants parts of the national parks and wildlife refuges for shooting ranges. The stockmen perennially want the range lands and national forests transferred to the states, knowing that the states cannot resist pressure as well as the federal government can. But the old days of the easy-going Land Office are evidently past.

In 1956, when Secretary of the Interior Douglas McKay was reported to have cleared the title to a few hundred acres of excellent timber on a long-pending mining claim said to be based on questionable ore samples, there was much excitement and a Congressional investigation. Back in 1900 such occurrences were commonplace; much of the conservation effort during the first ten years of the century involved struggles in and with the Land Office about just such claims.

Chapter 3

THE COMING OF THE PROPHET

"Gifford Pinchot is the man to whom the nation owes most for what has been accomplished as regards the preservation of the natural resources of our country. He led, and indeed during its most vital period embodied, the fight for the preservation through use of our forests. He played one of the leading parts in the effort to make the National Government the chief instrument in developing the irrigation of the arid West. He was the foremost leader in the great struggle to coordinate all our social and governmental forces in the effort to secure the adoption of a rational and far-seeing policy for securing the conservation of all our national resources. . . . Taking into account the varied nature of the work he did, its vital importance to the nation and the fact that as regards much of it he was practically breaking new ground, and taking into account also his tireless energy and activity, his fearlessness, his complete disinterestedness, his single-minded devotion to the interests of the plain people, and his extraordinary efficiency, I believe it is but just to say that among the many, many public officials who under my administration rendered literally invaluable service to the people of the United States, he, on the whole, stood first."—Theodore Roosevelt's *Autobiography*. Charles Scribner's Sons, New York, 1920.

A hundred years before Theodore Roosevelt's presidency the eighteenth-century efforts at conservation had been generally forgotten by the American people in the excitement of their break-through into the West. The idea of protecting scarce resources had to be rediscovered.

In the nineteenth century the first noticeable action looking toward conservation came from the Navy about 1820. In those days all ships were built of wood, and the best timbers, especially knees, were of American live oak, found along the southeastern coast. In 1819 John Quincy Adams, Secretary of State, was negotiating with Spain for the purchase of Florida, and an important reason for wanting that territory was to get the coastal live oak and to keep foreign navies from getting it.

Adams was an enthusiastic tree planter, and as soon as he became President in 1825 he took a keen interest in an oak-planting project on the Santa Rosa Peninsula near Pensacola. This project failed, but it was a real attempt by the government to produce timber for the future needs of the Navy.

While the Navy was worrying about live-oak knees for wooden ships, the opening of the Erie Canal in 1825 began to have a powerful effect on the future of conservation. It brought the great pine forests of Michigan and Wisconsin within reach of the eastern markets. The lumber business, which had centered first in Maine, then in New York, and then in Pennsylvania, spread into the Great Lakes states, where most of the land was in the public domain. The growth of railroads also helped make possible the sale of vast amounts of cheap lumber from these virgin forests. In the Great Lakes states the legendary Paul Bunyan grew from the mere champion strong man of the Maine lumber camps to the fabulous giant who could roll up a square mile of land and tuck it under his arm, and pick his teeth with a 150-foot pine tree.

In 1853 the authorities in their safe offices in Washington decided that it was time to make an effort to stop the timber poaching in Michigan. They sent Isaac Willard, representing the Land Office, to enforce the law. He began by seizing a quantity of lumber that had been stolen from the government and offering it for sale at auction. But local public opinion was hostile to him. No one at the sale dared to buy. He then tried to arrest the timber thieves. He was nearly lynched, and one of his deputies was killed.

Then Willard got the USS *Michigan* to come to Manistee, a town on the eastern shore of Lake Michigan and the main center of the disorder. The sailors landed and arrested many of the offenders, most of whom were actually convicted and fined. For the moment it looked as if federal law had come to Michigan.

But Westerners all along the frontier were enraged, and their voices penetrated eastward to Washington. Commissioner Wilson of the Land Office, who had encouraged Willard to carry the law to the wild woods, was sacked. His successor announced that there would be no more special agents, but that the local land offices, on top of their regular duties, would look after the government's timber. During the next dozen years all was sweetness and light and no questions were asked. In 1865 the General Land Office reported that it had reached a compromise. It would charge reasonable fees for cutting on the public lands instead of trying to keep the lumbermen out. This was a sensible rule on paper, but there was no intention of enforcing it.

For the time being the frontier had defeated the federal government, but times were beginning to change. For one thing, between 1861 and 1865 the federal government won its war with the seceding Southern States, and the question at issue had been whether federal law was to be supreme in the land. When this second American Revolution failed, the early American dream of the wild, free frontier defying a distant and tyrannical sovereign began to fade. Even though the American people had thrown off the distant authority of the King in London, they could not forever defy the authority of the federal government in Washington. The United States was to be accepted as a legitimate American power entitled to respect, even along its border.

Moreover, as the frontier moved westward the settled area of the country grew and the federal government's power to govern also grew.

In 1873 Congress appropriated $10,000 for protection of public lands against depredation, and in 1877 Carl Schurz, the Civil War hero, was appointed Secretary of the Interior by President Hayes. He proclaimed the end of "compromise" and appointed regular agents to enforce the laws with the cooperation of the local land offices and United States attorneys. He set out to civilize the frontier, but he aroused a storm of protest, and there was another compromise. The Act of June 15, 1880, allowed trespassers to escape legal penalties by purchasing the land where they had poached timber, at $1.25 an acre.

Meanwhile the public was beginning to show an increasing concern with the waste of natural resources. One of the earliest signs of it was the publication, in 1864, of George P. Marsh's remarkable book, *The Earth as Modified by Human Action*.

Marsh pointed out the danger of human enterprises that "interfere with the spontaneous arrangements of the organic and inorganic world" and the need for "the restoration of the disturbed harmonies." He told of the Roman Empire, that in classic times ruled a rich territory more than half of which had since become desert. Harbors had silted up and famous rivers that once were navigable had now shrunk in the dry season to mere brooks. He called the sonorous and pitiful roll of the provinces of that great empire, now turned into deserts, from North Africa and Syria, Arabia and Mesopotamia, to Greece, Sicily, and parts of Italy and

Spain. All these sorrowful changes, he said, had come from ignorant disregard of the laws of nature and by way of misrule, tyranny, and war.

Marsh's book gives a foretaste of practically all the modern ideas about conservation. Marsh urged the planting of shelterbelts to break the force of the wind and protect the soil, and along seacoasts to reduce the effects of the sea winds. He urged that people stop killing song birds—a relic, he said, of the old reaction against feudal game laws. He defended snakes as eaters of rodents and insects. He knew that forests help maintain the flow of springs, and he knew how they replenish the groundwater. "The vegetable mould does not cease to absorb water when it becomes saturated, for it then gives off a portion of its moisture to the mineral earth below, and thus is ready to receive a new supply." Many years later Walter Lowdermilk had to struggle hard against the skeptics who scoffed at the water-holding effects of forest cover, on the ground that the leaf mold, once wet, would hold no more water. He had to prove by elaborate tests what Marsh had been trying to tell people half a century earlier.

Marsh noted that Americans had long regarded stealing trees as no crime, but now they were beginning to respect the law in the East, and it was important to rouse them to the danger of indiscriminate cutting. It had often been proposed, he said, that the state declare the remaining forests the inalienable property of the commonwealth, but that suggestion originated, in his opinion, "rather in poetical than in economical views of the subject." That idea had merit for parks, he pointed out, but for general policy a forest, "economically managed, would without injury, and even with benefit to its permanence and growth, soon yield a regular income." That was the practical answer, but it was too soon for general adoption in the United States. Conservation had to go through its stage of simple opposition to all cutting of trees before Gifford Pinchot could bring a new attitude by demonstrating the value of commercial forestry in North Carolina and New York.

The tree-planting movement was crystallized by Governor Sterling Morton of Nebraska in the institution of Arbor Day on April 10, 1872. It was a natural development in Nebraska, since trees will not readily grow there unless they are first raised in a nursery to such a size that their roots can reach down to moisture in the dry season. The next year Congress passed the Act of March 3, 1873, under which any citizen could get 160 acres of government prairie land if he would plant 20 acres of it to trees. Most of these trees, in the dry states, died because the special techniques of shelterbelt planting had not yet been sufficiently worked out. But thousands of communities throughout the United States took up the custom of Arbor Day, with tree-planting ceremonies and speeches. This custom, as much as any other, has been influential in overcoming the pioneer hatred of trees as the natural cover for Indian raiders and replacing it with the feeling of affection that people have for something they have planted. Both extremes of feeling were to be parts of the American experience before a practical conservation policy came into being.

In 1872 Congress created Yellowstone National Park. This was not a public forest for timber production, but later, in 1891, the Yellowstone Park Timberland Reserve, of 1¼ million acres, was set aside as a timber-producing federal forest.

Also in 1872 James Arnold left $100,000 to Harvard University to set up a notable tree collection, the Arnold Arboretum, and in the same year New York State established a Forest Commission. There were already recently formed state commissions to study the forest situation and advise on legislation, in the pine states of Maine, Michigan, and Wisconsin.

In 1873 the American Association for the Advancement of Science sent a memorial to President Grant, as a result of which Congress three years later authorized the Department of Agriculture to employ an adviser on forest policy. Dr. Franklin B. Hough, who had sparked the original resolution in the AAAS, was appointed to the job, with an appropriation of $2,000 for his salary. This small beginning grew slowly into the Division of Forestry, which occupied itself inconspicuously in collecting statistics.

In 1876 legislation was sought to create national forest reservations around the headwaters of streams to protect their flow. The bill failed, largely because its proponents, ignorant of conditions in the West, inserted requirements that were easily discredited. The idea of headwater protection was destined to come up later in more realistic form, in the Weeks Law of 1911 that resulted in the creation of the eastern national forests. In 1878 a bill was introduced to reserve all the forested parts of the public domain and operate them by selling the timber rights under restrictions; but the time was not ripe, and the bill failed to pass.

In 1875 the American Forestry Association was formed at a meeting in Chicago. It soon became the most powerful agency of those who were working to save the forests. Dr. Bernard E. Fernow became its secretary. In 1886 he was appointed head of the Division of Forestry in the Department of Agriculture.

The American Forestry Association promoted state legislation for the protection of forests, though the ideas about what ought to be done were still somewhat vague. Forest fires, which were especially disastrous in the pine country, served to win public support for state fire laws. During the 1880s the Association also urged Congress to create federal reservations in the remaining forests on the national domain. This effort was suddenly and unexpectedly successful in 1891, when Congress rather casually passed an appropria-

tion act with a rider that authorized the President to withdraw public lands by executive order and set them aside as
forest reserves. The President was left free to choose any
lands he might think proper for this purpose. This Congressional action had been quietly promoted by Secretary of the
Interior John W. Noble and Edward A. Bowers of the Land
Office. President Benjamin Harrison approved the act. Then,
with the advice of the Geological Survey, he set aside the
Yellowstone Park Timberland and went on to create a total
of 13 million acres of forest reserves.

This was the beginning of the present-day national forests. The land was simply withdrawn, so as not to be distributed under the various land laws, but there was no protection against fire, disease, or even theft, for the Land Office could not spare enough men to guard the timber. And
there was no provision for selling the timber. Those trees
were locked up, by law; they could be made to serve local
needs only by stealing. The Westerners would not long en-
dure having such vast resources locked up. There would
have to be laws that would let them build roads, and run
cattle, open mines, and even cut trees, on conditions that
would reasonably protect the public interest. All these laws
have come in due course, but the process was necessarily
slow.

As the nineteenth century drew to a close the times were
growing ripe for the right man to preach a new gospel of
prudent care of all the resources—the forests, the waters, the
land, the minerals, and the wildlife.

The opportunity arrived when Theodore Roosevelt, a man
of action who loved the outdoors, became President. And
the prophet was at hand—Gifford Pinchot, who had become
head of the obscure Division of Forestry in the Department
of Agriculture. Pinchot was a man with a mission, and he
needed only a president who would take fire with enthusiasm for the message that the young forester would deliver.

By birth and training Gifford Pinchot was well suited to the role he was destined to play. He began with one branch of conservation, forestry, and with one aspect of forestry that had been almost unknown in this country, the commercial management of forests for permanent yield. Many voices had been crying against the waste of resources, but, as it happened, the way to break through the indifference of the people and launch a nation-wide program of conservation was the way pioneered by Pinchot alone, during the ten years before Theodore Roosevelt came to the White House.

In the summer of 1885, when young Gifford was about to enter Yale, his father surprised him by asking how he would like to be a forester. Gifford had no clear idea of what a forester was, but he was open to suggestion. He was already an ardent camper, hunter, and fisherman, and had decided that he wanted to be a naturalist. As he says in *Breaking New Ground*, "Of course a youngster with such a background would want to be a forester. Whatever Forestry might be, I was for it."

In 1885 there were practically no forests under forestry management in the United States. But there had been forestry for centuries in Europe, where everyone knew that forests were a valuable resource, worth protecting and maintaining. The Pinchot family had come from France to Milford, Pennsylvania, in 1816. In Milford they went into lumbering, cutting timber to be rafted down the Delaware to the Philadelphia market, so they knew something of American forests and their depletion. They had not forgotten France either, and after three generations in America they could still speak French fluently and often visited the old country. James Pinchot, Gifford's father, was familiar with managed forests in France and other parts of Europe, and he was deeply concerned with the widespread devastation of American forests. It is not surprising that a man with his background and knowledge should have wished that the European type of forestry could be introduced into America.

What is extraordinary is that he had the faith and courage to advise his son to stake his future on the belief that he could make a career as a forester in this country. Though the opportunity was coming, it was not yet in sight, and the two Pinchots, father and son, met no encouragement from their family and friends. But James Pinchot could see further ahead than the others, and his son trusted his vision.

So young Pinchot went off to Yale, where he studied botany and geology and meteorology, since they all had some relation to forests. There was of course no teaching of forestry as such, but there would be time later to go abroad for technical training. When he was graduated in 1889 he was chosen to make one of the ceremonial speeches, for which he carefully prepared a manuscript. When his time came to speak, however, with characteristic uninhibited enthusiasm he disregarded his prepared address and burst forth into a plea for forestry. Then he went to see the few American authorities on trees and forests and asked their advice. It was all negative.

Most of the organized "forestry" movement in the United States at that time was occupied with going to meetings and passing indignant resolutions deploring the devastation of the forests. The practical lumbermen were contemptuous of the movement; they were sure that the forests were inexhaustible. In 1889 the time was not yet in sight for a workable compromise between the preservers—often called "denudatics"—and the carefree lumbermen. That was a problem for Pinchot himself to tackle later.

The leading tree experts in the United States could not see much hope for a young man who wanted to be a forester in this country. In their opinion it offered no career suitable to a man of wealthy family with plenty of other opportunities. Professor Charles S. Sargent of Harvard did not believe there was a future in tree-cutting forestry in the United States. Dr. George B. Loring, former Commissioner of Agriculture and a leading "denudatic," saw little point in trying to bring forestry to the United States, since the country had "no centralized monarchial power." He assumed that without national control no effective forest management would be possible—and that was hitting close to the center of a struggle that would occupy Pinchot and his successors to the present day.

Bernard E. Fernow, head of the insignificant Forestry Division in the Department of Agriculture, was a German by birth and a forester with European training, but he also saw no prospect for a young forester in the United States. He advised Pinchot to go into landscape gardening or the nursery business, and perhaps work in some forestry as a side line.

Nevertheless, Pinchot set out in the autumn of 1889 to see what he could learn in Europe. He started on the right foot in London by going to India House for advice. The British had introduced a forestry program in India with notable success, and this experience, as it turned out, held the clue to the problem of selecting the exportable features of European forest practices. The man who had founded the successful British work in India was a German, Sir Dietrich Brandis, then living at Bonn. Brandis was an inspiring teacher, and he also had a good knowledge of the American situation. He welcomed Pinchot and took charge of his training program. He advised him to go first to the French Forest School at Nancy, and gave him a letter of introduction to the director. There he was to learn about silviculture—the growth and treatment of forests—and forest economics, "how to get out of the forest the most of whatever it is you want." That schooling took up the winter of 1889–90.

In the spring Brandis sent Pinchot to Switzerland to spend a month with the Director of the Sihlwald, the municipal forest of Zurich. The Sihlwald had been a scientifically managed forest for four hundred years and was yielding a good supply of timber and a good profit in money. After a month in Switzerland Pinchot joined the Nancy school study trips in the Vosges and the Alps and finished with a memorable walking tour with Brandis and a group of English students.

From observation and the advice of his mentors Pinchot learned in one year of European study what he felt to be the necessary elements of his future work as a forester.

Brandis taught him the importance of a flexible policy adapted to the country and the people where it was to be used. He was emphatic that to succeed a forestry program must have the understanding and support of the local people. And it must give enough scope to individual foresters to bring out their talents under unforeseen conditions in a new country. These principles had been the foundation of Brandis's outstanding success in India.

Pinchot was impressed with the necessity of government control over private cutting. That was the lesson of forestry in Germany and France, where governments had built strong control systems with traditions dating back to feudal times. The question for an American was whether a democracy could hope to set up controls strong enough to be of practical value. Switzerland seemed to have an answer to that. The Swiss had been faced with the fact that most of their forest land was so steep that if denuded of forest cover it would soon slide into the valleys, and they were using government regulation to prevent irresponsible cutting. The lesson seemed to be that when the American people should decide that their future welfare depended on certain restraints in lumbering they might find ways to impose those restraints by democratic authority. Pinchot never forgot that lesson.

Finally, all the teachers of forestry emphasized the fact that no real progress would be possible until someone had demonstrated that a scientifically managed forest would pay a commercial profit. Commercial forestry at a profit would be the key to a reconciliation between the preservers and the lumbermen. In general it was true that where virgin forest was within easy reach of markets the price of lumber might not yet be high enough to pay for growing new forests. But there were probably opportunities in the eastern states to start demonstrating the commercial value of scientific forestry. The job, as Pinchot saw it, was "not to stop the ax but to regulate its use." Scientific forestry had to be separated from landscape gardening and the management of parks and arboretums. The main job of forestry was to grow trees as a crop—a crop like corn except with a longer growing season.

So in December, 1890, Gifford Pinchot returned to the United States to try to tell the carefree American people, especially the lumbermen, that their forests were not inexhaustible and that their treatment of them was all wrong. No bands met the young crusader on the pier, but he went around and talked to the leaders of the existing forestry movement "from Boston to Washington." Note the geography. These men were not to be found between Wisconsin and the West Coast. Pinchot read a paper on "Government Forestry Abroad" at a joint meeting of the American Forestry Association and the American Economic Association in Washington. His paper was printed, and within a few days he got a job.

Phelps, Dodge & Co. hired Pinchot to examine some of their forest holdings in Pennsylvania and in Arkansas, and then sent him to the Pacific coast. These trips taught him something of the United States beyond the eastern seaboard. Later he traveled extensively in the West, and hunted and fished in western forests.

In December, 1891, Pinchot was appointed manager of the Biltmore Forest near Asheville, North Carolina. Biltmore was the estate of George W. Vanderbilt. Its development was under charge of the great landscape architect Frederick Law Olmsted and the plans included a large arboretum and a game preserve as well as a managed forest. The forest was not to be merely an ornamental park, but a demonstration of a paying business.

As a paying business the Biltmore Forest looked like a poor gamble. The land had been occupied for a couple of hundred years by mountain folk who cut and burned the woods, planted corn on the sloping land until it lost its topsoil, and then let the clearings go back to scrub oak and sassafras. Dr. Fernow told Pinchot that the Biltmore project was "an impracticable fad," and wrote: "if you can make forestry *profitable* under the conditions at Biltmore within the next ten years, I shall consider you the wisest forester and financier of the age." As it turned out, Pinchot made forestry profitable at Biltmore from the start.

The 7,000-acre estate was made up of rolling hills and bottom lands along the French Broad River, a tributary of the Tennessee in western North Carolina, at an elevation of some 2,000 feet. About half the land was in woods, and by no means all the woods were scrub. There were some good areas, containing a wide range of species from white oak to yellow poplar. But the mixture was generally poor, since many of the best trees had been cut out, leaving weed trees and spreading, defective specimens to cumber the ground and discourage new growth.

What the forest needed was "improvement cutting" to take out the old trees, good and bad, and make room for the young ones to grow into a good stand of timber. Cattle had to be fenced out, for one of the principal causes of the bad condition of the woods had been overgrazing. Also fire had to be prevented, for even a ground fire burning the dead leaves and trash would kill the young trees, the hope of a future forest. And all this improvement and protection work had to be confined to the areas where it would not cost more than the income expected from sales.

The woodsmen, including foremen, had to be educated into new ways. They had to be taught to fell the marked trees carefully, so as not to knock down too many young specimens of desirable species, and to get the logs out with as little damage to the woods as possible. It was a general belief among the lumbermen that if old trees were cut young ones of the same species would never grow up to take their place, even though they were visibly doing so wherever an opening in the forest let in enough light. The idea of giving care and consideration to the young trees was therefore hard to introduce to old hands who thought they knew all about lumbering.

Altogether, Pinchot's first forestry demonstration was difficult. It called for decisions on a hundred points where European forest science was only loosely fitted to the American varieties of trees, soils, and climate. Pinchot, after a long day in the woods, restudied his books at night, and hoped for the best when he had to invent new answers for himself. But the first year's work showed a small profit, and the woods were better than they had been at the beginning. From then on, while nothing was easy, there was light ahead.

One evening at Biltmore, Pinchot was sitting before the fire with J. A. Holmes, the State Geologist of North Carolina, when Holmes remarked that the federal government ought to buy a big part of the mountain country thereabouts and manage it on forestry principles. This idea fitted in with what Pinchot had learned in Europe, where the problem of regulating the treatment of the forest had often been solved in a particular area by taking it over into government ownership. Both men always remembered this historic conversation. Nearly twenty years later, after Holmes had devoted a large part of his life to that project, the Weeks Law was passed. From it have come the important and successful eastern national forests that we have today in the Southern Appalachians and the White Mountains.

In 1893 the Biltmore Forest put on an exhibit at the Chicago World's Fair. The exhibit showed photographs of the forest and how it had already been improved, and emphasized the fact that it had made a profit. There were models of European forests to show what could be done under long-term management. There was a pamphlet by Pinchot for free distribution, describing his work and showing the balance sheet for the first year. The pamphlet was mailed to thousands of newspapers and drew favorable comment from all over the United States. This was not bad progress for a young man two years out of technical school, trying to start in a new profession in a wholly skeptical country.

One result of this publicity was a crop of young men seeking positions in order to enter the profession of forestry. Pinchot at first offered them no encouragement, feeling that the few who would fight their way into the profession against all odds would be enough to start the next stage of the crusade. He also received applications from European foresters who wanted a fresh start in the fabulous land of America, but these he refused on the ground that thoroughly educated European foresters were not likely to be able to see the woods in the complicated economic and political setting of the United States.

The Biltmore contract did not require Pinchot's full time. In 1893, hoping to widen his field of action, he opened an office in New York as "Consulting Forester," taking into partnership one of his brightest young followers, Henry Graves. On the face of it this action seemed overconfident, considering the intense lack of enthusiasm for commercial forestry among the old hands in the American forestry movement. But here and there the owner of a private forest was beginning to think about managing it, and some of them asked the only consulting forester in America for advice. There were also many opportunities to write and speak on forestry.

Charles S. Sargent, head of the Arnold Arboretum and publisher of *Garden and Forest* magazine, had recommended in 1889 that the President appoint a commission to advise on the control and administration of the public forest lands. This proposal had a checkered career for several years. In

December, 1894, Sargent met with several others, including Pinchot, to work out a bill for a forest commission. By the following June the idea had grown into a proposal for a commission of the National Academy of Sciences. Hoke Smith, of Georgia, who was President Grover Cleveland's Secretary of the Interior, was persuaded to write Dr. Wolcott Gibbs, head of the Academy, asking the Academy to advise the government on the following questions:

1. Is it practicable for the government forest lands to be protected from fire and maintained as a permanent source of wood?

2. How much protection is justified by the influence of the forests on climate, soil, and water conditions?

3. What new laws are needed?

Dr. Gibbs, to no one's surprise, accepted the assignment, which he had inspired in the first place. He appointed a commission, with Sargent as chairman, and six other distinguished scientists, plus young Gifford Pinchot. This was in 1896, and Cleveland was coming to the end of his second term. He was strongly in favor of forest preservation and welcomed the chance to get a report with powerful scientific backing. He advised the commission to concentrate on the organization of a workable forest service and to avoid scaring Congress with big talk about more reserves. He wanted the report by November so that he could refer to it in his final annual message. The commission failed to follow Cleveland's advice. It was unable to agree on plans for a forest service, but it did recommend a number of new reserves and also the Grand Canyon and Mount Rainier National Parks. No statement was made to ease the minds of the Westerners who opposed locking up these resources against commercial use, and for that reason Pinchot disagreed strongly with the commission's report.

On the commission's recommendation, Cleveland withdrew 21 million acres of western lands on February 22, 1897, ten days before going out of office. The West was enraged, and the Senate passed an amendment to the Sundry Civil Appropriation Bill to restore Cleveland's reserves to the public domain.

In the House, with Pinchot lobbying vigorously to save the reserves, an amendment to the same bill was passed that authorized the President to license the cutting of timber on the reserves, essentially the system now in use. In conference both amendments were dropped, but the bill finally gave the President power to keep or cancel any part of any reserve. This meant that a hostile president could wipe out the reserves set up by his predecessors. Cleveland pocket-vetoed the bill, leaving the problem to the next President, William McKinley.

McKinley was in favor of saving the reserves Cleveland had set aside. Some of the Westerners, led by the Homestake Mining Company, were willing to agree to the reserves if they could get licenses to use the resources in them. After some months of maneuvering, an amendment introduced by Senator Richard F. Pettigrew of South Dakota was passed, authorizing the Secretary of the Interior to administer the reserves. The Secretary could make rules and establish services "to regulate their occupancy and use" and "to preserve the forests therein from destruction."

With the Pettigrew Amendment to the Sundry Civil Act of 1897, the legal base of the present national forest system was completed. The Act of 1891 had permitted the President to set aside a good area of forest reserves, and the new law allowed them to be managed for sustained production. The early period of trying to save the forest by fencing out the woodcutter had ended and the period of regulated use of publicly owned resources, for the purpose of maintaining the general welfare, had begun.

McKinley appointed Pinchot to be head of the Forestry Division, and he took office on July 1, 1898.

Chapter 4

THE FOREST SERVICE

The old Forestry Division in the Department of Agriculture had not been designed as an "action agency." At the beginning when Congress authorized the department to "appoint a competent person" to study the forest situation it specified a man "well acquainted with the methods of statistical inquiry," not necessarily with forests. Dr. Hough, who was chosen, was a scholar who happened to be interested in forest preservation. Dr. Fernow, who ran the division from 1886 to 1898, was a forester, to be sure, but he had had no experience in practical lumbering. He was devoted to thorough scholarship, which in practice meant that no one should pretend to manage a forest until he knew all about the biology of the individual kinds of trees.

During Fernow's time, therefore, the Forestry Division had contented itself with study and with the printing of helpful bulletins on such matters as the uses of forest products. There were no bulletins telling how to manage an American forest for the production of timber. Eventually Cornell University decided to open a school of forestry and invited Fernow to be its head. He resigned his government post and it was offered to Pinchot.

Pinchot and his partner, Henry Graves, were busy with their consulting work and at best they had a robust contempt for the feeble Forestry Division. But the Secretary of Agriculture, "Tama Jim" Wilson of Iowa, promised Pinchot to back him in building a new kind of forest agency. Pinchot took the job and Graves consented to be his assistant. Wilson changed Pinchot's new title from "Chief of Division" to "Forester." Washington was full of chiefs of division even then, but there was only one Forester. Pinchot set out on what he calls in his own account of it "a halcyon and vociferous time."

When the new breeze blew into the Forestry Division's two-room office the total staff, including the Forester, numbered eleven people, some of them good. There were three pieces of outdoor equipment: a folding caliper, a tape measure, and an increment borer to take a core out of a tree for a study of the rings. The budget appropriation was $28,500 and there was little hope of getting any more until some kind of demonstration should have changed the attitude of Congress.

The natural way to demonstrate was to get some government forestry started in the woods, but all the federal forests were under the Interior Department. There were a few state forests. The greatest opportunity lay in giving free consulting service to individual forest owners, the same kind of work that Pinchot and Graves had been doing as private consultants.

On October 15, 1898, therefore, the division got out a bulletin offering to help lumbermen and farm-woodlot owners to manage their forests. The division offered to send someone to examine the property and to supply full working plans and directions for conservative lumbering. The owners of large tracts were asked to pay the expenses but not the salaries of the government men, and during the first year they did contribute over $2,000 out of a total cost of about $6,000 for this work. A dollar stretched far in 1898. By the end of the year 108,000 acres of private forest were under good management with the division's advice. As Pinchot says: "It wasn't gilt-edged, wire-drawn German Forestry by any means. It wasn't even what we could have made it with more men and more time. But it did pay, it did stop forest devastation, and it did provide for a second crop."

Moreover, by the end of the year 123 requests had come in for help on 1½ million acres distributed over thirty-five states. The division cultivated a growing mailing list, which included two thousand newspapers. The people who had been given service were pleased and the word spread. Demand built up faster than the force could be increased, partly on account of budget trouble and partly because there were fewer than a dozen American foresters at that time, and even they were not all available. The men were overworked, lean, hungry, and full of crusading zeal.

Fortunately Secretary Wilson recognized the value of protecting Pinchot from the patronage hunting of senators and representatives. Everyone in the division was in the civil service, but there were loopholes, as there are to this day. A minor executive, unless he has strong Administration support, must let in some political hacks who will eat up his budget with no corresponding benefit to his program. Pinchot could not afford any parasites, and Wilson gave him strong and effective backing. Gradually he was able to bring in one American forester after another. As for civil service examinations, no one in the government knew how to write one on forestry, or to mark the papers, except Pinchot and Graves. So it was a good team; and from that good start the federal forest organization down to the present time has been conspicuous for high morale, technical competence, and honesty.

On a winter trip to the Adirondacks early in 1899, Pinchot was taken by a friend to Albany to visit Governor Theodore Roosevelt overnight. T.R. had known about Pinchot and had got him elected to the Boone and Crockett, a club of big-game hunters that he had founded, but this was their first conversation. They got so far as to try a bit of wrestling, which T.R. won, and some boxing, in which Pinchot reports that he "had the honor of knocking the future President of the United States off his very solid pins."

As Pinchot's first year in office began to draw to a close enough work had been done, and enough good feeling had been created among timber owners, to cause Congress to vote the division an increase of $20,000 in its budget. That was something, but it was still a shoestring operation. To stretch the money, Pinchot offered to let a number of college students come in as apprentices at $25 a month. He was at once flooded with applications. By July 1, 1900, out of a total force of 123 people in the division, 61 were student assistants, as they were called. The students were carefully selected, and they prided themselves on their ability to work in cold and heat and water and in company with black flies, mosquitoes, and chiggers. They also were good for the morale of the division.

Another budget-stretching device was the appointment of outside experts as collaborators or, as we should now call them, consultants. These were scientists and college professors with specialized knowledge that could be of use in forestry, and with a willingness to help the good cause. They were paid a nominal fee of $300 a year, and of course enjoyed the prospect that the government might print their scientific papers.

On July 1, 1901, the division was promoted to be the Bureau of Forestry. It now had a budget of $185,440, and 179 people working for it, of whom 81 were student assistants and about 25 were collaborators. The rate of growth indicated that for the time being the Forestry Division had escaped arousing any serious opposition and had made friends who were speaking well of it to their congressmen.

Meanwhile, in November, 1900, Pinchot and his chief assistants had formed a technical association, the Society of American Foresters, which was a useful agency for nourishing a professional spirit and winning public respect for forestry as a profession. The Society met weekly at the Pinchot house on Rhode Island Avenue.

As the work progressed and became more widely known, it was inevitable that the peculiar situation in the federal forests should be noted. The Interior Department had all the forests and Agriculture had all the foresters. In the winter of 1899–1900 Pinchot carried on a campaign to get the forest reserves transferred from Interior to Agriculture. This effort soon led to a war that has flared up, off and on, down to the present day.

One reason that Pinchot was determined to get the reserves away from the Interior Department was that the Land Office was corrupt and he saw no way in which it could be reformed.

The Land Office had grown up with the public land laws and had adapted itself to them. Its traditional job was to give away the national domain without too much fussing over little matters of law. Its standards of recruitment and behavior did not fit the job of handling forests that must not be given away and ought not to be stolen. When Pinchot traveled in the West in the summer of 1899 he made a point of visiting the public forests, and what he found shocked him.

The field men of the Land Office were political appointees; the field service had been found to be an ideal spot for dumping useless relatives and hangers-on who were not presentable enough for jobs in Washington. Several were local incompetents related to the Land Office Commissioner, who happened to have come from Oregon. Others were protégés of senators or representatives from other sections who were sent out West to get them out of sight.

There was graft. One superintendent charged a personal fee for free-use permits that he had to issue under the law. A supervisor drew his salary and reported regularly that he "patrolled out and looked over" the reserve. This was true. He ran a saloon, from which he regularly "patrolled out" onto the front porch and took in the excellent view across the near side of the reserve. Many rangers were invalids, and others worked as watchmakers, bookkeepers, or veterinarians and never did anything for the government except to pick up their salary.

The Westerners were not violently averse to timber poaching, but they were averse to graft and laziness and they felt contempt for the forest reserves and the Interior Department. Pinchot wanted no part of the Land Office forest organization with Interior Department management attached to it.

Eric Biddle, who worked with Pinchot when the latter was Governor of Pennsylvania, says that Pinchot once told him quite categorically about his position in this matter. Pinchot emphatically stated that his opposition to Interior as controller of the forests was by no means limited to distrust based on that department's tradition of giving away the public domain. The Department of Agriculture, he pointed out, was answerable to a massive, alert, and articulate constituency—the farmers whose best interests were served by a vigorous conservation policy. The pressure of this constituency, he believed, was the best and surest safeguard for the progressive development of a sound and effective forest policy. It was for this reason that he had wanted to bring about the transfer of the reserves from Interior to Agriculture.

In Pinchot's opinion it was unlikely that those whose interests were opposed to conservation would succeed in getting one of their friends appointed Secretary of Agriculture. About the Secretaryship of the Interior he did not feel so sure. With the wrong kind of Secretary in that department there would be danger of damage to the public domain, and the forests in particular might suffer.

In 1900 McKinley was reelected with a new Vice-President, Theodore Roosevelt. McKinley was assassinated the following year and Roosevelt came into the White House ready for action on all fronts.

As soon as the new President reached Washington Pinchot went to see him about his forthcoming Message to Congress. With him went his friend F. H. Newell, who was promoting the idea of a United States Reclamation Service to build irrigation systems. Roosevelt welcomed the two crusaders and commissioned them to draft parts of his message. They proceeded to set forth what they wanted to see done, and Roosevelt accepted practically all they gave him.

In particular, the President declared that the forest reserves ought properly to be put under the Bureau of Forestry. He also pointed out that in the West it is water that measures production and the water supply depends on the forests, supplemented by storage dams. He suggested that large irrigation works should be built by the federal government. Roosevelt's message gave notice that Pinchot and his friends had direct access to the White House, and their ideas were beginning to include more than simple forestry.

The American Forestry Association called an American Forest Congress in Washington in January, 1905, at which were gathered public officials, lumbermen, stockmen and irrigation men, miners, and other interested citizens. It showed a gratifying growth of sentiment in favor of forestry among lumber interests and even among woolgrowers. The resolutions adopted at this meeting recommended transfer of the reserves. The Transfer Act was passed and was signed by the President on February 1, 1905. So the reserves came under control of the Bureau of Forestry, and their name was soon changed to national forests. In the Agricultural Appropriations Act of March 3, 1905, the bureau was renamed the Forest Service.

But all was not peace in the wild West. There was opposition to government controls and it grew rapidly after the foresters got the power to set up real controls in the federal forests. There had been a foretaste of the trouble

to come, several years earlier, in the case of the Chippewa
Indian lands in Minnesota. Representative Knute Nelson
of Minnesota had got a bill through in 1889 under which
the government would take over the Chippewa timber lands,
sell them, and give the Indians the proceeds. There was evil
intent back of that bargain, for the Indian Office was no
better than the Land Office, and the lumber companies stole
and cheated under cover of their purchase contracts. There
were local protests from public-spirited citizens, especially
from the Minnesota Federation of Women's Clubs. Some
of those who objected to the looting wanted to set up a
national park, but the chairman of the federation's Forestry
Committee spoke up for a forest reserve, carried it through
to Washington, and finally got Congress to pass a bill creating the reserve. The bill gave the Bureau of Forestry the
job of controlling the cutting on this reserve.

The lumber interests were violently opposed to any real
control, and this would be no easy Indian Office or Land
Office control. There was plenty of disorder, and every political trick was tried. The one loss came when the State of
Minnesota laid claim to a part of the best pine land under
the old Swamp Land Act of 1860, in face of proof that the
land was not a swamp. Minnesota got away with that, which
means that the lumbermen got away with it; but the major
part of the reservation was saved, and in due course it became an excellent example of what could be accomplished
by honest and intelligent management.

After all the reserves were transferred to the Department
of Agriculture and came under control of the Forest Service,
the same kind of trouble spread through the West. Several
western senators set out to undermine the Forest Service,
which they said was made up of dreamers and theorists.
There was some oratory and, in 1907, some action. The
Agricultural Bill, which the President would have to sign,
carried a rider taking away the President's power to create

any new national forests in six western states, and reserving that power to Congress. This was a blow.

During the years since 1898 Pinchot and his men had gone over the ground and selected many tracts that they thought should be reserved out of the public domain. The crippling amendment was passed on February 25 and Roosevelt had to sign the bill by March 4. Pinchot saw the President and between them they hatched a plot. T.R. would hold the bill until the last minute, and the Forester could have all the reserve proclamations he could write in the meantime.

The forest men burned the midnight gas in Washington and scorched the telegraph wires to their offices in the West. Pinchot strode to and fro between his office and the White House carrying maps and proclamations. Altogether they added another 16 million acres to the national forests. Then Roosevelt heaved a satisfied sigh and signed the bill taking away his power to make such reservations.

Of course Theodore Roosevelt could not last forever, but while he lasted conservation succeeded in putting down roots that have never been torn up.

Chapter 5

AMERICAN FORESTRY TECHNIQUES

~~~~~~

In 1900 American knowledge of native forests was crude.
Much that was done by guess and common sense needed
to be pointed up by scientific knowledge, and the science
had to be brought outdoors and applied to actual woods.
Evidently German forestry, or even Swiss forestry, could
not be American forestry, as Pinchot had recognized when he
cut off his studies after only one year abroad.

Pinchot happened to start his work at the Biltmore Forest
with selective cutting, a complicated technique of which
he knew only the European methods. In a different forest
he might have tried cutting 95 per cent of the trees and leaving a few for seed, or cutting in strips, or some other system,
of which, as applied to American conditions, he knew only
the rudiments. But he had to use such technical knowledge
as he possessed, and then piece it out with calculated risks.
At the same time he started to write a *Primer of Forestry*,
which would tell enough about the woods to guide the beginning forester or the lumberman wanting to adopt some
features of scientific forestry. The *Primer* was developed
gradually and was published in two parts in 1899 and 1905.
But meanwhile forest practice had to go ahead, and technical
knowledge was built up by constant observation and also
by special studies.

There are numerous difficult questions that a forester must answer with some show of confidence in taking charge of a forest before he can decide which trees to cut.

A sapling in a forest may be thriving, and it may be of a good species with commercial value, but will it do well if the big trees are cut, giving it room and light? Each species has its preferences, for wet or for well-drained soil, for sunny slopes or for north slopes where it will not start to leaf out too soon in the spring; and above all each species has its own preference for conditions of light.

One of the main distinctions among kinds of trees is whether they can start as seedlings and grow comfortably in the shade, or whether they depend on wind or fire or the lumberman to remove the forest and let in full sunlight before they can make a start. Northern spruce, for instance, likes to start under dense blackberry and bayberry, protected from wind and sun. Ten years later it will be poking through the tangle into full sunlight; after which it will grow tall and kill off its nurse plants. But if it grows up with fast-growing aspen it may become discouraged and grow only slowly, until the short-lived aspen dies. A pine forest, after it is cut, may turn into a forest of scrub oak because the young oaks get ahead of the pine seedlings, which will not tolerate the shade. Some authorities even recommend carefully controlled burning in the longleaf pine areas of the South to give the pine a chance to seed the land and start a new forest. Everyone who has any experience in the woods knows a few such facts, but a good forestry program calls for a fairly comprehensive knowledge of what is likely to grow after the forest is cut. Many kinds of trees are of no value in the market, and some of them may take possession of the land in a second-growth forest if not held back by weeding.

Another typical question is when to weed or thin a close-growing forest of saplings. Some kinds take care of themselves. They prune themselves naturally if they are thickly crowded, killing off the lower branches before they can make big knots. They then grow up smooth and straight, killing off the weaker trees and leaving room for the survivors to grow into good clear sawtimber. Other kinds may fail to do battle to the death and thus may stay for years overcrowded and sickly, too slender to be worth cutting. When should the forester let the forest alone and when should he go to the expense of thinning? Someone needs to know if the managed forest is to prove successful.

Planting is another problem. If the land is already covered with high weeds, bushes, or scrub trees, only certain kinds of seedlings will stand the shade and the competition for water in dry weather. It is expensive to cut the weeds and brush, but it may be even more expensive to plant the land and have the trees fail. In the eastern United States there is a vast amount of scrub forest where the chance of ever again getting a good forest depends on the answer to this question. In the dry belt from the Dakotas to Texas the main problem is to keep the young trees from dying in heat, wind, and drought.

In some types of forest the best way to get a new crop is to leave seed trees while cutting out all the rest and letting in the sunlight. But the seed trees have grown up dependent on the rest of the forest for protection from the wind. If they are left exposed, will they blow over before they have done their job of reseeding? And how far will the seeds travel? Some seeds have wings and travel far; other seeds, such as nuts and acorns, travel only when a squirrel or some other creature carries them.

When part of the forest is cut and the sun and wind get in, the remaining trees may be killed by blowdown, by drying out, or by fire getting into the slash and dry weeds. Forests that are necessary to protect watersheds against erosion must be cut with special skill so as to leave the forest cover undamaged and assure full protection over the forest floor. On the other hand, if the mature trees are not cut they may blow over, causing dangerous openings and possibly fire or landslides.

All these general principles were of course well known in Europe, and Pinchot was well grounded in them before he went to work at Biltmore. The details regarding each variety of tree were what he had to guess from his immediate observation.

The principal enemies of the forest can be easily listed, though how to fight them is not so easy to work out. Fire, insects, fungi, and wind are imposed by nature even in the absence of men. The virgin American forests showed the results of thousands of years of conflict between these enemies and the recuperative efforts of the forests. Even the California Big Trees, surviving all enemies for several thousand years, show the marks of forest fires that scorched their thick, fire-resistant bark. If we wanted only to maintain the virgin forests untouched we might leave them to fight their own battles, but we should need nature's patience to wait for their slow regrowth after each disastrous fire or epidemic. In our forests, where we want to interfere with nature by cutting down some of the best trees, we have to support nature's efforts against even the natural fires set by thunderstorms, as well as against those set by campers and motorists.

The man-made enemies of the forest—bad cutting practices, fire, and overgrazing—are urgent problems, and much of the science of conservation is the science of fighting these enemies.

The first detailed forestry text in this country was a book named *The White Pine,* written by Pinchot and Henry Graves and published in 1896. This was the result of a special study financed by several friends. Most of the field work was done in Pennsylvania. It showed that white pine could make a satisfactory second growth, and it discussed also the effect of interest, taxes, and other expenses on the possibility of a profitable operation.

Next came *The Adirondack Spruce,* written by Pinchot in

connection with an Adirondack forest job that he did in 1896–97. This was intended as a handbook for lumbermen and forest owners. Besides growth tables and other information on the biology of northern spruce, it included a simple description of forest management and of the difference between European forestry practices and what was possible in America.

After Pinchot took charge of the Division of Forestry, along with his new program of help for forest owners he carried on constant research into problems of practical forest science. The division made studies of eastern hardwoods, Maine balsam fir, and western yellow pine and sugar pine. Pinchot's men also went into the difficult problem of tree planting in the plains country. There had been, for instance, some fairly successful planting in the sand hills of western Nebraska. Box elder, black locust, black cherry, and hackberry had been used as nurse trees to shelter various kinds of pine. After a study of this experience, Pinchot got Theodore Roosevelt to set aside the Dismal River and Niobrara Reserves in Nebraska for further experiments. In 1946 Pinchot reported that these plantations, started in 1903, had developed into successful pine forests.

One point that the foresters emphasized was the folly of the old armchair belief in planting a tree for every tree cut down. They pointed out that even under favorable conditions it took half a dozen seedlings to replace one sawtimber tree. For one thing, some of the seedlings would die. For another, in order to make good clear lumber they should grow up crowded so that competition would kill off all but the strongest, or they might have to be thinned, and in either case the survivor would be finally the one to replace the tree that was cut.

When the forest reserves were transferred to the Department of Agriculture in 1905 the Land Office also transferred over five hundred employees, many of whom were frustrated but honest workers who could be used if given suitable instruction and freed from excessive red tape. In a few months the Service had prepared a book for the instruction of these newly acquired workers called *Regulations and Instructions for the Use of the National Forest Reserves.* This handbook, known as the *Use Book,* defined the purposes and methods of the Forest Service. It made plain that the national forests were to serve the people and that the forest officers were not only to protect the forests from abuse but to help and advise the public in the use of forest resources. The *Use Book* became the bible of the Service and was helpful in building up good will toward the Service among the suspicious Westerners.

In 1908 one of Pinchot's best foresters, Raphael Zon, proposed the establishment of forest experiment stations for research and educational purposes. The first one was set up in the Coconino National Forest in Arizona during the summer of 1908, a small affair that pioneered in a limited way. Today the Forest Service has a series of regional stations that cover practically every important type of forest in the country, and there are also stations in Alaska and Puerto Rico. The experiment stations have done notable work on planting techniques, methods of cutting, the use of forest and other range lands, protection against fire, insects, and diseases, and the influence of forests on stream flow. Recently they have experimented with breeding better types of forest trees. They maintain a nation-wide forest survey as a basis for national policy. Earle H. Clapp, who in later years was to become Acting Chief Forester under the second Roosevelt, was mainly responsible for managing the nation-wide development of research by the Forest Service.

An important aspect of forest management is the discovery of more and better uses for the products of the forest. There was some research on wood in the Division of Forestry under Dr. Fernow, but the modern forest products work began in 1901. The new program was intended to support and promote practical forestry rather than to be a substitute for it, like Fernow's "timber physics" research. The bureau collaborated with Dr. Harvey W. Wiley, Chief of the Bureau of Chemistry of the Department of Agriculture, in setting up a laboratory to study tree chemistry. It also investigated the method of tapping southern pine trees for turpentine, and in 1902 commissioned Dr. Charles H. Herty to complete a study he had already started and to develop his "cup-and-gutter system," by which the sap is collected with the smallest possible cutting of the bark. Dr. Herty reported in 1903. His new system, which is much less destructive than the old-fashioned "box" chopped into the side of the tree, was soon adopted by most of the operators, with good results on the forests of the South.

The forest products work grew rapidly, and in 1909 a central Forest Products Laboratory was established at Madison, Wisconsin. This laboratory has made notable contributions to present-day wood technology. For example, the laboratory developed improved methods of bleaching southern pine kraft pulp that allowed the industry to make a pulp suitable for white papers such as bond and high-grade printing papers. It also pioneered in the technology of wood preservatives, in dry-kiln seasoning of lumber, and in glued plywood.

In experimenting with hot chemicals to kill the borers in southern oak lumber, the laboratory discovered a treatment that makes the oak plastic while hot. The technology of such "modified woods" is still progressing. This, like the new developments in plywood and wood pulp, may do much to create uses for trees that are now regarded as weeds, making it easier to pay for improving a mixed and crowded forest.

As forestry got under way in the United States the fact became evident that this country needed some forestry schools. Retraining Europeans would not do and on-the-job training of bright young Americans was not enough. The first school was started at Biltmore and was followed by one at Cornell. Both were run by Germans, and Pinchot felt the need of something more purely native. Therefore, he persuaded his family to finance the beginning of a school of forestry at Yale in 1900 and released two of the best men in his Forestry Division to give it a start. The Yale school was the pioneer of present-day American forest education. Many of its graduates helped to found the flock of other forestry schools that soon grew up in American universities.

The science of forest management and the allied sciences of range management, soil conservation, and water control have developed along many lines since 1900, but not much faster than the problems of resource management have grown. It was fortunate that a good beginning was made as early as it was.

Chapter 6

THE GOSPEL OF CONSERVATION

In 1905, when the Forest Service took over the forest reserves, it was not the only government agency dealing with
natural resources. There were more than twenty others,
and they cooperated if their chiefs happened to be friendly.

The Geological Survey, for instance, did the mapping on
which the Forest Service based its requests for new national
forests, and the cooperation was good because Pinchot and
Henry Gannett, head of the Geological Survey, were friends.
F. H. Newell, head of the Reclamation Service, also was
Pinchot's friend. But there was no friendship between Pinchot and the Land Office, from which he had wrested the
public forests and which had been forced by the President
to adopt some reforms that it knew had been suggested by
the Forester.

The Interior Department had control of the national
parks, which in some ways are similar to national forests;
Agriculture at that time dealt with wild animals, and Commerce with fish. The Bureau of Animal Industry in the Department of Agriculture was inclined to resent the Forest
Service's control of grazing in the national forests.

Forestry was technically related to the work of the Land
Office and to the management of grazing, fish and game,
minerals and water, and the faint beginning of the study of

soil erosion. These too had logical relations with one another, but forestry had the inside track at the White House, and so it was Pinchot who struggled with the rivalries and inconsistencies among the different bureaus. It was a natural result that after fifteen years in the practice of forestry, followed by this work as government coordinator, he should have come out with the new idea of a national policy to integrate the prudent use of all resources.

As soon as Pinchot had talked over his new idea with his associates he took it to the President, who immediately adopted it as his own policy. In later years Theodore Roosevelt said that launching this movement was the most important achievement of his Administration.

The new idea had to have a name. Pinchot and his men talked it over exhaustively. Finally they fixed upon the fact that the British in India had large forest reserves called "conservancies," with men in charge called "conservators." There was a word "conservation" in the dictionary. It meant preserving, and putting up preserved fruit, and keeping bees. They decided to take over the word for their purposes, and were successful in doing so. It seems clear that in the excitement no one recalled that Marsh had used the word in its modern sense nearly fifty years earlier.

The conservation of natural resources normally becomes necessary as the population grows, for the danger of running out of raw materials grows at the same time. Wherever people are scarce and raw resources are plentiful—as in pioneering days—the people will naturally save their own labor as much as they can at the expense of a lavish use of the local raw materials. As the population increases and raw materials begin to grow scarce, the people finally will have to pay a high price for the preservation and increase of these valuable materials. During the transition from the pioneer stage to the crowded stage, the more prudent citizens will begin to call for more economical management of resources and the less prudent will resist, not wanting to pay the price for something that does not seem to them to be necessary. This difference in viewpoint necessarily leads to controversy. The details are not so simple.

A second reason for the necessity of conservation is the development of technology that increases the demand for raw materials. In the United States the strain on natural resources has come not only from the growth of population but also from the rise of the standard of living. A century ago railroads and factories were demanding more and more coal and iron. Today radios, automobiles, plastics, and other new products call for raw materials that our ancestors never knew about. High-speed tools and jet engines require alloys of rare metals, many of them coming from far parts of the world which may not always be open to our buyers. We depend on resources of more and more kinds and in greater quantities per person. It is easy to say that science will find substitutes for anything that becomes scarce. But the trend has been for science to require more different raw materials rather than fewer.

Technology not only makes conservation more necessary, it also tends to make it seem less necessary to many of the voters. Much of our ingenuity is devoted to inventing methods for getting raw materials faster. Where our ancestors used pick and shovel and one-horse plows, we use bulldozers and gang plows drawn by tractors that eat petroleum instead of hay. We have invented techniques for smelting low-grade ores, so that we can use up deposits of metals that were safe from the crude mining efforts of our ancestors. We can squeeze the orange harder and get more juice more quickly. The effect of these new ways of getting the last drop is temporarily to make the resource plentiful, often also reducing the cost and increasing the profits of the producers. But the end will come sooner too. Every advance that lets us mine a leaner copper ore or sink the oil wells to a deeper level uses up some reserve that otherwise would have been left for Americans of the twenty-first century to discover. In the meantime both producers and consumers are tempted to take for granted that the engineers can go on finding new techniques and opening up new resources forever.

During the period when resources are only beginning to be scarce a business system like ours does not lend itself readily to the prudent use of resources, mainly because of the behavior of prices.

The usual trouble with prices during the wasteful period is that they are too low to pay the private operator for conservation. Lumber prices will pay for the cost of cutting, manufacture, and distribution with a good profit as long as the companies can get virgin timber from the government at a nominal cost, but the price may not cover the cost of protecting and restoring the forest. The farmer can grow wheat or cotton on virgin soil and make a living, with no surplus, however, to invest in terracing and grass or tree planting. The zinc miner can afford to carry on even when prices are low provided he can "pick the eyes of the mine," taking only the richest ore and leaving the rest perhaps to be flooded and abandoned as hopelessly unprofitable.

Such waste cannot be stopped by preaching alone, for businessmen are likely to feel that they cannot afford to stop the waste at the prices they are able to get in competition with others who are assuming no such expense. That is where the government is often asked to come in with some kind of subsidy, on the ground that the private operator needs a price increase or help of some kind before he can be expected to pay the cost of conservation. But as a rule, too, he needs strong persuasion to take the necessary action instead of spending the added income. Even some compulsion may be needed, and of course that is where the controversy is liable to be the most violent.

In 1955, for instance, the farm problem was in one of its frequent spasms, with farm income down since 1947 from 10.3 per cent of the national income to 6 per cent. Secretary of Agriculture Ezra Taft Benson had been trying to cut down the frightening mass of surplus farm products, largely by reducing the level of price supports. Unless the market situation could be improved there was danger that thousands of small farmers would be reduced to desperation.

In June Secretary Benson called a referendum of wheat farmers, according to law, to see if they would accept a positive limitation on the acreage to be planted to wheat. The farmers voted to cut back from 78 million acres to 55 million, in return for a government guarantee of $1.81 a bushel, instead of $1.19 without the cutback.

This action meant that every wheat farmer in the 36 wheat-growing states had to limit his plantings or pay a penalty, and a government inspector had to come on each farm and check on the wheat acreage. This threat of discipline called forth a blast of defiance from a woman farmer in Pennsylvania, Miss Elsie Mumma, that deserves quotation as a good example of the traditional American feeling about land-ownership. As reported in the press, this embattled farmer told the court:

"My ancestors pioneered this land in 1624 * and as long as I own the land, pay the taxes, pay my debts, and ask for no aid from the government, the land is mine, to have, to hold, to govern, to protect, to plant, to harvest, and no one has a right to enter upon the land without my permission or without a warrant of law, and I will die to defend my right."

These are moving sentiments that cannot fail to arouse an echo in every American breast. And yet—what socialist tyrant was this who was threatening to invade the sacred ancestral rights of an old-time American landholding? Only Secretary Benson, Republican, of Utah, carrying out the will of the majority of wheat farmers, as authorized by an Act of Congress that had been upheld by the Supreme Court.

* Miss Mumma assures me that her ancestors came from the German Palatinate in 1624 and settled where she now lives.

Shocking as it has seemed to several outraged landholders who have taken their protests to the courts without avail, the fact is that the majority of American farmers would rather suffer acreage controls than glutted markets and ruinously low prices.

The farmer is no longer a settler merely raising food to eat. He is a commercial producer for world markets. If he is to be financially strong enough to treat his land as a permanent capital asset, he may have to submit to production controls and accept government subsidies. More and more people are coming to believe that the nation cannot indefinitely let farmers neglect to treat their land as a permanent resource. But no one can help wincing when the machinery rolls over a Pennsylvania Dutch farmer whose land has been well conserved with no government help for three hundred years.

On principle, the American people disapprove not only of government controls but also of subsidies. As taxpayers they disapprove of letting special interests "get their snouts into the public trough." In particular cases, however, they have always used government subsidies to promote special interests that seemed to be useful and to need help. Hence there are many arguments in which those who oppose the subsidy stand on high moral ground and those who favor it on low practical ground, without a meeting of the minds.

The main reason for subsidies is that ordinary business operations sometimes cannot supply an essential service at a price that the users will pay. There is little use asking why. It is a habit of consumers in a free market to refuse to buy some things at prices that will cover the costs. A common example is transportation. The government has had to subsidize highways, canals, railways, ocean shipping, and airways. For, if rates were raised to cover costs and a fair profit, most of these transportation agencies would lose traffic and business in general would suffer. Subsidies are adopted whenever the public wants a service that cannot make expenses as a purely commercial activity.

Sometimes, too, for practical reasons of management, the government will buy out an owner who cannot afford to operate his property according to the public interest, instead of giving him a subsidy and regulating his use of the property. For example, there is some cutover forest and marginal farm land that can most easily be turned into productive forest if it is taken over by a government, federal, state, or local.

As both Gifford Pinchot and Theodore Roosevelt were by nature men of action, and as the beginnings of conservation policy were mainly concerned with resources owned by the federal government, it was natural for both men to take it for granted that the federal government must act. On public lands they took the action of reserving the resources and leasing them for use under government control. On private lands the conservationists were ready to go beyond education and appeals if necessary. They were ready to resort to regulation of land use, to subsidy, and sometimes to outright purchase to bring the treatment of resources into public control.

The first official recognition of the new conservation policy came on March 14, 1907, in connection with the appointment of the Inland Waterways Commission, promoted by Pinchot and his friends and vigorously approved by the President. In the letter creating the commission Theodore Roosevelt said:

"It is not possible to frame so large a plan as this for control of our rivers without taking account of the orderly development of other natural resources. Therefore, I ask that the Inland Waterways Commission shall consider the relation of the streams to the use of all the great permanent natural resources and their conservation for the making and maintenance of prosperous homes."

The commission was made up of interested senators and representatives, the head of the Army Engineers, and four other officials, including Gifford Pinchot. Roosevelt did not ask Congress for any appropriation, leaving the commission free to report as it thought best without Congressional instructions. This it did in less than a year. In the meantime its activities were such as to draw public attention to the new doctrine. The most effective of these was an inspection trip down the Mississippi as guests of the Mississippi Valley Improvement Association, and with President Roosevelt as guest of honor.

The Inland Waterways Commission made history by stating that every river system ought to be given scientific study and treatment from its sources to its mouth. And since the river flow pays no attention to political boundaries, the principle of unified river basin management calls for a type of organization that goes beyond the lines of states or Congressional districts.

The commission declared: "Hereafter plans for the improvement of inland waterways . . . shall take account of the purification of the waters, the development of power, the control of floods, the reclamation of lands by irrigation and drainage, and all other uses of the waters or benefits to be derived from their control."

This principle, simply a concrete statement of the new doctrine of conservation, was strong medicine then, and it is strong medicine today. It is by no means acceptable to the opponents of conservation policies. In particular, while the principles of unified management and multiple use were, in the extraordinary circumstances of 1933, embodied in the Tennessee Valley Authority, they have been bitterly and successfully fought off in the Missouri Valley and the other great river basins of this country.

The Inland Waterways Commission pointed out the vast stretches of land that might be reclaimed for agriculture by irrigation or drainage (in those days the limitations on such reclamation were not so well understood as now). It called attention to the loss of a billion tons of fertile soil per year by erosion, a matter that Dr. Hugh Bennett was beginning to study at that time in an obscure bureau in the Department of Agriculture.

In transmitting the commission's report to Congress, T.R. warned strongly against monopolies of resources, especially of waterpower sites. He said: "Among these monopolies, as the report of the Commission points out, there is no other which threatens, or has ever threatened, such intolerable interference with the daily life of the people as the consolidation of the companies controlling waterpower." There he was declaring a war that was to go on long after his time.

The Forest Service was not satisfied with the power policies that had been previously followed on the forest lands. On taking charge of the forests it established a policy of demanding a rental for land used in a power installation and also a "charge for the conservation of water supply and the use of advantageous locations and other privileges." These rules became the foundation of the present federal waterpower policy in cases where private companies are granted permits to develop power on public land. Pinchot recommended that permits be limited to ninety-nine years, but Secretary of Agriculture Wilson cut it to fifty, and Pinchot admitted that fifty was right. Fifty it has been ever since, though in 1955 there were signs of a questionable legal device by which 40-year-old permits could be consolidated with some new ones and a new 50-year permit wrapped around the combined system.

When the Forest Service announced its new power rules the companies were opposed to having to pay rentals and conservation charges. Legally the charges rested only on an interpretation of the law by the Attorney General, but the interpretation was never successfully challenged. Bills were introduced in Congress to open the national forest sites to condemnation by state courts and to open all sites to the first comer, with no time limit. There were special bills to grant permits over the head of the Forest Service. Roosevelt, in vetoing the James River Bill, announced that he would veto any bill that failed to provide for a rental and a time limit. He accused the companies of "acting with foresight, singleness of purpose, and vigor to control the water powers of the country."

The new gospel of conservation extended to an awakened interest in the condition of the farm population. T.R. was deeply influenced by Sir Horace Plunkett, the founder of rural cooperatives in Ireland. Plunkett had come to America and was raising cattle in Montana when Roosevelt as a young man was ranching on the Little Missouri. In 1908 Roosevelt brought Plunkett and Pinchot together. At their suggestion the President appointed the Country Life Commission to look into what might be done to improve living conditions on the farm. The Department of Agriculture, which had done good work on the improvement of crops, had not hitherto taken a deep interest in farm income, comfort, and social life, the poverty of which had most to do with causing bright young people to move to the cities.

The Country Life Commission made a wide swing around the country, held thirty public hearings, and sent out thousands of questionnaires. It found poor education for country living, poor roads, widespread soil erosion, no leadership, and the obvious disadvantages of unorganized farmers in dealing with well-organized city businessmen.

The commission recommended that the farmers organize cooperatives to strengthen their bargaining position, and that they take a more active interest in politics, education, and social life. These recommendations were not cordially regarded by people who were accustomed to doing sharp business with the farmers, but they started a line of events that would eventually bring new services into the farm country, including rural electrification.

During the last year of his administration T.R. hastened to spread the knowledge of conservation as widely as possible through a series of great conferences. At the end of his term conservation was fated to fall on evil days, but the blight would not be fatal. So much public support had been gained before Roosevelt was through that the men who came into power with Taft could not wipe it out.

The first of the great conservation conferences was that of the governors of the states. The President told the governors that this conference "ought to be among the most important gatherings in our history, for none have had a more vital question to consider."

All the governors accepted the President's invitation. In addition, the presidents of about seventy national organizations concerned with resources were invited. All the members of the 60th Congress, the Supreme Court, and the Cabinet were invited, and of course the Inland Waterways Commission. There were some fifty other guests, including such men as Andrew Carnegie, William J. Bryan, and James J. Hill. It was as distinguished a company as the President of the United States could find within the national borders.

Behind the scenes the conservation men—chiefly Gifford Pinchot, F. H. Newell, and W J McGee—prepared the agenda, chose the speakers, and wrote most of their speeches, for the ideas were new and most of the governors had no clear knowledge of them.

Roosevelt, in his own speech, proclaimed that the time had come when the lavish resources of the nation were in danger of exhaustion if the old wasteful methods were permitted to continue. He could already see the beginnings of a timber famine. In the past, he said, we had "admitted the right of the individual to injure the future of the Republic for his own present profit. The time has come for a change." He declared that it was time to assert the national right and duty of protecting ourselves and our children against the wasteful development of our natural resources.

That was laying down the law, and the governors listened. The conference adopted a Declaration of the Governors, a notable hymn to conservation in which they all joined. The words were largely written by McGee and Governor Newton C. Blanchard of Louisiana, who was chosen by the steering committee because of his interest and his understanding of the problems. What was remarkable was the unanimity. The effect on public opinion in the United States and abroad was profound. It stamped the doctrine of conservation on the minds of the American people. This conference in the spring of 1908 was the official installation of conservation as the central policy of the Roosevelt Administration.

To carry forward the campaign the Governors' Conference recommended an inventory of natural resources and the promotion of conservation by state commissions cooperating with a national commission. Some forty out of the forty-six * states soon created conservation commissions, and about as many national private organizations appointed conservation committees before the end of 1908.

In June, 1908, Roosevelt appointed the National Conservation Commission, including many senators and representatives, government officials, and private experts, and directed it to make an inventory of natural resources. It was divided into four sections: to study waters, forests, lands, and minerals. Pinchot was chairman of the commission, and his friends were strategically placed as secretaries of the sections, directing the actual work of the inventory. By Executive Order, all federal agencies were required to provide all the information possible "not inconsistent with express provisions of law."

As usual, Roosevelt told them to do not merely all the law required but everything needful that the law did not forbid. It was this particular attitude toward the law that William Howard Taft reversed when he became President

* Arizona and New Mexico were not admitted to the Union until 1912.

the next year, thus letting himself in for a controversy that was later to end in his defeat for reelection.

The inventory was made with no Congressional appropriation, much of it by overtime work in executive and legislative offices that cost the Treasury nothing. The four sections brought in their reports early in December, 1908, and discussed them at a general meeting of the commission. This was the first attempt at a national resources inventory, and it has had a world-wide influence down to the present day.

Conservation having been well and truly preached to the Americans, and within a miraculously short time after it was conceived, the next step was to preach it abroad, to North America and then to the world at large. So on December 24 the President wrote to Lord Grey, the Governor-General of Canada, and to President Porfirio Diaz of Mexico, proposing a conference in February, for Roosevelt's term would end in March. The letters were carried by Pinchot, who could explain details that might not be clear at first sight.

When the Canadian Premier, Sir Wilfrid Laurier, told the Parliament that the Government was accepting President Roosevelt's invitation, the leader of the Opposition arose to say that he had no amendment to offer. Conservation already had a good name north of the border. Mexico and Newfoundland also accepted, and the delegates met at the White House on February 18, 1909.

At this conference the spirit of prophecy continued to guide the words of the men who took part, and the germs of a future Marshall Plan, Point 4, and various United Nations technical institutions began to form. The conference recognized the interdependence of nations and the need for conservation practices that would cross political boundaries. It accepted and proclaimed the main principles of conservation: the duty of private owners to conserve their forests, the dangers of monopoly in water resources, and the need for regulation of grazing and for the restriction of waste and monopoly in minerals. As Pinchot felt free to say thirty-seven years later, if the world had followed the advice of this conference it would certainly have avoided some unfortunate kinds of waste and possibly might even have avoided war.

The North American Conference recommended to the President of the United States that he call a world conference on "the subject of world resources and their inventory, conservation, and wise utilization." The President, not having long to stay in the White House, had already sounded out the principal governments of the world about such a conference, and the replies were all favorable. The Netherlands consented to act as host country and invitations went out from Washington to fifty-eight nations to meet at The Hague in September, 1909. Carrying through with the conference, of course, would not be a job for Theodore Roosevelt, nor for Pinchot either, unless they should be appointed as delegates by the new President, William Howard Taft.

The conservation men could not openly admit that by the following September they might be political outsiders, but they were beginning to feel the ground slipping from under their feet. Mr. Taft, nominated for the Presidency with Roosevelt's strong backing in 1908, had been elected. During his campaign he had made a good speech on conservation, which Pinchot had written for him, but after election day he avoided the White House and consorted with Roosevelt's political enemies.

On December 8, 1908, the conservation men got a severe shock. A conservation meeting was to be addressed by Roosevelt and Taft, among others, and President-elect Taft was invited to act as chairman. Taft was introduced by Pinchot, and rose to his feet. His first words were:

"Mr. President, Ladies and Gentlemen: There is one difficulty about the conservation of natural resources. It is that the imagination of those who are pressing it may outrun the practical facts."

Later in the meeting it was time for Mr. Taft to make a speech, and a manuscript had been supplied. Laying the manuscript pointedly aside, he said, with his famous chuckle: "How many parts of the speeches that have been delivered Mr. Pinchot has written I am unable to testify for others." He then went on to talk without looking at the manuscript.

So the prophet was given notice that he was going to be without honor in the new administration. It is an experience that has happened to many less authentic prophets in American political life, even when the new administration is of the same political party as the old. There were going to be new faces in the White House. The Taft wing of the party was coming into power.

The Roosevelt wing of the party could hardly be so frank as to drop the project for an International Conservation Conference, but at home they hastened to batten down all the resources they could. The conservation men worked days and nights in preparing papers so that President Roosevelt could withdraw every possible acre of the public domain that would be better used in public than in private ownership. They were afraid that Taft's friends might try to grab these properties. But they wanted to make sure that, if Taft allowed such actions, it would require an open repudiation of Roosevelt's conservation policies, with all the political penalties that might follow if it should turn out that Pinchot and Roosevelt had gained the support of the people. That was what the future was going to have to work out.

So came March 4, and Taft was President. The international conference died.

Part Two

REACTION, WAR, AND
"NORMALCY"

Chapter 7

TAFT AND BALLINGER

The battle that was to bring Pinchot and finally Roosevelt into direct conflict with Taft had its roots in the old-fashioned ideas of Richard Achilles Ballinger, Taft's Secretary of the Interior. Ballinger believed in the traditional Land Office policy of getting the national domain into private ownership as fast as possible so as to promote development. Pinchot believed that the government ought to keep what was left of its domain and license the use of the resources rather than sell the land. On each side of this argument there were many honest and intelligent men. But one side was the nineteenth century, dying hard, and the other was the twentieth, fighting to take its place. The two sides had to fight it out; and they are not yet through fighting.

Ballinger first came to Washington in T.R.'s time. He was a conservative lawyer from Seattle, who had made a good record as Mayor and had a wide circle of friends in the business community. He favored the development of Alaska, Seattle's great hinterland, and many of his friends were investing in Alaskan properties.

Ballinger had gone to college with James Garfield, who became T.R.'s Secretary of the Interior in March, 1907. Garfield supported Pinchot and the conservation men, but he was nevertheless pleased to get his old friend, the conservative ex-Mayor of Seattle, to be head of the Land Office. When Ballinger arrived, Pinchot, Newell of Reclamation, and Richards, the outgoing commissioner of the Land Office, interviewed him and found to their distress that he was not in favor of leasing the publicly owned coal lands of Alaska but thought they should be sold outright. It was the Alaska coal fields that were later going to be the cause of the great controversy.

In Alaska the Morgan-Guggenheim Syndicate was actively engaged in getting control of as much of the Territory as possible. The syndicate was backed by J. P. Morgan & Co., the American Smelting and Refining Co. (Guggenheim), Kuhn, Loeb & Co., and other New York banking interests. It owned the great Kennecott copper mines, an Alaskan railroad, the biggest Alaska steamship line, and assorted fisheries. It needed local coal. Coal from Washington State was of poor quality and it cost up to $15 a ton delivered in Alaska. Seattle businessmen were not hostile to the syndicate's plan to get Alaskan coal. On the contrary, many of them had investments that were in line to be benefited by the project.

One of these investors, Clarence Cunningham, had begun to stake out coal claims in 1902, about 25 miles inland from Controller Bay, where a good harbor could be built. Before these claims could be recorded and paid for at the legal rate of $10 an acre, the law of 1904 was passed. The legally allowed size of claim was 160 acres for each individual. Under the 1904 law not more than four men could form an association and combine their claims to 640 acres, one square mile. The law was absurd, for even a square mile of coal land in that location would not pay for the cost of building a railroad and seaport to get out the coal. But it was the law, and any attempt to put together a coal property large enough to be practical was open to charges of being an attempted evasion.

Cunningham and his associates had thirty-three claims to

taling 5,280 acres, enough to make a good business proposition. The law required each claimant, except for an association of four, to swear that his entry was made "in good faith for his own benefit, and not directly or indirectly, in whole or in part, in behalf of any person or persons whomsoever" and, further, that he had no intention of consolidating his claim with any others. The total value of the Cunningham claims was estimated at anything from $20 million to $300 million, and the price Cunningham and his friends would pay the government at $10 an acre would be $52,800.

Pinchot and the conservationists had no objection to a mining project of suitable size, but they wanted the government to keep the lands closed until Congress could pass a proper leasing law that would yield royalties to the government and would give it some control of the treatment of the resource. The existing law, impractical as it was, could serve to block the transfer of the lands until the conservationists could get a proper leasing law through Congress. The heart of the controversy, therefore, was ownership or rental, not any question of whether or not the coal should be developed. But behind the immediate dispute about whether the land ought to be sold or only leased, there was an economic, social, and moral dispute about whether the Morgan-Guggenheim Syndicate ought to be allowed to acquire a coal property that might tighten its stranglehold on Alaska. For Cunningham's natural customer for the property would be the syndicate. This conflict over monopoly powers gave bitterness to the whole controversy.

In 1905 the local agents of the Land Office reported that the Cunningham claims were on the way to Washington and that they were "fraudulent." By the time Ballinger took over the Land Office in 1907 three Land Office agents had reported unfavorably on the claims, including one who was afterward to become a storm center, Louis R. Glavis.

On July 20, 1907, however, the Morgan-Guggenheim Syndicate took an option on the Cunningham claims and on

December 7 took up the option. The deal provided for a $5,000,000 corporation with half the stock going to the Cunningham group.

Then Horace T. Jones, the first of the Land Office agents to question the claims, was transferred from Alaska to Salt Lake City. Cunningham reported to Daniel Guggenheim that Ballinger had said everything would be cleared up within ninety days. Glavis and Jones got together and sent a special report to Ballinger, but he did not reply. Glavis went to Washington and saw Ballinger. He was told to go to Alaska and examine all coal claims in the Territory, and a week later Ballinger talked with ex-Governor Miles C. Moore, who was representing the Cunningham claimants, and immediately ordered the claims to go through.

At that point Glavis rebelled. He telegraphed a protest, which arrived just as the papers were ready to be signed. The telegram could not be disregarded, and the signing had to be held up. Ballinger shifted the action to Congress by trying to get a bill passed validating the Cunningham claims. He testified that the proposed bill "does not call for proof of good faith of the original entrymen." He also recommended that existing claims be allowed at the original price of $10 an acre, but that future ones should be charged for at their actual value, which would give the syndicate an advantage over any future competitors. Secretary Garfield opposed the bill and it failed.

A year after his appointment Ballinger resigned, saying he could not sympathize with Garfield's public land policies, and Garfield agreed. Ballinger went home to Seattle and became attorney for the Cunningham group, pressing their claims personally on Garfield, but in vain.

In March, 1909, when Taft took office, he appointed Ballinger to succeed Garfield as Secretary of the Interior. Later, one of the Seattle coal claimants told Glavis that he and his friends had brought pressure through their senators to pre vent the reappointment of Garfield because of his stubborn attitude about Alaska coal.

The new Secretary of the Interior lost no time in starting to undo some of the conservation policies of his predecessor. Garfield had withdrawn nearly four million acres of water-power sites just before March 4, to give time for the government to provide for their proper use. Ballinger declared the withdrawals illegal, on the Taft principle that anything not positively required by Act of Congress must not be done. He gave orders to reopen the power sites as soon as possible. Pinchot went to the President and protested. Taft ordered Ballinger to withdraw the power sites again, which he did. This was a temporary victory for the remaining influence of T.R., who was off to Africa to hunt the big game of that continent.

But on other points Ballinger came out ahead. For example, early in 1908 the Forest Service had made an agreement with the Indian Office to manage the Indian forests, which were rapidly being stolen. This arrangement was abolished by Ballinger in July, 1909, on the ground that there was no legal authority for it, and the Indians were left unprotected.

By the middle of 1909 the newspapers were full of headlines saying that Taft was disciplining Ballinger and might even remove him from office. The general opinion was that this was a battle between Ballinger on one side and Pinchot, as representative of T.R., on the other, and that Taft was taking the side of T.R. and Pinchot. The intense interest in the press indicated that the efforts of T.R. and Pinchot to arouse public support for conservation had succeeded. All the papers, even those in Washington State, evidently assumed that the public would not stand for any betrayal of conservation.

Pinchot, who was still Forester, took time to make speeches extolling the Roosevelt policies. Ballinger also made speeches. Pinchot felt that the public response was in his favor.

As for the Alaska coal lands, they were not forgotten. As soon as he took office Ballinger ordered the Land Office to expedite all Alaska cases, but since he had been counsel for the Cunningham group he "dissociated" himself from their claims, leaving them to be handled by the staff. This satisfied nobody. The Cunningham people were disappointed not to get immediate help from a sympathetic Secretary of the Interior. The conservation people felt that as ex-attorney for the group the Secretary knew better than anyone else that the government might be cheated unless he should step in to enforce the law.

Then Glavis found out that the Cunningham claims were being pushed through and he began to fight. He came to Washington, talked with Ballinger, and was not satisfied. He began going outside the organization. He saw Attorney General George Wickersham and got an opinion adverse to the claims, which checked their progress for the moment. He appealed to the Forest Service, for most of the claims lay in a national forest. The Forest Service could not legally refuse mineral rights, but the Secretary of Agriculture had a right to look into the dispute, so there was more delay.

Glavis, who was beginning to annoy Mr. Ballinger, was ordered off the case. It was turned over to another agent, who increased the awkwardness by also reporting against the claims.

By this time Glavis was thoroughly aroused. He went to Pinchot, and Pinchot gave him a letter of introduction to the President. Pinchot also wrote to Taft saying that these claims were so well known that if they should be allowed the ensuing scandal would be immense.

Glavis saw Taft at his summer home in Beverly, Massachusetts, on August 18, 1909, and gave him a statement of about fifty pages, mostly official documents. Taft read them immediately. He told Glavis to go back to Seattle, and sent the Glavis report on to Ballinger for reply.

Ballinger prepared a long reply, with masses of documents attached. It later took Louis D. Brandeis more than ten days to read this material, and he was well used to reading difficult stuff. On September 6 Ballinger went to Beverly with his reply and the supporting documents. With him he took Oscar Lawler, an Assistant Attorney General and his close friend. Lawler was unfriendly to Glavis, who had once accused him of land frauds in California.

After an evening of discussion Taft took the material and examined it until about three in the morning. The next day he authorized Lawler to prepare for him an opinion "as if he were President," one that would uphold Ballinger's position. Lawler and Ballinger went back to Washington and drafted a 30-page letter for Taft to sign, and Lawler and Attorney General Wickersham took it to Taft on September 12. Taft revised it, added a defense of Ballinger's actions regarding waterpower sites and Indian forests, and signed it. The letter directed Ballinger to fire Glavis, which he did.

Taft also wrote a polite letter to Pinchot, enclosing a copy of the Ballinger letter and urging him not to take hasty action in Glavis's cause, and not to think of resigning as Forester. Pinchot at that time was on a vacation in the West, and he took occasion to meet Taft at Salt Lake City on September 24. Taft was on a speaking trip. Their conference was amicable, but Pinchot was worried by Taft's repeated reference to insufficient legal powers, and his hope that Congress would decide the conservation questions "one way or another." As Pinchot said, "I wanted it settled one way only."

Pinchot complained to Taft that the newspapermen were pursuing him, since they interpreted the Ballinger decision as a defeat for Pinchot. So the President issued a friendly statement exonerating him too. Then Pinchot issued one more or less exonerating the President.

A few days later Taft wrote to his daughter and mentioned Pinchot, saying that Pinchot and Roosevelt "sympathized much more than he and I can, for they both have more of a socialist tendency."

Senator Jonathan Dolliver of Iowa is credited by Pinchot with having originated the famous description of Taft as "that ponderous and pleasant person entirely surrounded by men who know exactly what they want." The kind of men Taft liked were those who let him sleep while they went about their business. Pinchot, who wanted an active president, was a nuisance to Taft. As Mr. Dooley, the famous philosopher of the time, said: "Taft knows th' brakes well, but he ain't very familyer with th' power."

In that autumn of 1909 there was to be not much quiet sleep for the pleasant person in the White House. Glavis wrote to the President that he deemed it to be his duty to make the facts known, thus plainly indicating an intention to stir up trouble. Then he visited numerous influential men, and on November 13 he published an article in *Collier's*, entitled "The Whitewash of Ballinger."

While Pinchot was on the West Coast, Overton Price and Alexander Shaw, holding the fort in the Forest Service, took the liberty of passing out to the press information in their official possession on the Alaska coal claims. This was, of course, highly improper but useful to the cause of conservation; so when Pinchot came back he officially reprimanded them and privately patted them on the back. He told Agriculture Secretary Wilson that he thought the reprimand was enough.

Meanwhile, Congress decided to investigate both the Interior Department and the Forest Service. At that point Ballinger wrote a letter to Senator Wesley L. Jones of Washington complaining of the "pernicious activity" of certain Forest Service officers, which Jones read from the Senate floor. Then Senator Dolliver asked Pinchot for a letter. Pinchot's letter vigorously defended Price and Shaw, and of course by implication made it clear that in Pinchot's opinion Ballinger had fooled the President. Dolliver read the letter in the Senate on January 7, 1910, and Taft fired Pinchot the same evening. But in his place he appointed Pinchot's close friend and one-time business partner, Henry Solon Graves.

In 1909 conservation underwent a slight shift in emphasis in order to withstand the reaction against it. From the beginning there had been both scientific and moral implications in this doctrine. As an engineering matter it called for the best technical treatment of resources to avoid waste. As a moral matter it might involve action to prevent monopoly control of resources and the gouging of the public. Both these aspects have been constantly familiar to the friends of conservation down to the present time, but the emphasis changes according to circumstances. By the end of 1909 Pinchot's mind had less room for technical forestry than for the crusade against monopoly.

In a speech on December 27, 1909, Pinchot declared that the conservation issue was a moral issue. "A man in public life can no more serve both the special interests and the people than he can serve God and Mammon." He set aside for the moment the peaceful problems of forest management to emphasize that when a few men get possession of one of the necessaries of life and use that control to extort undue profits they are guilty of a moral wrong. This was going to be the theme of the great battle of 1910 and it was on the moral issue that the public would give the verdict for Pinchot.

The Joint Committee to investigate the Pinchot-Ballinger fight was to be made up of six senators and six members of the House, with the Republicans, as the majority party, having four of each. Since Vice-President James S. Sherman and the Speaker, Joseph G. Cannon, were both of the Taft wing, it was a foregone conclusion that the committee would decide in favor of Ballinger, but that was not all that mattered. Taft was really on trial, and the public would give the final decision. Pinchot and his friends believed that the public was with them and acted accordingly.

In those days the Speaker of the House, "Uncle Joe" Cannon, ruled with an iron hand, appointing all committees and deciding what bills should be considered by the House. Not all the members were content with his reactionary policies. There was a rising revolt of young Republicans, who called themselves Insurgents. Robert La Follette the elder and George Norris, afterward Senator and father of the TVA, were leaders of the Insurgents, and they were all friends of Theodore Roosevelt. When the House came to consider the Joint Resolution creating the investigating committee in the Pinchot-Ballinger affair, Norris observed that the resolution provided that the six House members would be appointed by the Speaker. But he had a plan.

At noon, when the Chairman of the Rules Committee went out to lunch, Norris asked for two minutes of time, in which he moved to amend the resolution so that the committee members would be elected by the House. The Democrats and Insurgents outvoted the Taft Republicans, and Norris got his amendment. This in itself was a historic moment, for it was the first time Cannon had been successfully defied; and before the Insurgents were finished with Cannon his dictatorship was overthrown.

So the House elected three Cannon Republicans, two liberal Democrats, and one Insurgent, thus making it sure that there would be no unanimous whitewash of Ballinger. The two Senate Democrats, though hand picked by the Vice-President, were influenced by the two House Democrats. Seven Taft Republicans, four Democrats, and one Insurgent opened the hearings on January 26, 1910.

Pinchot retained George Wharton Pepper as his counsel, but the lawyer who finally won the laurels was Louis D. Brandeis, counsel for Glavis.

Glavis and Pinchot testified about the questionable nature of the Cunningham claims and the failure of Ballinger to defend the national domain against the Morgan-Guggenheim Syndicate. They did not accuse Ballinger of graft, but of neglecting the public interest. The majority of the committee, however, plainly agreed with Taft that Ballinger had done all that the law required of him. They did not believe, with Pinchot and T.R., that an official should go out and resist monopolists as far as he could stretch the law. Ballinger and Taft obviously believed that to refuse the Cunningham claims would have been to stretch the law. No one could have accused Taft of wanting the law evaded, and no one actually accused Ballinger of corruption.

It was a moral disagreement that was apparently doomed to lead only to confusion, since both sides were evidently sure they were right. If there was to be a victory, it would come through an accidental slip by one side or the other. Such a slip came when the Administration made the mistake of distorting some of the evidence presented to Congress and got caught at it.

Congress had asked the President for "any reports, statements, or documents upon which he had acted in reaching his conclusions." In reply the President sent a mass of documents which the committee had a right to suppose contained the material, the whole material, and nothing but the material used by the President before he exonerated Ballinger.

Now, as it happened, Attorney General Wickersham had conferred with Taft while the President was considering what to do with Ballinger. Apparently Wickersham was afterward asked to put his advice in writing, and did so. His report, dated September 11, 1909, was included in the papers that Taft sent to Congress. September 11 was two days before the date of Taft's letter to Ballinger, and so the Wickersham report seemed to fit properly into the materials used by Taft in reaching his conclusions.

But Brandeis read the Wickersham report and knew it was too well finished a document to have been written in the available time. It must have been written later and falsely dated. But he had to prove it. Then he discovered that at one point Wickersham had given arguments against a statement of Glavis's that Glavis had not made until his *Collier's* article in November. So the President had not had the Wickersham report when he made his decision in September. Was it possible that he did have some other report that had not been included in the file sent to Congress?

Ballinger at first denied knowing anything of a missing document, but Brandeis finally made him admit that Lawler had brought the President "a sort of résumé of the case." The majority members of the committee may or may not have known that this résumé was the letter that Taft had told Lawler to draft "as if he were President," but at least they knew that Brandeis was getting warm, and they tried to change the subject. But before he could be shut off, Brandeis had got Ballinger, Wickersham, and Lawler to deny that they had copies of any such document.

Then there came on the scene Frederick M. Kerby, later a distinguished newspaperman in the Scripps-Howard organization. Garfield had brought Kerby into the Interior Department, and he had stayed on as a secretary in Ballinger's office. Kerby had been present all during the night when Ballinger and Lawler made the draft, and he knew that parts of it were contained in the letter that Taft had published. He told another of Garfield's men about it and so finally came to tell Garfield and Brandeis.

For weeks thereafter Brandeis tried to get trace of the Lawler draft without calling on Kerby, but everyone denied everything. At last Kerby decided to give his story to the newspapers and take the consequences. The story broke in the afternoon papers on Saturday, May 14, and Kerby was fired on Monday.

Meanwhile the Administration team had become badly tangled in its own feet. The President heard of the story on Saturday afternoon while he was playing golf on the Chevy Chase links. He sent instructions to the White House to "deny it absolutely; state that there is not a word of truth in it."

But Wickersham had a copy of the Lawler draft in his safe. He had only recently told the committee there was no such document, but now he panicked. He sent his copy to the committee, saying it had been "inadvertently overlooked." It was embarrassing for the President when he got home that afternoon. But Justice Brandeis told Pinchot in 1939 that what had won the fight was the discovery that the Wickersham report was falsely dated. In his opinion the Lawler draft would not have been very damaging if everyone had not tried to conceal it.

Thus the great conservation battle of the day was settled for the time being in the public mind by the almost irrelevant fact that the Administration had been caught trying to conceal evidence.

The committee itself was divided in its verdict. The seven Taft Republicans gave Ballinger a clean bill of health. The four Democrats condemned Ballinger and praised Glavis and Kerby for sacrificing their jobs in defense of the national interest. The one Insurgent gave a more detached analysis of the evidence and concluded that Ballinger "was not a faithful trustee of the interests of the people." All that was about what everyone expected.

The surprising feature was that the majority of the committee, after patting Ballinger on the back, recommended legislation to take all the Alaska coal claims out of his hands and turn them over to a federal court for decision. Finally, the majority declared that "it would be the height of unwisdom to permit these great coal fields to be monopolized," and recommended that, instead of selling, the government should lease these lands at fair royalties and in large enough blocks to justify the necessary investment. This was all that Pinchot had wanted when he and Ballinger had first met and disagreed three years earlier.

As for the verdict of the people, it appeared to be against

Taft and Ballinger. Roosevelt was alienated, and lacking Roosevelt's support Taft lost favor with the people. The House went Democratic in 1910. Ballinger hung on for a while but resigned under threat of impeachment, in March, 1911. Taft appointed in his place Walter L. Fisher of Chicago, vice-president of the National Conservation Association, of which Pinchot was president. Under the new Secretary the Cunningham claims were canceled and the land was returned to the public domain.

Taft ran for reelection in 1912, but T.R. ran too and got 88 electoral votes to Taft's 8, throwing the Presidency to Woodrow Wilson. It was eight years before another Republican was elected President. Harding appointed Taft Chief Justice of the Supreme Court. Before that, however, Woodrow Wilson had appointed Louis D. Brandeis to the Court and he was confirmed after a bitter fight, with the powerful help of the Insurgents. Senator Norris recalled in 1934 that the reputation Brandeis made in the Pinchot-Ballinger affair had a great deal to do with his appointment by Woodrow Wilson to the Court.

To fill out the changing pattern of history, when after 1933 Harold Ickes as Secretary of the Interior besought F.D.R. to transfer the Forest Service to his department and was refused, he suspected, not without cause, that his old friend Gifford Pinchot was once more influencing a Roosevelt. He published a violent article in the *Saturday Evening Post* attacking Pinchot and upholding Ballinger. He also wrote Pinchot a 22-page letter, never published, but now available in the Library of Congress, in which his well-known vocabulary was at its best. Pinchot had almost as good a vocabulary, which he unlimbered briefly, but in the end nothing came of that skirmish.

Chapter 8

INTERLUDE

After the battle between Pinchot and Ballinger the conservation movement went on developing in relative quiet for nearly twenty-five years until its next outburst of expansion after 1933. Taft had helped to quiet the political storm by his appointment of Henry S. Graves as successor to Pinchot in 1910, and in 1911 by accepting Ballinger's resignation and appointing a good conservationist, Walter L. Fisher, as Secretary of the Interior.

In 1909, when the National Conservation Commission died off with the coming of Taft to power, Pinchot and his friends had decided to carry on with a private organization. They formed the National Conservation Association, with President Charles W. Eliot of Harvard as honorary president. Pinchot was active president, and Fisher was vice-president. With this organization to focus the widespread influence of the conservationists, they went ahead to campaign successfully for legislation under both Republican and Democratic Administrations.

In January, 1911, Pinchot wrote that the opposition to conservation was confined to a single class: the representatives of special interests. He recommended that for the next few years the friends of conservation should concentrate on the prevention of forest fires, the creation of national forests in the Appalachians and the White Mountains, the reduction of stream pollution, and the saving of waterpower from monopoly control.

The principal immediate project was the establishment of an Appalachian national forest, the dream Dr. Joseph A. Holmes, State Geologist of North Carolina, had unfolded to Gifford Pinchot at Biltmore in the early nineties. National forests in the East could not be carved out of the public domain because there was none in the original states. The only way that eastern forest lands could get into public ownership was by the acquisition of private lands through purchase, gift, or tax delinquency. By 1909 New York State had acquired 1,611,817 acres and Pennsylvania 863,000 acres, but public pressure was strong in other eastern states to get the advantages of federal ownership and Forest Service management. The constitutional basis for the proposed legislation for federal purchase of eastern forests soon came to rest on the protection of the watersheds of navigable rivers.

For several years eastern lawmakers had been trying to have such legislation passed. In 1906 Senator Frank B. Brandegee of Connecticut and Representative James W. Wadsworth of New York had introduced bills authorizing the purchase of forest lands in the South and in the White Mountains. The Wadsworth bill was defeated by such conservatives as Speaker Cannon, James A. Tawney of Minnesota, Chairman of the Committee on Appropriations, Champ Clark of Missouri, and John Sharp Williams of Mississippi. The defeat aroused strong feelings along the East Coast. These feelings were shared by eastern conservatives such as John W. Weeks, banker and Member of Congress from the suburban 12th District of Massachusetts.

Cannon liked Weeks, and put him on the Agriculture Committee, where he was able to work for the forest project. Years later Weeks told Pinchot that he had warned Cannon that he, Weeks, would oppose him on the purchase of forests, and Uncle Joe had benignantly told Weeks to go ahead and try to convert him. He promised Weeks: "If you can frame a forestry bill which you, as a businessman, are willing to support, I will do what I can to get an opportunity to get it consideration in the House."

President Roosevelt's Message of December 3, 1907, recommended the purchase of as much forest land as possible in the Appalachians and the White Mountains. All the private conservation organizations went into action. The House in January, 1908, asked its Judiciary Committee to report on a purchase bill introduced by Representative Frank D. Currier of New Hampshire. The committee reported that the bill was unconstitutional because it did not clearly show that the lands to be acquired "have a direct and substantial connection with the conservation and improvement of the navigability of a river." So Mr. Weeks brought in a new bill to buy forest land "for protecting navigable streams and promoting navigation." This bill was not limited to any part of the country.

The next line of opposition came from a minority in the Agriculture Committee who wanted the government to confine itself to teaching the hill farmers soil conservation, and leave the rest to the states. So the next Weeks bill, to placate this minority, included an authorization of subsidies to states for cooperation in the protection of forested watersheds feeding navigable streams. Thus the principle of federal-state cooperation slipped into the conservation program almost by accident. It was hardly noticed in the debate. Speaker Cannon helped the bill, and it passed the House on March 1, 1909, but in the Senate some of the western senators filibustered it to death. After other minor vicissitudes, the Weeks bill was finally passed by the next Congress, on March 1, 1911.

The Weeks Law was a triumph for many citizens and groups of citizens, including J. A. Holmes and the great conservation organizations, inspired principally by the energy of Gifford Pinchot. Among the members of Congress,

the credit for sticking with the bill through all its defeats
and bringing it to final victory goes chiefly to the man from
the Boston banking firm of Hornblower and Weeks. Weeks
became a senator in 1913, but was defeated for reelection
in 1918. Later he was Secretary of War under Harding. His
son, Sinclair Weeks, became Secretary of Commerce in 1953.

The Weeks Law led to the creation of greater national
forests than the original dreamers had ever hoped. The federal-state cooperation clause that was inserted to quiet some
of the opposition turned out to be unexpectedly valuable.
To get the benefit of the federal subsidy a state had to have
a federally approved fire-protection system. The state's Forestry Department would spend the money, and the federal
Forest Service took over the job of inspection and advice.
The effect was a great stimulation of state fire-protection systems and the promotion of contributions from private owners to the cost of protecting their property. Within a dozen
years the recorded expenditures for fire protection rose from
$265,000 a year to more than $2,500,000, with the federal
contribution amounting to only one-eighth of the total. This
was the first federal aid law in which the government had
offered to contribute to state programs on a 50-50 matching
basis, and its success in stimulating state and local contributions in excess of 50 per cent was gratifying.

As to the constitutional issue, the Weather Bureau and
General Hiram M. Chittenden of the Corps of Engineers
had questioned the "direct and substantial" relation of upland forests to the behavior of navigable streams. These
doubts were calmly disregarded.

Woodrow Wilson, who came to the White House in 1913,
was a "liberal," but not an outdoor man nor one deeply
versed in the Roosevelt-Pinchot ideas on conservation. When
he appointed Franklin K. Lane of California, who was not
strong for conservation, as Secretary of the Interior, the war

between Pinchot, now a private citizen, and the Interior Department resumed its normal course.

Lane called attention to the numerous federal agencies working in Alaska and suggested that Alaska ought to be governed by an appointed board, whose members would live in the Territory and report solely to the Interior Department. This proposal was at first denounced by the Seattle businessmen, but later, as a correspondent reported to Pinchot, they embraced the idea, feeling confident that they could nominate friends to the board. Pinchot was not, of course, in favor of turning Alaska over to the Interior Department in cooperation with Seattle businessmen. Nothing finally came of Lane's proposal.

It was under Woodrow Wilson that the National Park Service was established, in 1916. There had long been national parks, starting with the Yellowstone in 1872, all created by Congress out of the public domain. Many of the parks contained good timber, some of it magnificent. There were perennial pressures from the lumbermen to get sections of the parks opened to "settlement" or transferred to the national forests, where cutting could be licensed. But the most dangerous and successful attack, one that was the turning point of national park history, was the Hetch Hetchy Dam project in 1913.

The Hetch Hetchy Valley in the Yosemite National Park was almost as beautiful as the Yosemite Valley itself, but San Francisco decided it wanted to build a reservoir there to supply water and power for the city. The project roused violent protests from nature lovers, led by the great naturalist, John Muir.

When the question of permitting this use of the national park came before Congress, the proponents of the dam argued that a beautiful lake would actually improve the valley. They even hired an artist to make pictures showing the expected beauties. John Muir replied with a scathing description of the future reservoir, of how in the summer "it would be gradually drained, exposing the slimy sides of the basin and the shallower parts of the bottom, with the gathered drift and waste, death and decay. . . ." That, in fact, is how it appears today, and people looking for camping places generally go elsewhere.

There was some confusion among the conservationists about the Hetch Hetchy. There were other less beautiful valleys where San Francisco could have found good water supplies. But the Hetch Hetchy Dam would be cheaper, and it would produce more hydroelectric power, a point that appealed to those who favored public power. The cause of the nature lovers suffered from the fact that the private power and water interests were fighting on their side, though from quite different motives. Besides, in those days the United States population was only 95 million, and the pressure for outdoor recreation space was not so great as it is today. It was hard for many of the devotees of conservation to see the time coming when Yosemite would be crowded and the lost Hetch Hetchy would be desperately missed. So, in the absence of a united opposition from the conservation forces, Congress in 1913 decided to let the dam be built, and it was built.

Once the valley was irretrievably spoiled there was a revulsion of feeling, and in 1916 Congress passed the act establishing the National Park Service. In the act Congress declared its purpose to preserve the natural beauties so as to leave them "unimpaired for the enjoyment of future generations." Never since that time has Congress let a dam be built in a national park, though there have been innumerable requests.

In 1918 the conservation of game birds took a notable step forward in the Migratory Bird Treaty with Canada, and the Migratory Bird Treaty Act by which the federal government took control of the hunting and protection of migratory birds. All other hunting is controlled by the states, though the Lacy Act of 1900 prohibited interstate traffic in birds killed for market. Under the treaty Canada and the United States were able to stop the spring shooting of wild ducks and other migrants.

This treaty, which under the Constitution transferred some powers from the states to the federal government, has always been a sore point with certain types of hunters, especially with those who are accustomed to use influence to modify or disregard with impunity the state game laws. It was the original cause of the attempted Bricker Amendment which would take away any such federal powers, leaving the government helpless to bargain with any foreign country on matters normally coming under state jurisdiction.

The Mineral Leasing Act was passed in 1920. Its purpose was to stop the sale of mineral lands from the public domain and instead grant leases, as proposed by the conservationists. The bill covered nonmetallic minerals, including oil, gas, coal, potash, phosphorus, sulfur, and soda. As originally written the bill did not allow leases in the naval oil reserves, which Wilson had set aside at the behest of Secretary of the Navy Josephus Daniels. Pinchot favored this bill until an amendment was tacked on to include the naval reserves, which were made subject to lease at the discretion of the Navy. Pinchot accused Lane, as a Californian, of favoring the amendment. The amendment was passed, and led some years later to the Teapot Dome affair.

In Woodrow Wilson's time the Forest Service ran into a controversy about federal regulation of forest practices that is still continuing in one form or another. By 1911 the people in the eastern part of the country were definitely worried about timber scarcity, and even some of the lumbermen had begun to think about the need for growing new timber. The Weeks Law stimulated federal-state cooperation for fire controls, helping to make tree-growing seem less risky. But Pinchot and his followers had no confidence in the ability or willingness of most of the forest owners to adopt sound cutting methods that would reproduce the forest. Pinchot was then and always for federal regulation of cutting on private land. To promote that cause he organized a Committee for the Application of Forestry.

On the other side of the argument was the American Forestry Association, whose president from 1916 to 1923 was Charles Lathrop Pack. Pack had made a fortune in southern pine and had decided to devote himself to the restoration of the forests. But he believed the states and private owners would do the job without federal compulsion.

Senator Arthur Capper of Kansas was on Pinchot's side. Early in 1920 he sponsored a resolution asking the Forest Service to make a full report on the forest resources of the country. The service had been collecting data, and Earle H. Clapp, in charge of research, was able to get out the Capper Report on June 1 of the same year. It was an impressive document, showing how the timber shortage was already troubling many industries and consumers.

The Republicans, who were destined to win the election in 1920, were evidently impressed with the importance of conservation. It had a place in their platform, and Warren G. Harding spoke of it in his "front porch campaign." As for Calvin Coolidge, nominated for the Vice-Presidency, he went down the line in good style. In his acceptance speech on July 27, Coolidge said:

"Diminishing resources warn us of the necessity of conservation. The public domain is the property of the public. It is held in trust for present and future generations. The material resources of our country are great, very great, but they are not inexhaustible. They are becoming more and more valuable and more and more necessary to the public welfare.

"It is not wise either to withhold waterpower, reservoir sites, and mineral deposits from development or to deny a reasonable profit to such operators. But these natural resources are not to be turned over to speculation to the detriment of the public. Such a policy would soon remove these resources from public control and the result would be that soon the people would be paying tribute to private greed. Conservation does not desire to retard development. It permits it and encourages it. It is a desire honestly to administer the public domain. The time has passed when public franchises and public grants can be used for private speculation."

Not all Coolidge's hopes were realized in Harding's Administration, but he at least was on the side of conservation.

Among the conservationists there continued to be dissension about federal regulation of forests.

On May 1, 1920, William B. Greeley had been appointed chief forester. He was more in sympathy with the lumber and paper men than with Pinchot. In the next few months he organized a National Forestry Program Committee representing the American Forestry Association and all branches of the industry. In December the numerous state foresters whose jobs had been created by the Weeks Law met at Harrisburg, Pennsylvania, and organized the Association of State Foresters. Pinchot spoke in favor of federal regulation, and Greeley took the other side, urging "control of fire and of cutting operations in the hands of the individual states under the leadership and with the financial and technical assistance of the federal government."

On December 22, 1920, Representative Bertrand H. Snell of New York introduced a bill embodying the ideas of the Greeley committee, with an authorization of $1,000,000 a year to subsidize the states in fire-control work. The Snell bill received wide support but made little progress in Congress.

Senator Capper, meanwhile, had introduced a bill embodying Pinchot's idea of federal control, but that also made no progress. Both bills were reintroduced in 1921 after Harding had come into office, and the argument went on, with neither Pinchot nor Snell winning.

Then Senator Charles McNary of Oregon entered the field in search of a program that everyone would accept. Everyone was agreed about fire protection by cooperative effort, already working well under the Weeks Law, so McNary started from there. In January, 1923, a Senate committee, with McNary as chairman, was appointed, and during that year it traveled around the country holding hearings. Harding died, and President Coolidge, in his first Message to Congress on December 6, called for more effective forestry legislation. The Senate committee reported in January, 1924.

The resulting Clarke-McNary Law, passed June 6, 1924, extended further the cooperation started by the Weeks Law. It enlarged the fire-protection work, provided for free distribution of seedlings for farm woodlots, and set up a forestry extension service to give advice to individual forest owners. There are now extension foresters in nearly all states and territories.

The Clarke-McNary Law was a victory for Forester Greeley and the idea of voluntary cooperation of federal and state forest services with private owners. Pinchot's belief, that without federal compulsion the majority of private forest lands would not be handled in such a way as to grow a good second crop has, to be sure, been confirmed by time. But the pressure of the industry, led by men who were prepared to practice forestry on their own lands, added to the natural prejudices in favor of states' rights, prevailed. Much progress followed the Clarke-McNary Act, especially in fire protection; but, as Pinchot had insisted, it fell far short of a satisfactory treatment of the whole national forest resource.

The constant pressure of Pinchot and his many ardent followers for government control was undoubtedly an important spur to the big forest owners, driving them to think seriously of putting their estates in order. The great Weyerhaeuser interests, for example, having done their share of devastation in the Great Lakes states and having moved to the Northwest, were already in 1920 consulting with David T. Mason, one of the strongest advocates of private sustained-yield forestry.

In 1928 the American Forestry Association—by that time closely affiliated with the industry—collected $200,000 and launched an educational fire-prevention program in Florida, Georgia, Mississippi, and South Carolina. Special trucks with films and lecturers visited the country schools, no matter how rutty the roads. The missionaries, called "Dixie Crusaders," also addressed women's clubs, 4-H groups, and the workers in lumber and turpentine camps. They traveled more than 300,000 miles before the drive ended in 1931. By 1933, when the CCC boys came to plant trees and fight fires, local sentiment had already changed in favor of trees and against those who set fires. Much of the later improvement in southern forestry and in wood-using industries is credited to this campaign of the Dixie Crusaders. The American Forestry Association reports that the State of Georgia, which was spending $18,000 of state money for forestry in 1928, had a forestry budget of $1,981,000 in 1955; its trained foresters had increased from six to sixty-one, and its area under fire protection had grown from less than a million acres to more than twenty million.

Only future history will show whether federal regulation of the forests in private hands will have to come. But at least there is evidence that pressure for federal regulation has been a stimulus to the adoption of good practices on many of the larger holdings.

In 1926 Earle Clapp, head of research in the Forest Service, published through the American Tree Association *A National Program of Forest Research*. This appeal led two years later to the McNary-McSweeney Act for the expansion of research. In particular the act authorized the Forest Service to make a comprehensive inventory of American forest resources. It has made several nation-wide reports since 1930 and many special reports for limited areas. The act also authorized nine regional forest experiment stations for the study of forestry problems.

By 1933, when the second Roosevelt came to power, bringing new vigor to governmental operations, the Forest Service was ready with expansive ideas. When the Senate called on it for a plan, it came forward with proposals for a large extension of public forest ownership and management, federal, state, and local. The time was still not ripe for federal regulation on private lands, but at least it could be applied to some lands by acquiring title to them.

During the interval between the two Roosevelts the Interior Department continued to nurse the hope that someday it might recover its lost forests, cruelly seized by Agriculture in 1905 through the machinations of Gifford Pinchot. And Interior wanted to take the Forest Service, too. Pinchot, though out of the federal service, never forgot to watch over his offspring and to defend it.

One of the earliest signs of the future conflict came in 1911 when the Secretary of Agriculture obtained a memorandum, probably written by Pinchot, giving detailed reasons for resisting such a transfer. Forests, it said, are a crop, classed under agriculture by colleges and foreign governments. Forest science depends on close contacts with other agricultural sciences, such as soil conservation, range management, and the control of insects and disease. As for the fact that the national parks and Indian reservations need forestry, that means only that they need to be in Agriculture. All lands needing government management should be in Agriculture, leaving to the Land Office of the Interior Department only those that need to be sold.

That was the doctrine. But behind it, of course, was the belief that the prudent management of public lands could not be had in Interior. This memorandum came after the Ballinger affair, but Pinchot's opinion of land management in the Interior Department had been low long before that. There was an attempt to promote a transfer under President Harding, when Secretary of the Interior Albert B. Fall persuaded the President that Interior ought to have the Forest Service and the national forests. Fall had been a stockman in New Mexico and felt that the Service had not given him all the grazing privileges he should have had. Pinchot went to see Harding, who freely admitted that he favored giving Fall the forests, but that he could not do it in face of the opposition that Pinchot was capable of stirring up. When Coolidge came to power he, too, was urged to transfer the Service, but found strong pressures against the transfer and refused to act.

When the depression came in the 1930s there was pressure on the government to find work for millions of the unemployed. And in 1933 came the second Roosevelt, who was naturally inclined to favor conservation. Many of the public works that he sponsored were designed to conserve forests, land, and water, as well as human beings.

Part Three

~~~~~~

1933 AND AFTER

Chapter 9

FORESTRY MARCHES ON

Franklin D. Roosevelt was a country landowner who loved trees. While he was thinking about how, if he became President, he would tackle the depression, his uncle, Frederic Delano, engineer and city planner, suggested the idea of hiring thousands of unemployed young men to plant and tend the forests. After the 1932 election, Gifford Pinchot sent F.D.R. a detailed memorandum on American forest conditions and needs, to which the President-elect replied that it was just what he wanted for a project that he had in mind. His project, which later took the form of the Civilian Conservation Corps, was first of all a forest enterprise, though it also spread out into soil conservation. It set forestry ahead many years.

The CCC lasted about ten years, until World War II wiped out the unemployment of healthy young men. During this period between 1933 and 1942 the Corps numbered between 300,000 and 500,000 boys, and they did much useful work. They planted or seeded about 2 million acres of forest and thinned nearly 4 million acres of overcrowded growth. They fought numberless fires, repaired half a million miles of fire-protection roads and trails, and built more than 100,000 miles of new roads. They cleared 56,000 miles of firebreaks. They fought the bark beetle, gypsy moth, and blister rust. Not only was their physical work useful, but the CCC boys were also a powerful educational force in behalf of good forestry.

The other thing that happened to the forests almost immediately was the NRA. The National Recovery Administration was a mistaken experiment in the "corporative state," as Mussolini called the Italian version when he carried it to its logical development as a system of government. Under the NRA business, labor, and government were to join in ruling industry by means of "codes," under which the leaders of industry and labor could unite to exercise monopoly powers over output, wages, and prices. The American instinct for free enterprise strongly resisted this unwholesome system, and in a couple of years the Supreme Court declared it unconstitutional. But the effect of NRA on forestry happened to be good and of far-reaching consequence.

As soon as the act was passed in 1933 the lumbermen met in Chicago to devise a lumber code. They wanted a schedule of minimum prices and a limit on the hours each sawmill could run. They knew the Administration would require a floor under wages as well as under prices. Greeley, the former Chief Forester, who was there, reports that he told the meeting: "President Roosevelt is almost certain to want something in this code on *forestry*. Let's beat him to the draw. It will help us get the rest." The others agreed, and the lumber code had an article committing the industry to cutting practices that would leave its cutover lands in good condition for reforestation.

The Forest Service was naturally gratified. The President received the lumbermen at the White House and beamed upon them. Everyone was happy. As Greeley says in his *Forests and Men,* it reminded him a bit of the mass baptism of armies of Franks and Gauls in the Middle Ages by simply having them wade through a river.

But simple as the baptism was, the lumbermen were so pleased with it that many of them really tried to do more tree growing. On the West Coast, for instance, they set up a Joint Committee on Conservation that published a *Handbook of Forest Practice*. It told in plain language how to leave seed trees in blocks that would not blow down, and how to keep fire out of the new growth. While the NRA lasted the lumbermen put strong pressure on lagging members to catch up with the code. By the time the Supreme Court killed the law many of the lumbermen had decided that good forestry was worth carrying on for its own sake.

In 1937 the Norris-Doxey Law was put through Congress at the instance of the Association of State Foresters with the help of the American Forestry Association. Their purpose was to expand the technical advisory services to individual forest owners and to encourage tree planting. The Administration favored the law mainly as a means of paying for the shelterbelt program, which had been limping along on relief money. During World War II the demands for lumber became so heavy that the Forest Service also sent men into the field in the Timber Production War Service. This action led to a conflict with the State Foresters, who considered direct service to forest owners as their exclusive job. Public technical service to private owners had come a long way from the time when Gifford Pinchot first activated the somnolent Bureau of Forestry by offering forestry advice to anyone who would take it.

A perennial regulation problem is that of grazing on the public lands. The Forest Service established from the start its right to regulate grazing in the national forests and to charge a small fee per animal, thus maintaining the principle that no one had a right to graze his cattle or sheep there without permission. The Land Office was much slower to set up a system of regulation for the unreserved public domain, which therefore became badly depleted and eroded.

When too many animals tramp over the land, the soil is compacted, less water can be absorbed and more runs off.

Small animals and birds that keep down insect pests are killed or driven away. The cattle or sheep crop the good forage plants too short, and with the loss of vegetation the soil starts to erode. Certain poisonous plants that are normally choked out by grass are found to spread if the range is overgrazed.

Once a range has been damaged, the cure is expensive. The vegetation must be built up, even at the cost of reseeding the land. Often the cure requires complete rest for some years, with no animals admitted, but in the end it is worth the cost. When the range has been restored to good condition a proper amount of grazing is good for it. It keeps the grass short and thus reduces the fire danger. In a forest, except when the young trees are small, the animals may do more good than harm. They keep down some of the plants that compete with the trees for water.

The moral is that grazing is a good use for most of the western lands, forested or not, but that someone has to watch over the different kinds of range and regulate how and when each area can be used. Cattlemen and sheepmen are often shortsighted and reluctant to limit their operations, but they make more money in the long run if they are not permitted to injure the range.

After many years of argument, the Taylor Grazing Act of 1934 gave the Interior Department the right to divide the open range into districts for regulated grazing. Some 140 million acres of public land thus came under regulation. With Indian and national forest lands the total federal range under control is more than 300 million acres. Some 60 million acres are in more or less well-regulated state and county lands, and about 375 million acres of range are privately owned. Many of the public and private lands are interlaced. Fencing is an improvement over the old-fashioned open range. By fencing, the cattle belonging to different owners can be separated and the owners can more easily be held responsible for whatever damage they may do to the range.

For many years the Forest Service has encouraged the stockmen to form local associations through which they can cooperate in range management and can take up any complaints about the regulations. In 1950 the Granger-Thye Act was passed, covering a number of "housekeeping" points in connection with the national forest ranges. At the insistence of some of the stockmen, a section of the act gave them the right to elect official local advisory boards, but not many have done so, and legalizing the advisory groups is reported to have made no appreciable change in the relations between the stockmen and the Forest Service.

Naturally some of the stockmen try from time to time to shake off government control. They make perennial attacks on the Forest Service, accusing it of arbitrarily locking them out of lush and nourishing feed that ought not to be wasted, and they are constantly trying to get the Interior Department's range lands turned over to them or to the states.

After 1933 the normal efforts of Interior to get possession of the Forest Service and its lands were intensified under the redoubtable Secretary Harold Ickes.

In 1934 when the Taylor Grazing bill was before Congress, Senator Henry F. Ashurst of Arizona proposed an amendment transferring the Forest Service to Interior. The amendment was later withdrawn but Pinchot and the American Forestry Association stood to their arms all that year, fearing a sudden raid.

In 1937, when the President was considering a reorganization of the government, his Advisory Committee, under the chairmanship of Louis Brownlow, recommended that the Interior Department should be renamed the Department of Conservation. Its job was to be (1) to advise the President on conservation and (2) to administer the public lands, national parks, Indian reservations, and Territories, and to enforce the conservation laws "except as otherwise assigned." Although the lands recommended to be controlled by In-

terior were only those that it already had, Pinchot suspected
that this might be a subtle attempt to prepare the Interior
Department to devour the Forest Service.

Mr. Brownlow has stated, however, that at that time there
was no thought of transferring any part of Agriculture to
Interior, but two years later, after the Reorganization Act
was passed, he took part in a discussion at the White House
in which a possible transfer was mentioned. But the President did not ask for Brownlow's advice on that point, and
he did not feel free to offer any.

There is a well-authenticated story that F.D.R. once called
in F. A. Silcox, the Chief Forester, and offered to make him
chief of a combined Forest and National Park Service, to
be located in Interior, but Silcox refused. F.D.R. seems to
have tried the idea at least one other time, on some of his
friends in Congress, who would have none of it. Ickes undoubtedly thought that Pinchot had a hand in this disap-
pointing outcome, in which he was correct. Pinchot and
many other friends of the Forest Service were using all the
influence they could muster.

The temptation for F.D.R. to move the Forest Service to
the Interior Department illustrates a common difficulty in
the government—the uneasy feeling that all recent presidents
have had, that if only they could get the sprawling federal
administration arranged in some logical system they could
make it more efficient and save a great deal of money. But,
as Charles Beard used to point out in the days of the Brownlow Committee, if an agency has four important features,
you can classify it according to any one of them and be three
times as wrong as right. It is this natural impossibility of
finding any perfect arrangement of agencies that leaves the
way open for various interdepartmental raiding expeditions.

Marion Clawson, head of the Bureau of Land Management of the Interior Department before 1953, points out
that in view of rising population and pressure on the land
more and more careful management of public and private

land is becoming necessary and some new institutions may be required. For example, the pressure for outdoor recreation is overloading the national parks and may have to be relieved, partly by steering tourists and campers to the national forests and other federal lands and partly by increasing the acreage of state and local parks. Forest management on both public and private land will have to be far more intensive, as it is in the crowded countries of Europe. Clawson is inclined to expect that a federal corporation may be found necessary to manage the public lands and provide an over-all coordination of land-use policies. In his opinion, if Gifford Pinchot were forty years old today he might well favor some such device for carrying forward the work of conservation under the new conditions.

The planting of shelterbelts, which had been started back in the 1880s, had a strong revival after 1933. The early shelterbelt plantings in the United States succeeded only in the most favorable locations, largely because of ignorance about what trees to plant and how they should be treated. When the second Roosevelt announced a great shelterbelt project there was naturally some skepticism among people who knew the prairie country, since their grandfathers had seen the plantings fail in so many places. Roosevelt's opponents were moved to ridicule. There were cartoons of F.D.R. pulling a rabbit from a hat and it was said that he thought he could make a tree where God couldn't.

The shelterbelts were planted within a strip of land about a hundred miles wide stretching from North Dakota to Texas. Each belt of trees was five to ten rows wide, with tall-growing trees inside and shorter trees and bushes to windward.

The main secret of making trees grow in the shelterbelt zone is to plant them with roots long enough to reach moisture in dry weather. East of the shelterbelt area, a seed falling on the land and sprouting may, with luck, get its roots down far enough so that it will not be killed by the next dry spell. West of this area there is not enough moisture except along the river bottoms to support a thrifty growth of trees at all. But in between, if the right kinds of trees and bushes are chosen, and are grown to the right size in the nursery, and then are protected from cattle by fences and cultivated to keep down weeds, they can flourish.

So long as there was public works money to spend, the shelterbelt program went ahead at a great rate. The landowners did most of the field work and undertook to care for the plantings; the government supplied the planting material and the supervision.

The management and research for this project were under the direction of Paul H. Roberts. Earle Clapp regards this as one of the best forestry jobs on record. The foresters had to overcome an extraordinary series of difficulties, including a run of dry years, but only about one-tenth of the plantings had failed by 1944.

The program lasted seven years, during which more than 200 million trees were planted on some 30,000 farms, making more than 18,000 miles of shelterbelt. Thereafter the fate of the plantings depended on the willingness of the farmers to cultivate them and keep the fences mended. In 1954 a survey found 18 per cent of the shelterbelts in poor condition, usually because cattle had been allowed to get in, and another 5 per cent had been entirely removed. The rest were flourishing.

The shelterbelt program was never on a sound financial basis since it depended on a kind of government help that was bound to be temporary. By 1937 the relief funds were rapidly diminishing and had to be pieced out by the Norris-Doxey Act. With the coming of the war the project was closed. But as the trees have grown and the farmers who took care of them have been rewarded by the benefits of their shelter, a considerable amount of new planting has occurred. More than 2,000 miles of new shelterbelt are reported to have been planted in 1955.

The increase of government spending in 1933 helped to speed the war of the Forest Service against insects and tree diseases. Fire, pests, and diseases take more than a tenth as much out of the forests as do all human uses and human waste. Some of the pests such as the bark beetle and the spruce budworm, and diseases like the white-pine blister rust, can do heavy damage over a wide area, even to the extent of wiping out a species. The fight to protect the forests has often been hampered by budget trouble, even after 1933.

For a time the CCC was able to fight the white-pine blister rust with some success by pulling up the wild gooseberry and currant bushes that harbor the disease. But in one part of West Virginia, after about $100,000 had been invested in getting an area half cleaned up, the money ran out and work had to be stopped, leaving the field to the enemy.

The chestnut blight was first recognized in 1902, and a fight was started but was lost because of a budget cut. Almost all the sweet chestnut trees in the eastern United States have died, but a new effort to restore them is under way. There are a few almost immune trees that still survive, with spots of blight but no sign of dying. The Department of Agriculture carefully saves the nuts from these trees and they are planted by the TVA and several experiment stations. In another fifty years a new blightproof race of chestnuts may be spreading across the land, if Congress provides the necessary money.

The new blights that challenge the budget makers include the Dutch elm disease and birch dieback in eastern Canada and the United States. One of the worst seems to be the oak wilt, which attacks all kinds of oaks. Diseases and pests may be more dangerous than fire as forest destroyers because they are hard to detect until they have already gained a wide foothold.

The most useful methods of fighting disease are quarantine, destruction of diseased trees, and the search for immune specimens. For insect pests, DDT is sometimes sprayed over the woods from airplanes, though with serious danger to the birds and insect-eating animals that are the regular defenders of the woods against the pests. There has been some success with the introduction of enemies that will eat the insects, and also with virus and fungus diseases that attack them.

Congress helped in 1937 and 1940 by authorizing federal funds to be used for fighting tree diseases on private lands. In 1947 the Forest Pest Control Act was passed, authorizing federal aid for surveys and for pest-control work on public and private territory.

Today the tendency is to look to further research and better forestry—such as cutting out weaklings that offer easy harborage to pests—and to the more intensive protection of valuable forests. So far there is little hope that scrub lands can all be treated, because of the expense. These areas will remain as reservoirs of bugs and diseases until someone is ready to plant them to real forests and put them under management.

Since the passage of the Clarke-McNary Law the system of fire protection has been greatly developed. In 1924 the Forest Service estimated that $10 million a year could be profitably spent on "adequate protection" for all state and private forest lands. The estimate in 1951 was $40 million, partly because of price increases but also partly because of new inventions that cost money but are worth the cost. The job is now mechanized with tank trucks, bulldozers, walkie-talkies, and parachutists to drop in where vehicles cannot go. As a result, tree farming has become more certain of profitable returns. There are even forests that can get fire insurance.

The foundations of the present-day tree-farm system were established when fire protection under the Clarke-McNary Law began to take hold, and as more and more states adopted the new forest yield-tax laws. Under a typical yield-tax law the landowner can register his cutover land for reforestation. His land is then taxed at a low rate as long as the trees are growing, and he pays a stumpage tax when they are cut. This system tends to reduce the pressure for premature cutting and puts a premium on restoration of cutover lands— that is, on tree farming.

About 1939 the Weyerhaeuser Timber Company had a tract of 120,000 acres of cutover fir land that would grow a new crop if fire could be kept out. They hunted for some way to persuade hunters and berrypickers not to start fires. A local newspaper editor suggested calling the land a tree farm, and putting tree-farm signs around it. He pointed out that people are not so likely to set fire to anybody's farm as they are to a mere piece of cutover berry patch. The company found that the name was effective, and with a small investment in fire protection the tree farm was profitable.

The Timbermen's Joint Committee on Forest Conservation took up the tree-farm idea and made a campaign of it. The committee set standards of continuous production and protection and offered certificates to owners who could pass inspection. Tree farming not only was profitable under the new tax laws and improved fire protection—it also was a way of avoiding the pressure for government regulation. Soon the National Lumber Manufacturers Association and the American Forest Products Industries were spreading the word. In each state some well-known agency, private or public, inspects the would-be tree farms and issues the certificates. By 1954 more than 30 million acres were registered in tree farms belonging to some 5,000 owners.

This seems like a goodly bit of land, but it needs to be

viewed in proportion. The Forest Service, for instance, is managing more than five times as much acreage as all the private tree farms combined, and private owners have more than ten times as much commercial forest land outside tree farms as inside. But it is a good start.

The lack of a market for small quantities of logs is an obstacle to the practice of good forestry on many small woodlots. In some areas there is no sawmill or other timber user within reach. In others the only available buyers will take nothing less than a license to clear-cut the woods all at once. But there are some encouraging developments. In some parts of New England, for instance, the farmers have formed cooperatives to dispose of selected logs from well-managed woods.

Another system for small woodlot owners is that of "pine tree banking," which was started in Arkansas by two former members of the staff of the Wisconsin Forest Products Laboratory. The farmer deposits his land in the "bank" where, with other deposited land, the total forest amounts to enough for sustained-yield cutting. And any one farmer who needs cash in a hurry can call up the bank and turn some of his trees into money.

The Forest Service itself has greatly increased its output of timber since it was first established. The first forest reserves were hastily withdrawn to save as much of the publicly owned forests as possible, but by then the most accessible forested lands had passed into private hands. Much of the reserved land was rugged and far from any road. Much of the accessible reserved land had been cut over. So, although it was always the policy of the Forest Service to license the cutting of ripe trees wherever possible, for a long time it was unable to sell enough timber to meet its expenses. Its enemies could easily accuse it of "locking up" needed resources, since a large part of its acreage was not being harvested because of lack of roads.

At present the picture is quite different. Stumpage prices have risen so high that it pays to go far in search of timber. Many of the needed roads have been built. In the year ending June 30, 1956, the Forest Service harvested 7 billion board feet, for which it received nearly $100 million, making a neat profit over all expenses.

According to law, one-quarter of the gross income from national forest timber is granted to the states, since they cannot tax federal land. In addition, the Forest Service provides fire protection, roads, trails, and other improvements that the state would have to supply if the land were privately owned. A study reported in *Land Economics* magazine for August, 1955, estimated that the states get about twice as much in money and services from this arrangement as they would if the property were privately owned and taxable.

There is good evidence that the forest resources of the United States have been improving since the Forest Service was established in 1905, and especially since the Capper Report of 1920. The rate of tree growth in the nation appears to have doubled since 1920, and it seems to be increasing. The growth of sawtimber was reported in 1955 to have almost caught up with the rate of drain from cutting, plus fire, insects, and other natural losses. On the other hand, it must be said that one reason the growth is catching up to the drain is that much smaller logs are today accepted as sawlogs. Another is that the timber famine that Pinchot predicted has long since caught up with the American people, and prices are high. The average American now thinks twice before buying the boards for a set of bookshelves, and when he does they are too often not what his grandfather would have used except in the barn.

As for small timber, we are doing better because it takes so short a time to grow. We now have a steady and increasing supply of pulpwood, mine timbers, and fence posts.

Most of the improvement has taken place on the large

landholdings, public and private. Many of the great lumber companies are practicing good forestry. They are growing new timber and are making more kinds of products, so as to use thinnings, weed trees, broken trees, and tops that in old days were wasted. They are severely guarding their woods against fire. As the companies who cannot change their old ways finally cut out and close down, their cutover lands are often bought by others who want to grow trees. The old-fashioned wasteful lumber baron seems to be passing from the scene.

The Forest Industries Council, defender of the lumberman, declared in 1944 for the following policies:

1. Practices on all forest lands to ensure the continuous production of timber.

2. Private ownership (rather than public) for all lands that can be profitably managed for continuous production of forest crops.

3. Public regulation when necessary or desirable, to be administered under state law; the need and scope of such regulation to be determined by the people of each state.

Gifford Pinchot would not have been satisfied with these policies, but the recommendations bear the marks of the hammer of Forest Service insistence on federal control. For the time being they represent an improved technical and moral position for an industry that fifty years ago had no observable scruples about the policy of cut out and get out. Even so, the organized lumber industry owns only a small part of the forest lands in the United States. The bigger part is in small, poorly managed woodlots.

There are changes still on the way, and how they will balance out only the future will show. The principal change is the rapid growth of the United States population. Fifty million more people in this country, in the next twenty years, will need at least 12 million more houses. Their cities, suburbs, and roads will occupy more space. They may even need to clear some forest land to grow food, unless farming efficiency keeps ahead of the demand.

Additional pressure can be expected from a continued rise in living standards, calling for more raw materials per person to make the things people want. On the other hand, the present scarcity of sawtimber and the high price of sawn lumber will probably lead to more substitutions and reduce the relative demand for lumber. We have already almost entirely given up wooden boxes for packing and substituted corrugated paper. We use steel and concrete in many places where our ancestors used boards and planks. That change will probably go further.

Technology, which has already given many new paper and plywood substitutes for sawn lumber, will go on finding uses for small trees and for species that have not previously been used. These technical changes will open the way for cleaning up millions of acres of scrub forest and bringing it into production of more useful material.

Chapter 10

SOIL CONSERVATION

~~~~~~

"Thou shalt inherit the Holy Earth as a faithful steward, conserving its resources and productivity from generation to generation. Thou shalt safeguard thy fields from soil erosion, thy living waters from drying up, thy forests from desolation, and protect thy hills from overgrazing by thy herds, that thy descendants may have abundance forever. If any shall fail in this stewardship of the land, thy fruitful fields shall become sterile, stony ground and wasting gullies, and thy descendants shall decrease and live in poverty or perish from off the face of the earth."—Walter Lowdermilk, in a radio address, Jerusalem, 1939.

Soil erosion in the United States began to attract wide public attention after 1933. Most of the American people had never known about the work of George Washington and Thomas Jefferson to halt soil erosion in Virginia. They had been deaf to occasional voices of protest and warning, such as that of George Marsh in the 1860s, pointing out the growing gullies in Georgia and Alabama. There was always new land to the westward. It was the forests that drew the earliest attention, mainly because their destruction was more spectacular, especially in the great fires. Gullies, too, can be spectacular, but the bad ones were local disasters that few people ever saw or heard about.

Yet a few scientists in the Department of Agriculture were quietly studying soil erosion. Dr. Hugh Bennett, who under the second Roosevelt was to become head of the Soil Conservation Service, began to survey soils under the old Bureau of Soils in 1903, and for twenty-five years he tried without success to arouse interest in the destruction that he saw going on. In 1928, however, the department issued a bulletin, *Soil Erosion a National Menace,* prepared by Bennett, which aroused some comment, and in 1929 Congress appropriated some money for soil conservation research.

With this money Bennett set up ten research centers. There began the first scientific study ever made of soil conservation. The experiment stations developed several new techniques, including strip cropping, and grassed waterways to dispose of surplus runoff. But the depression had started and until Roosevelt was elected there was no money for a program of action.

The new President was less familiar with soil problems than with forests. But he was easily persuaded that soil conservation was a good cause, and he established the Soil Erosion Service in the Interior Department on September 19, 1933, with Hugh Bennett as its Director. One state agricultural college, Wisconsin, sent some of its men to help Bennett get started.

Secretary Ickes, who was also head of the Public Works Administration, gave Bennett an allocation of $5 million of public works money, soon followed by another $5 million, and by spring of 1934 Bennett had his men out on the land helping farmers to lay out terraces, build dams in the gullies, and install other conservation practices. The small force of technicians began with those farmers who were ready to cooperate, and they liked the program.

Congressmen began to hear praise of the conservation work. After accepting another $10 million from Ickes in 1934, Bennett refused a suggestion from Congress that he come and get $125 million. For there were not enough trained men to use that much money without danger of poor work and washed-out structures, and he declined to overextend himself.

By 1935, however, Congress was back in its normal state of resistance to increased appropriations. Then came a day when Bennett had to go before a Senate committee and ask for extra funds to swing his young organization into a war against the advancing dust bowl. There had been stories in the papers about the dust storms and about how the farmers were moving out. But many of the senators came from states where wind erosion was no problem. They were more worried about erosion of the federal budget and seemed none too eager to accept the recommendations of this bureaucrat.

Hugh Bennett was in the position of Moses when Pharaoh refused to let his people go: he needed a miracle. Sure enough, as he sat at the hearing the sun over Washington was blotted out by a great western dust cloud.

Bennett stood up before the senators. He pointed out the window and said: "There, gentlemen, goes part of Oklahoma now." And there they saw it, driving past on the wings of the wind.

He got the money, and his men went out to fight the marching desert. They showed the remaining dust-bowl farmers how to replant the land with buffalo grass and other hardy grasses, and even, if necessary, with weeds, and how to cut the sorghum high on the stalk so that the stubble would shield the land from wind. When the dry period came again in the high plains, ten years later, those rescued lands held firm. The dust blew from other lands, farmed by men who had not learned what the soil conservation experts had taught years before.

The dust storms illustrate one of the common reasons for soil erosion—the wrong use of land, especially the raising of crops where the climate and soil call for grass. Wheat can be grown on the high plains in good years, and if the price of wheat is high the profit may be large. But there will be dry years. In the dry part of the cycle the wheat on sandy soils fails to hold against the wind. This land would have stayed in place under grass, if not overgrazed.

Grass is often the best medicine for land that when cultivated suffers erosion by either wind or water. In the southeastern states, for instance, the crops causing the most erosion are corn (maize), cotton, and tobacco. These are row crops with bare soil between the rows and between the plants in the rows; they do not protect the land against washing. Much of the soil conservation in those states consists of techniques for getting the row crops off the more sloping land and replacing them with grass or trees.

Another common cause of soil erosion is deforestation, especially when the cutover land is burned. Much harm is also done in the United States by road building because of the tendency of road engineers, with generous appropriations to spend, to cut through hills when they could go over or around. Many a hill has been undercut, drained of groundwater, and exposed to the danger of gullies by engineers who thought of nothing except to smooth the way for higher traffic speed.

These various causes of erosion, together with the many different varieties of soil, slope, and climate, create complicated problems for the conservationists. Some problems are entirely scientific, such as the spacing and grading of terraces, the art of planting in strips, and the choice of crops for different slopes and crop rotations. Others are economic, such as finding satisfactory ways to pay the cost of protecting the land owned by a marginal farmer. Others range from economic to political, including the irresponsibility of tenants and sharecroppers, and the powerfully organized demands of cattlemen and woolgrowers. It is not enough to recognize that all these forces and influences threaten the soil. The scientists have to know how to pinpoint exactly what needs to be done on each piece of land and how to get the landowner or tenant to do it.

The practice of soil conservation, in other words, is much like the practice of medicine. Medicine deals sometimes with simple injuries that can be treated with a bandage and some antiseptic, and sometimes it deals with cancer or tuberculosis, which are not so simple. Some of the rules of hygiene and first aid can be learned from a schoolteacher, but the common schools do not try to teach the pupils how to treat a major illness. Soil erosion may be a simple wound, or it may be a deep-seated wasting disease like tuberculosis or a devouring enemy like cancer. Most of the political troubles of the soil conservation movement have been caused by people who could not see any need for working experts but regarded soil conservation as merely an educational movement.

The Soil Erosion Service, when it got under way in 1934, made rapid progress. Hugh Bennett, Walter Lowdermilk from the Forest Service, and other men who had long been working on the causes and cures for erosion were able to lay out useful projects as fast as they could get the workers to carry them through. They took on the simplest kinds of work first, while they pushed ahead with needed research.

The Civilian Conservation Corps, with hundreds of thousands of young men available for unskilled labor, could be used for planting millions of seedling trees where they were needed for holding the soil. The Corps also built thousands of check dams of rocks and brush in gullies to catch the silt and stop the deepening of the wash, setting the program far ahead of what could have been expected by ordinary means. Much of this work was done on private as well as on public land.

When the dust started to blow, the soil experts recognized at once that they needed special dry-land grasses to replant those parts of the plains that should never have been plowed.

They set up nurseries to grow seed of the native western grasses that had supported the buffalo herds in the old days before the cattlemen and the wheat planters came. They found these old kinds of grass along railroad rights of way. They invented a sort of carpet sweeper to harvest the seed of these wild grasses and again got the CCC to help with the job.

This was something the experiment stations of the state colleges had not thought of doing, and they were not too happy to see the new Soil Erosion Service taking the initiative. Years later, when the Extension Service men allied to the state colleges came to power in the Department of Agriculture, one of their first acts in 1953 was to cut off the Soil Conservation nurseries, which were still engaged in finding and producing supplies of seed and seedlings for soil-holding work.

The original Soil Erosion Service, founded in 1933 in the Interior Department, was transferred to Agriculture in 1935 and renamed the Soil Conservation Service. In its early days the research was under the direction of a central staff attached to the Washington office. There was also an office in each state to do research and to direct the application of soil conservation practices in the state. But this system did not work well. Washington was too far away from the states to have the feel of local problems and there were not enough experts to man an effective scientific-engineering staff in every state.

The Service therefore moved most of its technical staff into eleven regional offices, later reduced to seven. These were close enough to the problems of their regions to handle them effectively, and they were few enough so that good men could be found to staff them. The regional offices not only served as effective centers for directing farm conservation planning and application, they also took care of the budgeting and accounting for the field service.

Although soil conservation from the first was "popular," there were plenty of backward farmers who thought it was a fad. A man who does not hold his own land can do great harm to his neighbors', either by sending down a flood of sand and gravel or by sending up a devouring gully from below, or both. The soil men expected trouble in persuading even the good farmers to adopt their methods unless they could be protected from bad neighbors. So, at the suggestion of Walter Lowdermilk, they recommended that the states authorize the farmers to form districts to handle the local aspects of the job, with police powers granted by the state to enforce whatever standards of conservation the majority in the district would adopt by democratic referendum.

President Roosevelt passed this recommendation along to the states, and they soon responded. The country is now well covered with soil conservation districts, except in a few states where the local Extension Service has worked successfully to prevent their formation.

In practice the police powers were not often found necessary. All the land is not yet under protection, but progress is good. The districts are organized to spread conservation ideas, to draw up agreements with the Soil Conservation Service for technical advice and with local contractors for construction work—and to put pressure on Congress whenever anyone attacks the program. The SCS is authorized to help the farmers with free advice from its experts and free maps of the cooperating farms. Since the first few years of introduction and demonstration most of the heavy work has been paid for by the farmers themselves.

In addition to this highly organized system the government has a more extensive but less definite line of subsidies, known as the Agricultural Conservation Program, for farmers who consent to adopt various conservation practices, such as changing sloping cornfields to pasture or woodlots. This system was adopted as a substitute for the original Agricultural Adjustment Administration of 1933, which had been set up to reduce farm surpluses by paying the farmers to plow under part of their cotton and slaughter little pigs. The Supreme Court declared the AAA unconstitutional in January, 1936, but somewhat the same effect was obtained by tying the payments to conservation, since most of the soil-destroying crops are the same cash crops that create market problems by being in surplus.

In essence, the "farm problem" in the United States is related to conservation mainly through the effect of government actions on the choice among various uses of land and upon the farmer's income and ability to pay for good practices.

Farmers naturally have a fluctuating income with a tendency to be lower than the average income of city people. If the farm is not profitable, the farmer cannot easily change his job. As a rule he has no other way to live except to go on farming. If prices fall, he cannot easily reduce his output as a businessman can do; he even has to plant more in the hope of making a living at low prices. So the farmers, except in wartime, usually get the worst of the bargain when they sell their crops and when they buy supplies. By these economic pressures they are often driven to plant the kind of cash crops that hurt the soil and to use for cash crops land that ought not to be so used.

The farmers have demanded government help to overcome their natural disadvantage in the market. The help has taken the form of price supports for certain staple crops that can be stored. The government buys enough to hold the price at an artificially high level. The farmers in return may agree to limit the acreage devoted to these crops, but then they can afford to pile on the fertilizer and produce more from fewer acres. The net effect is that the government holds large surplus stocks of many farm products. It cannot readily sell them or even give them away, at home or abroad, without upsetting markets and arousing strong protests.

As time goes on, perhaps the political situation may allow a more scientific handling of the farm price problem, and in that case the claims of conservation may be given more attention. Under President Eisenhower, in fact, the government showed a strong inclination to adopt two policies that would allow some consideration for saving the soil. Two earlier Secretaries of Agriculture had been associated with these policies, Charles Brannan and Henry Wallace.

The Brannan plan was to pay money to farmers directly in case of poor market conditions instead of helping them indirectly by a price support program. Consumers, especially the poorer ones, might then eat more, since the prices would not be raised artificially. Farmers entitled under the law to more money would get it directly, and other farmers would get none. The law would specify how a farmer would become entitled to a subsidy and in that way could have a purposeful influence on what kinds of farming would be worth carrying on. The rich farmers, who are now heavily subsidized by price supports, would get only what Congress found politically advisable to assign to them. The total cost to taxpayers and consumers would be less if the big farms were not allowed the full subsidy, and the government would not have to buy such awkward quantities of farm products.

Naturally there was powerful opposition to the Brannan plan, especially from the bigger farmers who benefit most by price supports. Though the Eisenhower Administration ventured to adopt it for wool, both political parties showed strong resistance against carrying it further. But if the Brannan plan could be combined with a well-designed soil conservation policy, strong pressure could be put on farmers to use their land only for purposes that do not injure the soil.

The Wallace plan, adopted in 1933, of paying farmers to take land out of use in order to limit production, is now known as the "soil bank" plan. It also could be directed toward conservation if well designed and administered. It could be a better-designed extension of the Agricultural Conservation Program, especially if combined with some form of Brannan plan so as to escape being too much governed by market requirements. These two plans, taken together, could provide a framework for a land-use control that in time would save most of the remaining soil. The Department of Agriculture has already made definite progress on a "soil capability" survey, showing the agricultural lands of the United States classified according to their best use. Such a classification is strongly advocated by Hugh Bennett as the basis for subsidies and for the withdrawal of lands from farming. The limitation of production could be worked in by squeezing or relaxing the limits of allowable use. Regulations for a "conservation reserve" were adopted in 1956 but were criticized by wildlife conservationists for failing to embody recommendations offered by the Fish and Wildlife Service.

In the meantime the price controls and the ACP payments could even now be better managed to discourage some well-known misuses of land, especially in the dust bowl section. In 1954 and 1955 there were signs in the Department of Agriculture of a demand that farmers who put the dry lands to uses that promote wind erosion should be cut off from all subsidies. The rough system of acreage limitation in connection with price supports has been criticized because of the absurd acreage allotments allowed on many farms in the dry areas. If the farm was ever used for wheat in the past it became legally entitled to plant wheat thereafter, with a subsidy, in spite of well-known dangers to the soil. The Soil Conservation Service has long wanted the right to veto allotments for wrong uses, the legal basis of which was merely a history of wrong uses in the past. A Great Plains Program designed to meet these requirements was adopted by Congress in 1956, and its administration was assigned by the Secretary of Agriculture to the Soil Conservation Service.

Finally, there have always been some lands going into public ownership because the farmers could not make a living and had to let them go for taxes. Most of those lands probably need to be forested and kept in public ownership. Some other marginal lands not yet tax delinquent could well be purchased, releasing the farmers to go to other jobs in agriculture or in the towns where they would be more productive. Federal and state money could be used in the retirement of such lands, since the local communities may be too poor to handle them usefully.

It appears possible that at some future date the improvements in agricultural technology may fall behind the growth of population. If that happens, it will take more land to feed the population, and the surplus problem will gradually be replaced by scarcity problems even in the United States.

City people often shrug off the idea of future scarcity by a vague trust that science can always keep ahead of the birth rate no matter what it may be. They think that we can grow food in tanks or comb plankton out of the ocean with some kind of domesticated or mechanical whale. It is true that science is wonderful and that conservationists have sometimes predicted early disasters only to be contradicted by some unexpected invention. No one can safely belittle the future triumphs of science, but that fact is a poor excuse for waste of resources that future science may want. Even synthetics have to be made out of something.

Hydroponics, the growing of food in tanks, is still a disputed subject. One expert writing for the *UNESCO Quarterly* says that large cities, such as New York and Calcutta, can grow all their vegetables in tanks, leaving the land farms to grow the cereals. He also believes that hydroponics will solve the food problem of India. On the other hand, the U.S. Department of Agriculture calls attention to the high cost of the tanks—$25,000 an acre or more—and the great technical skill required for operating them. The department seems to believe that at present tanks are appropriate only where the cost of bringing in fresh vegetables is unusually high, as, for instance, on a barren Pacific island used as an airline landing or a weather station.

From the viewpoint of conservation the chief objection to tank agriculture is that the plant food has to be all "store-bought." The necessary chemicals are dissolved in the water and are absorbed and carried away by the crops. Such chemicals usually come from mines where nature has concentrated the material in workable ores. The nitrates, to be sure, may be produced with electric power, but most of the power comes from coal or oil, which are not renewable resources.

Vegetables grown in a field, on the other hand, collect most of their chemicals from scattered particles in the soil that cannot be gathered for human use by any other known means at a reasonable cost. It is true that even for field farming the phosphate and potash fertilizers come from mines, but they are supplemented by phosphate and potash from the underlying rocks. Nitrates can be grown by plants in the field with no power but sunlight; plants collect not only scattered minerals but scattered sunpower. Sunlight can be collected for human use by mirrors and other mechanical devices, but only at a high cost.

The distinction between mining concentrated deposits of material to be scattered by use and cultivating organisms that collect scattered material not otherwise available to man is the same as the distinction between the use of "nonrenewable" and "renewable" resources. Nothing can be more inconsistent with prudent management of world resources than to invent ways of growing food entirely by using concentrated minerals that once used are dissipated forever, instead of growing it out of soil that is largely renewable and sunshine that comes new each morning.

Those who favor soil conservation point out that we do not yet know all about the chemical elements needed for health or about the biological conditions necessary for their effective use as food. The chance of getting everything that nature demands is better if we eat a variety of foods grown in many different soils than if we use a tank and supplement the plain water with those elements we know to be required. Knowledge increases, but there have been bad effects, too, from clever inventions, for example, that gave the people soft white bread with the nourishment left out.

In spite, therefore, of the contempt of those who look to science to feed countless billions of people with miraculous loaves and fishes, the devotees of conservation insist on trying to save as much soil as possible. In the United States they have good prospects of success, though not without a struggle.

Soil conservation is concerned not only with future supplies of food and fiber; it is also necessary as one factor in the protection of water supplies and in river management.

Groundwater from wells is widely used in the United States, and in many places it is used to excess. The wells have to draw from ever deeper and deeper levels, indicating that the underground reservoir is not being replenished as fast as it is being emptied. This situation is common in western lands that are irrigated from wells. If excessive pumping is continued too long, some land has to be abandoned because of the high cost of pumping or because of lack of water. In several coastal areas where the groundwater has been drawn down below sea level, salt water has come in.

As yet there is only scattered information about the whole American groundwater supply and the importance of falling levels in different places. But it is clear that with a growing population there will be more and more cases where the underground reservoirs cannot meet the demand for water.

Water seeps underground by various channels. Some of it leaks in from rivers, lakes, and swamps that have underlying beds of sand or gravel. Other bodies of water, with clay beds, may not leak at all. A large amount soaks down from forests and grasslands after the surface soil has become saturated. Not so much goes underground from cultivated fields, because the soil is easily stirred up by the rain and the muddy water seals the holes in the soil and then runs off over the surface. Terracing and contour plowing help to hold the water in the fields after a rain, and more of it has time to soak in. Soil conservation and forestry, therefore, are the principal ways of artificially increasing the amount of groundwater. There are other devices such as "spreading basins," where floodwaters are given time to soak in; they are used in some parts of California. But the main source of groundwater that can be improved by human action is the land where soil conservation and forestry need to be practiced.

The other most vital connection of soil conservation with water engineering is based on the growing need to keep silt from eroding land out of the rivers. Many dams that were built a generation ago with no thought of soil erosion in their watershed are now full of mud and of no further use as reservoirs. As more and more dams are built, the need for keeping the silt out becomes better known to the public. Mud does many other kinds of damage, such as killing fish and blocking river channels and harbors.

Early in 1936 the government published *Little Waters,* by Dr. Harlow S. Person, an industrial engineer who had much to do with giving form to the conservation movement of that period. Person had been acting as chairman of a Water Planning Committee of the National Resources Committee. His book put into readable form the facts about erosion along the headwaters of the streams and described what could be done to hold both land and water on the high ground. It has had an important influence on present-day thinking about soil conservation, water conservation, and flood control.

One result of this modern way of thinking has been that the Soil Conservation Districts have been promoting legislation to help them organize small-watershed projects for applying a coordinated program of conservation to a whole stream basin of small size. There have been many delays but by 1955 a few watersheds were under treatment. The New England floods of August, 1955, during the unprecedented rains of hurricane Diane, aroused interest in small-watershed management all over the country, for the worst damage was suffered in small valleys that discharged their runoff through the middle of some old mill town.

The soil conservation people point with pride to the valley of Sandstone Creek in Oklahoma, a fully treated valley that took a 9-inch rain in May, 1955, without a trace of flood. Whatever stops or greatly reduces the floods in little tributary valleys will stop most of the mud from getting into the great dams on the main streams, and nothing else will do it.

The opposition to soil conservation work differs from the opposition to forestry and grazing control in the fact that it arises not from business interests but from interagency conflicts. The Soil Conservation Service is resented by many of the state agricultural colleges and members of the Agricultural Extension System, with their political ally, the American Farm Bureau Federation. These educational institutions have a long and honorable history of spreading knowledge among American farmers. Their county-agent system is being widely imitated abroad in connection with Point 4 and the UN Technical Assistance Programs, for they are credited with much of the spectacular increase in the American farm output during the past hundred years. But many of their leaders have not grasped the complex technology of soil conservation, and they have resented having SCS agents telling the farmers what to do, in competition with their own county agents. They have preferred to believe that soil conservation is only a kind of education and that it therefore properly belongs in the agricultural education system.

In the late thirties the Extension Service men presented a

complete plan to the Secretary of Agriculture, Henry Wallace, to "make the conservation program move faster" by relieving Hugh Bennett of some of the arduous details and leaving him free to write and plan. All they proposed was that the appropriations and the field men be transferred to Extension. Bennett made a speech to Secretary Wallace about how the land-grant colleges had never offered him any help during his twenty-five years of lonely struggle, and he foresaw the same kind of energetic neglect of conservation if they should be given charge of it now. Wallace thought it over and turned thumbs down on the plan. He said it reminded him of the perennial efforts of the Interior Department to get the Forest Service.

In 1940 the Farm Bureau Federation declared that "the Extension Service should be responsible for the administration of the Soil Conservation Service."

The Farm Bureau and Extension Service men came to realize that if they ever should succeed in taking over soil conservation the regional offices would be an indigestible lump. There were no corresponding Extension offices into which the regional conservation staffs could be absorbed. Moreover, the regional staffs were giving scientific services that did not fit in with the kind of simple education work the Extension men proposed to do, by which the farmer would learn to treat his own land out of a pamphlet. So they felt that the regional offices had to be abolished. The Soil Conservation Districts were just as indigestible. In 1948 a bill in Congress to transfer the SCS to Extension was defeated by protests from the districts. That proposal and its defeat brought about a state of open war between Extension and the districts.

Extension came to power in 1953, for the new Secretary of Agriculture and all his principal assistants were Extension men by origin. They obtained a presidential plan giving the department full authority to reorganize itself, and Congress let the plan go into operation without exercising its right of disallowance. By September, 1953, the district leaders could sense that the reorganization was going to be painful to them. Waters Davis, head of the National Association of Soil Conservation Districts, led a delegation to Washington. When the plan for the SCS was announced on October 13, they were stunned.

The plan abolished the regional offices. It eliminated, at least in its first version, the specialists on agronomy, range management, woodland management, and wildlife, and scattered the remaining scientists among the states or pulled them in to Washington. No such thing as an organized soil conservation research program would be permitted. If anyone could organize his own knowledge well enough to discover the need for a piece of new research he could try it on a general research organization set up by the department or could shop around among the state colleges. The nurseries were abolished or transferred. Free map making was abolished, leaving it for the farmer to decide whether or not he wanted to pay for a map. If he could not see the need, the work could suffer accordingly.

The soil men were roused to fight. The districts put pressure on their congressmen. Hugh Bennett, who had retired and had become consultant to various Latin-American governments, rose in wrath and toured the country making speeches calling people to the rescue of soil conservation.

There was enough public response to lead to some softening of the attack. Secretary Benson declared that he had no desire to hurt soil conservation. All he wanted was to streamline it and bring it closer to the people, and he was not trying to combine it with Extension. Some of the dismissals of scientists were canceled.

But the regional offices were abolished nonetheless and Bennett was not pacified. In January, 1954, he published an article in the *Country Gentleman* entitled "They've Cut the Heart Out of Soil Conservation." Congressmen heard from home, and when they found that the proposed budget cut the funds for the SCS and increased those for Extension, they refused to go along. They shifted the items back. They also put back the item for free maps.

Early in July, 1955, President Eisenhower's Commission on Intergovernmental Relations issued its report, which plainly showed a reluctant yielding to public opinion. The majority recommended keeping the SCS "as presently organized," except that if any state should submit a satisfactory plan for taking over the program it might be allowed to do so, with grants in aid from the federal government. The report disclaimed any intention of merging the SCS into the Extension program at the state level. But eight members of the commission—senators, congressmen, and governors—strongly dissented. They wanted no tampering with the SCS at all.

At about the same time the Hoover Commission turned in its report on water and power, which recommended that upstream engineering be turned over to the Corps of Engineers of the Army. Both these reports, however, were taken calmly by the conservation men, as not likely to gain impressive support. In 1956, when the Army openly opposed the upstream program of the Soil Conservation Districts, the reaction was so strong that it hastened to camouflage its opposition in the form of suggested amendments designed only to cripple the program. These were defeated.

As early as 1955, when the Secretary of Agriculture announced the membership of an Advisory Committee on soil and water conservation, the official paper of the National Association of Soil Conservation Districts expressed pleasure at the composition of the committee. Most of the members were found to represent soil conservation districts or other conservation organizations.

A good summary of recent thought among soil conservation leaders is found in a list of their demands in the Great

Plains, as given by the president of the NASCD, in an interview with *Capper's Farmer,* published in March, 1957:

> Great Plains Conservation Leaders Want—
> Completion of soil survey and land classification of the Great Plains.
> More research on soil and water conservation.
> More aggressive campaign to acquaint farmers with proved methods of erosion control.
> Administration of Great Plains Conservation Program thru local soil conservation districts.
> Spreading of conservation payments for re-grassing cropland over a period of years in amounts to permit economic changes in land use.
> Change from present method of making acreage allotments which penalizes conservation farming.
> Long-term, low-interest credit to keep experienced practical farmers on the land.

The soil conservation program seems to be well rooted and capable of continued growth. For the population is increasing and, as the pressure grows, the need for saving the soil is likely to be more widely recognized every year.

Chapter 11

WATER, FLOODS, AND NAVIGATION

The problems of river use and water engineering came to the attention of the American people in reverse order of their present importance. Navigation was the first use of the rivers when the Europeans first arrived, for there were no roads, and on a broad river the explorers could penetrate far into the country with some protection from hostile Indians. As the country opened up, canals, rivers, and harbors preceded railroads in the "internal improvements" of the early nineteenth century. Still later, flood control began to take on increasing importance with the growth of cities and farms in the flood plains. Finally, with the increase of population and the development of modern industry, pollution and water scarcity became the most serious water problems.

The recognition of river management as a general problem of the United States began with Theodore Roosevelt's Inland Waterways Commission, which was so closely connected with the beginnings of conservation itself. Traditionally, before that time, however, individual river works had been chosen by Congress on political grounds, and there is still a strong tendency for Congress to decide on river projects for political reasons, although Congress takes the technical advice of the Corps of Engineers and has the Corps manage the construction.

The Corps of Engineers is the elite body of the Army, and takes only the highest ranking graduates of West Point. The Corps often calls itself "The United States Engineering Department" and also "the engineer consultants to, and contractors for, the Congress of the United States."

As a rule the Corps does not originate projects. A project is promoted by local interests and sponsored by their representative in Congress. After the congressman has obtained legislative approval for the Engineers to examine his proposals, the Army's local district engineer holds a hearing. The congressman and his constituents attend and submit their plans. The engineer can refuse a project as impracticable, for the Corps will not agree to build dams that may wash away. If the district engineer endorses the project, it is then checked at the higher echelons, and finally the Chief of Engineers may recommend it to Congress. Congress usually authorizes what the Corps recommends.

Conservationists are inclined to believe that the Engineers want to build things, whether a comprehensive river-development plan would include those things or not. They are therefore quick to attack the Corps at every weak point. For instance, they note that, though the Engineers' reputation as builders is good, the cost of Army construction has notoriously outrun the estimates. Congress has to put up the money for the deficit, since once a dam is begun it is a great waste of money not to finish it.

The Army's methods of justifying a project also have been criticized. The Engineers have been accused of justifying a navigation project by comparing the cost of shipping by water and by rail at the existing railroad freight rates, without looking at possible alternatives. The Youngstown "stub" canal, for instance, was recommended by the Engineers to haul coal for the steel mills. But Frederic Delano, then chairman of the National Resources Board and an old railroad man, found that the Interstate Commerce Commission could cut the rates on coal haulage by rail, which it did, making the canal unnecessary. It took six years to work out this solution after the Corps had recommended the job on the basis of a simple comparison of the railroad rates with estimated costs by water. In another case, the Engineers are reported to have recommended improving five competing harbors on the Florida coast. They justified each project on the basis of increased traffic that they estimated each harbor could get with its improved facilities—but only by taking business away from the other four.

Since Theodore Roosevelt's time the conservationists have wanted unified management of the river basins, to bring into use all the resources as harmoniously as possible. Such unified planning cannot be done by Congress; it has to be done by an authority or agency responsible to the Executive Branch of the government. Conservationists are inclined to take the side of the Executive whenever it is trying to establish unified river management and are opposed to purely local water projects that do not fit into a general river-use plan. Even when the Corps of Engineers plans a whole stretch of river at one time, with dams, locks, and levees in a well-designed order, the conservationists, on the basis of past experience, are afraid that these plans for navigation and flood control may fail to conserve other resources of the river, such as irrigation or waterpower.

By force of circumstances, the Engineers, whose job is to advise Congress, are in political fact the employees of Congress rather than of the Commander in Chief who sits in the White House. Conservationists are therefore generally opposed to the position of the Engineers in the governmental framework and are in favor of the efforts of the Executive to get more control of them and cut off their direct contact with the Congressional committees.

Congress, on the other hand, while not by any means wholly devoted to strictly local public works, is inevitably influenced by the pleas of members who are under heavy pressure to get approval of projects wanted by the home folks. There is also the traditional conflict between Congress and the Executive, resulting from the constitutional separation of powers. Congress, accordingly, has long resisted the Executive's attempts to divide it from the Engineers.

The story of the unsuccessful struggle of successive administrations to control the Corps of Engineers is long and complicated, but a summary of some of the high points will help to show why river management has been so slow to come.

In 1907 Theodore Roosevelt's Inland Waterways Commission recommended a Water Resources Authority. The only dissent came from the Chief of Engineers, who said it was premature, if not impractical—as it may have been at the time.

Senator Francis Newlands of Nevada, who has been called the father of reclamation, pushed repeatedly for a water resources planning commission, with the support of Presidents Roosevelt, Taft, and Wilson, but Congress would not create it. After 1933 the independence of the Corps of Engineers was attacked by F.D.R., the National Resources Planning Board, and the Bureau of the Budget, but the Corps appealed to Congress, and Congress stood by it.

In 1934, when F.D.R. was discussing general river planning in the Cabinet, Secretary of War George Dern said the Engineers could do any planning needed. Dern referred to the Corps as "acting in pursuance of law as an agency of the Legislative Branch," implying that what they did was no business of the President's. Congress, for its part, in passing various flood-control acts even at the height of F.D.R.'s power, pointedly ignored the Executive Branch. F.D.R. tried to make the Corps submit its projects to the Executive Office of the President before taking them to Congress, but the Corps insisted on recommending work to Congress even when notified that it was contrary to White House plans. Out of the 436 reports to Congress by the Corps favoring construction projects from 1941 to 1948, almost 10 per cent (42) were for projects that the White House had held to be contrary to the President's program. The Corps, nevertheless, recommended these disapproved projects and Congress passed nearly all of them.

In January, 1937, Roosevelt asked Congress for authority to reorganize the Executive Branch. Congress gave him an act with a proviso that exempted the Corps from any reorganization.

In 1945 President Harry S. Truman asked Congress for a Reorganization Act with no exemptions, but Congress provided in the act that the Corps must not be touched. The first Hoover Commission, set up under this act, recommended in 1949 that all water engineering should be consolidated in one Water Development Service, which the majority of the commission wanted to locate in the Interior Department. Nothing came of the commission's recommendation. Both President Truman and ex-President Herbert Hoover expressed themselves strongly about the resistance of the Corps to reorganization.

In recent years the Engineers are reported to be more inclined than in the past to give full consideration to all water uses, but it may take a long time for the traditional hostility of the conservationists toward the Engineers to fade away.

Meanwhile, the river waters of the United States are showing less and less ability to meet the demands made on them, even in the wetter parts of the country. The people of New York City had a lesson on water scarcity in the winter of 1949–50. A dry summer and autumn had left their reservoirs so far below normal that in December they were down to a two months' supply. New Yorkers managed to cut their use of water by one-quarter for a while, and got by without having to send crowds of people out of the city. But the publicity required to make New Yorkers use less water called their attention to the fact that it does not just naturally flow from faucets. Someone has to make the water run up out of the cellar to the faucet, and that someone may be far off in the mountains. Fortunately the forests in the Catskills are fairly well preserved and brooks there do not all dry up in dry weather, or the crisis would have been worse.

Twenty years from now, with another fifty million people in the country and fewer of them living in houses without plumbing, we can expect a real strain on the household water supplies in the eastern part of the United States as well as in the West. After that, if the population goes on growing, lack of water can be expected to be more and more the factor that limits where people can live.

The bulk of the water in the well-settled river valleys has to be used over and over on its way downstream. Along parts of the Ohio, at low-water stages of the river, about one-quarter of the flow has come out of sewers higher up. After purification and disinfection this liquid is sent through the city mains to be used for drinking and washing. Industrial wastes complicate the problem of purification; sometimes there will be an epidemic of poisoning from drinking water that is germ-free but contains too many chemicals.

Instead of taking a highly polluted river, filtering out the sewage, and doping the remainder with chlorine before drinking it, a better way is to treat the sewage before letting it run into the river. Sewage can be fermented in a treatment plant, yielding a sludge that when dried makes an inoffensive and valuable fertilizer. This is a sanitary way for a civilized community to salvage the mineral values that food crops have removed from the soil and to put them back on the land without infecting the next crop with disease germs. It costs money, and as a rule the sludge will not sell for enough to pay for the whole cost of the treatment. But something can well be paid for keeping the river clean, so that fish will live in it and so that people can sail boats on it without getting typhoid from the spray.

Some industrial wastes can also be kept out of the river by disposing of them inside the plant. This also is liable to be expensive, but the salvaged material often has some value.

A distillery, if forced to stop dumping its used grain in the river, may find that it can be sold for cattle feed. Paper mills often poison the streams and kill the fish, but their wastes have been found to have some uses—in making yeast, for instance. Scientists are still working to find profitable uses for lignin, the natural glue that holds the fibers of the wood together and one of the worst elements in paper-mill pollution.

Although science is trying to discover how all sorts of wastes can be utilized so as to pay for keeping them out of the rivers, scientists are working even harder to invent new synthetics and other chemicals. Some of the new processes give off wastes that are vicious and untreatable. Sometimes the only way to keep a river from being hopelessly poisoned is to keep the factory from being there at all.

A city gets practically no benefit from treating its own sewage, and a manufacturer may have no objection to spoiling the water for his rival downstream. But all concerned could enjoy the benefits of a pure water supply if all concerned would stop polluting the rivers, although few will act unless everyone has to act. That sort of situation is what government is for, and it must be a big enough government to cover the situation.

Most progress on cleaning up rivers was made during the depression when the Public Works Administration had money to lend and grant to cities for sewage-disposal plants. It was reported that the pollution in the lower Hudson River had so diminished that shad even began finding their way back in appreciable numbers. But a survey of the country in 1948 showed that more than two cities out of five were still discharging raw sewage into streams and that more than half the industrial plants producing poisonous wastes failed to treat them. In 1956 Congress passed a new Federal Water Pollution Control Act, authorizing $50 million a year for grants to states, interstate agencies, and municipalities to aid pollution control. The act offers support for research and federal technical assistance as well as for construction of sewage disposal works. Under this act the federal government can prosecute anyone who pollutes a stream, with the consent of the state where the pollution originates, or without its consent at the request of a downstream state that is affected by the pollution.

The growing scarcity of good water is bringing more and more urgency into the problems of water rights—the right to draw water from the streams, or even from wells. In the eastern states the English law prevails, under which the right to take water from a stream belongs to the owner of property along the bank. In the West the law comes down from Rome through Spain. There the water belongs to the man who first takes it for beneficial use; human and agricultural uses take priority over mining and industry. There is some overlapping of the two kinds of law, and in detail the rights are extremely complex. So far most of the legal problems have arisen in connection with irrigation, since the West is full of rich land that needs only water to be highly productive.

In the East, where cities, industry, and now irrigation projects are competing for water, the conflicts of rights are bound to grow more troublesome. The western law of the right of the first comer is bound to spread eastward, as cities, industrial concerns, and farmers go to court to claim a vested right to continue getting as much and as good water as they have had in the past. It seems certain that there will be less and less free water to be had even in the East.

There may be a good deal of government control in prospect, but traffic lights are the penalty of traffic density and the United States is becoming more crowded.

The flood problem is almost equally pressing. The actual size of floods has probably been increased, since the country was settled, by deforestation and soil erosion; and more and more buildings have been located in the flood plains where the land is covered at high water. It is not always clear that so many works of man ought to have been allowed where they are, but since they are there the federal government is expected to protect them. The main-stream protection works consist principally of dams and levees. The dams are placed where they will flood open country rather than big cities, and often there is criticism of the amount of good land they drown. The levees are placed so as to keep the river out of its natural flood plain. By squeezing the river together the levees cause the flood crest to rise higher, and that too is sometimes criticized.

A third device, sometimes used, is the provision of flood-ways, special strips of land protected only with "fuse-plug" levees that will let the water escape when it gets high enough to endanger the main levee system. A similar release valve is the spillway in the levee above New Orleans that can be used to turn the excess water into Lake Pontchartrain.

Walter Lowdermilk, retired from the Soil Conservation Service and acting as agricultural adviser to the government of Israel, writes that in his opinion the United States ought to make more use of "polders." These are areas of farm land in the flood plain kept free of ground-level houses and barns and designed to be flooded with muddy water whenever the river is high. The water will deposit a layer of topsoil from the erosion upstream, saving this rich material from being carried down and lost in the ocean. This is the traditional system of enriching the land of Egypt by the flooding of the Nile.

In 1933 Roosevelt began a serious effort to make nation-wide plans for a water engineering program. In that year he appointed a Mississippi Valley Committee, with Morris Llewellyn Cooke as chairman. The work was later taken over by the National Resources Committee, which got out a full-scale report on river basins and their engineering problems. Congress, however, was hostile to the idea of appropriating money for a committee that would tell it what it ought to do about river works and other politically nourishing public projects. The National Planning Board that F.D.R. set up with public works money in 1933 had to be renamed National Resources Board, National Resources Committee, and finally National Resources Planning Board, in a vain effort to evade Congressional enmity. Finally Congress killed it in 1943.

In January, 1950, however, President Truman appointed a new Water Policy Commission, with Cooke as chairman, to study the water resources of the United States and recommend what should be done about them. The final report of the commission is the most comprehensive and authoritative statement on the national water situation yet published. The report includes a detailed inventory of the nation's water resources so far as they are known; an elaborate description and codification of the water laws; and a volume setting forth the problems of water development and making recommendations for federal policies. There is room here for only a short summary of the recommendations, which represent the best thinking of the American experts at the present time. The commission recommended that:

1. The government should make a clear statement of purpose in relation to water resources, as a guide to planning.

2. There should be not more than 15 River Basin Commissions to coordinate the federal agencies in each of the important basins.

3. In each basin the governors of the states should appoint an advisory committee of 25 citizens, and this committee should elect two representatives to sit on the Basin Commission.

4. There should be a federal Board of Review to check on all projects.

5. Congress should be given a 20-year plan and asked to authorize projects six years ahead. The bookkeeping should

show annual resource budgets and appraisals of the investment values of the public work.

6. Standard principles should be adopted for collecting payments from those who benefit from government water works.

7. There should be a uniform accounting system, supplemented by annual reports from the River Basin Commissions and Board of Review.

In December, 1955, President Eisenhower sent to Congress a report on water resources policy, drawn up by a Cabinet advisory committee. Superficially, its recommendations looked somewhat like those of Truman's commission. The report called for a water resources committee in each river basin, but it would be made up of representatives of the states and of all the federal agencies concerned. There would be a top committee in Washington representing the departments that are interested in water problems, and an engineering Board of Review.

These proposals were greeted by leading conservationists with undiluted hostility, mainly because they did not call for a clear-cut national water policy but would leave the design of policies in the hands of local interests and competing agencies. Leland Olds, a former member of the Federal Power Commission, said of the report that "what it proposes to abandon is the whole concept of comprehensive multipurpose river basin programs." The Senate responded with a resolution reaffirming Congressional control and calling for a new study of standards for evaluating water projects.

Chapter 12

IRRIGATION AND WATERPOWER

Irrigation is an old art in North America. The Indians along the Rio Grande had good irrigation works before the Spaniards came. But the first English-speaking settlers to build large irrigation projects were the Mormons in Utah, starting in 1847. From then on all over the dry parts of the West settlers tried irrigation with more or less success, first by diverting water from the streams and in recent times largely by pumping the groundwater. Altogether about 16 million acres have been watered by private ditches or wells. The largest projects, requiring millions of dollars of investment, have been tackled by the federal government.

The first federal project came in 1868, when Congress appropriated $50,000 to irrigate land on the Mojave Indian Reservation in Arizona. In 1894 Congress tried to get the states to take over the job of irrigation by offering a million acres of arid land to them if they would put water on it. The scheme bogged down in legal tangles. When Theodore Roosevelt came in the time was ripe for the federal government to act. F. H. Newell easily persuaded him to take up the idea of a Reclamation Service; the Reclamation Act was passed in 1902, and Newell was put in charge of the Service, located in the Interior Department.

By 1950 the Reclamation Service had put water on more

than 5 million acres, and estimated that nearly 20 million more could possibly be irrigated—not counting supplemental irrigation in the East. "Possible" irrigation does not necessarily mean that it would be worth the cost.

The desert soils are often rich, because there is not enough rain to leach the plant food out of them as it often does in wetter climates. Water, therefore, makes the desert bloom, and the steady sunlight helps the crops grow. Irrigated lands can pay a good price for water. The federal irrigated lands are subsidized, however, for the water charge covers only the gradual repayment of the capital cost of the dams and other works, but no interest. As a rule the dams produce electric power that is sold and helps to pay for the project. But after the easiest reclamation systems are completed, the time comes when the cost of new development is questioned on the ground that direct repayments and the tax revenues derived from the farmers may not be enough to justify the cost.

The right to take water from interstate rivers is a politically important issue between the western states because the supply of water decides how many people can live in the state, and therefore how many members of Congress it can have. Any state with land along a stream can take water from it, except that it must not deprive another state, farther downstream, of water that that state has already appropriated for beneficial use. This point was decided by the Supreme Court in the Larimer Ditch case in 1922. Under this decision a state can take unappropriated water out of a river and through a tunnel to another river basin.

When big plans for federal water projects are under way there is still room for argument about what states are to get the water. The states along the Colorado River have had a long dispute over how the water ought to be divided by future structures, and Mexico also has a claim, since the

Colorado runs through Mexican territory into the Gulf of California.

The development of irrigation along the Rio Grande has also involved agreements with Mexico for sharing the water, much of which comes from tributaries lying inside Mexico. In the bargaining the United States has yielded some of the Colorado water in exchange for some Rio Grande water to be used in Texas, to the disgust of the Colorado basin states.

The recent Colorado River controversy that involves conservation policies arose from the interstate compact that divided the water between the upstream and the downstream states of the valley. According to the Santa Fe Compact of 1922, the Upper Basin states, Wyoming, Colorado, Utah, and New Mexico, would have the right to 7½ million acre-feet of water a year and the Lower Basin states of Arizona, Nevada, and California would also have 7½ million plus another million when available. The Mexican share, if necessary in a dry year, would be assessed from both basins.

Boulder Dam was built at the instance of the city of Los Angeles, which wanted to take water from the Colorado, and of the farmers of the Imperial Valley, who use Colorado water for irrigation. It was opposed by the private power companies, eastern members of Congress hostile to spending, and the state of Arizona, in which the dam is located. In the Supreme Court Arizona won the right to a royalty for water taken by California. But there was no similar dam in the upper Colorado by which the Upper Basin states could get the use of their allotted share of the water. They wanted a system of dams to tie down their right by actual use, lest California find a way to appropriate more than its share. California, on the other hand, was ready to find objections to any scheme for damming the upper river. From that basic conflict of interest there was destined to develop a dispute that would throw serious doubts on the future of desert irrigation in the United States. One of the most bitter controversies over irrigation in recent years has been the Upper Colorado dispute, often called also the fight over Echo Park Dam, though it began as mainly a contest between the Upper Basin states and California about water rights.

The Reclamation Bureau had laid out a series of dams in the Upper Colorado basin. Some were to store water for irrigation and others, lower down, were to produce power or to store water for delivery to the lower river under the Santa Fe Compact, so that water for irrigation would be available farther upstream. The division of opinion in Congress made it plain that the Upper Basin states wanted to make some use of their share of the river flow. California raised obstacles.

The defenders of the bureau's plan argued that the Upper Basin states had been neglected in the reclamation program and now deserved a chance to use their rightful water resources. The total cost of the new construction would be less than $2 billion, and tax revenues from the settlements in the irrigated territory would help to repay the investment. They pointed out that the irrigated lands would produce food that will be needed someday to feed an increased population.

The attackers swarmed in from all directions. Senator Thomas Kuchel of California spoke of the Supreme Court's decision that water rights are gained by "prior use" and referred to the Santa Fe Compact as "an attempt to substitute for the Supreme Court's ruling an agreement to apportion the water." The implication was that California still had hopes of getting some of that Upper Basin water.

The opposition of California was expected and discounted. But a more powerful attack, and the only one destined to succeed, came from those conservationists who had a special concern for the national parks and monuments, for an important part of the Reclamation Bureau's plan was the Echo Park Dam, which would drown out part of the Dinosaur National Monument.

The monument was originally a few acres containing dinosaur bones, reserved in 1915 to prevent their destruction. President Franklin D. Roosevelt enlarged the monument to 203,885 acres in 1938, "subject to all valid existing rights." The only private rights in the area at any time seem to have been those involved in an application for a power license made at one time by the Utah Power & Light Co., but that had been withdrawn before the 1938 proclamation. The proclamation itself had earmarked one site for a power dam, though far upstream from the Echo Park site, and the advocates of the project made much of that earmarking as a vested "right."

The conservationists pointed out that Congress itself had all the rights there were in the public domain as long as no private person had acquired any. It could put a dam in a national park or monument if it thought best, but in the past, after the unfortunate Hetch Hetchy experience, it had consistently refused to let such disruptive projects get into these reservations. The conservationists organized a nation-wide campaign against this dam. They called attention to more than a dozen other proposals for invading the national parks with waterpower projects, all of which were likely to go through if the barriers were once broken down. One of their most effective means of persuasion was to show a motion picture made by David R. Brower of the Sierra Club in the desolate Hetch Hetchy at low water and another made on the same day showing the Yosemite Valley crowded with people. This film was taken around to congressmen's offices and exhibited to drive home the lesson that Hetch Hetchy ought to have been saved for park space.

The Reclamation Bureau, once a full partner in the conservation movement, was in an awkward position. The awkwardness was increased by the fate of its arguments against substituting other dams for Echo Park when David Brower showed on a blackboard that the arithmetic of Reclamation's figures on relative evaporation was in error.

The conservationists turned out to be so powerful politically that in 1955 the advocates of the Upper Colorado plan had to yield on Echo Park Dam. On November 1, the governors, senators, and representatives of the area convened in Denver for a strategy meeting. Howard Zahniser, Washington representative of the Council of Conservationists, issued a statement saying in effect that if the proponents of the project could develop a bill that showed no place for any dam in a protected area, or any other violation of good conservation practice, the council would not oppose the revised project. In response the strategy meeting promised not to try to put Echo Park Dam back into the program. The Interior Department then agreed to find other reservoir sites instead of Echo Park. And so, in 1956, the revised project was passed by Congress. But during the debate the whole program had been subjected to a general attack on its economic soundness, an attack that portended for the future a much more critical examination of irrigation and power proposals.

Paul Douglas, Senator from Illinois and a respected economist, had decided to study the economic justification for irrigation and power in the Colorado River uplands. He began his attack in the Senate with an analysis of the costs of the power plants. He noted the figures for other public hydroelectric plants, starting with those in the Tennessee Valley, which cost an average of $166 a kilowatt, and so on down to $115 at Bonneville on the Columbia and $90 at Grand Coulee. The least expensive plant on the Upper Colorado would be at Glen Canyon, where the cost was expected to be $463, and the Echo Park plant would cost $640, according to the estimates. Further, he called attention to the unpleasant fact that the Reclamation Bureau, though having a world-wide reputation for outstanding engineering work on large dams, has not done so well on cost estimates. The Senator recalled the bureau's record of average costs running 106 per cent over the estimates—exceeded only by the Corps of Engineers, with its 124 per cent average overrun.

Some of the Columbia River power costs less than 1 mill per kilowatt-hour, but the Senator pointed out that Glen Canyon power would cost more than 4 mills and Echo Park power about 6 mills, even if the bureau's estimates should be correct. He noted the fact that there is plenty of coal and oil shale in the area and that, even if the government could find a market for power at 6 mills, some private company with a modern steam plant could undercut the price and take away the business. How, then, could the profits on power sales help carry the cost of irrigation?

But Douglas struck his heaviest blows against irrigation itself. He pointed out that, although the farmers do not have to repay the interest on the capital invested in the dams, the government must pay it. Interest is, therefore, a real cost to be considered in a discussion of whether the nation wants to open a new tract of land to irrigation. The estimated cost per acre in the Upper Colorado project for 18 inches of irrigation water a year would average $952 of construction expense, and $1,190 of interest. The land is at a fairly high elevation, from 4,500 to 7,500 feet above sea level. As a result, the valuable crops of the lower altitudes could not be grown on most of it. Douglas stated that in Illinois and Iowa some of the most fertile land in the world could be bought for no more than $800 an acre. Why, then, should the government create irrigated pasture out of desert land at more than $800 an acre?

The Department of Agriculture supplied ammunition for the attack. Its reports showed that practically every crop that could be grown on the newly irrigated lands is already a surplus problem, requiring government subsidy, and is likely to be so for some time to come. Besides, irrigation in the "humid" East is so inexpensive and profitable that many farmers use it with no subsidy from the government. Why, then, pay such high rates per acre to irrigate more land in the West? Although water supplies in the East are going to be increasingly required for much more profitable domestic and industrial uses, there are bound to be many places, especially in the Southeast, where water cannot be better used than for sprinkling the crops in dry weather.

The Upper Colorado project aroused strong support in Congress for a variety of reasons. Some of the friends of public power felt constrained to vote for it because it included several public hydroelectric plants. Others felt that the Upper Basin states had not got their share of government spending and ought to be given something. Others may have felt that making the desert blossom like the rose, or at least like the alfalfa, would be a worthy enterprise at almost any cost.

The final effect of all the argument on the Bureau of Reclamation is likely to be a more cautious questioning of the value of new irrigation. No doubt there are places where high-value farms can still be made out of sagebrush land by the bureau at a cost that will seem reasonable to Congressional critics. And certainly the bureau still has a vital part to play in supplying public power to the municipal and rural cooperative systems if the Interior Department will allow it to do so.

But where and when to open new lands to farming, and where and how to irrigate, will be more and more warmly disputed as long as the government is troubled by price support and crop surplus problems.

Some of the most far-reaching controversies over irrigation and its related hydroelectric power policies have long raged in the Central Valley of California.

The Central Valley is really two valleys formed by rivers that meet and discharge into San Francisco Bay. The Sacramento River, coming down from the north, has more than enough water. The San Joaquin River Valley, to the south, originally had a large supply of groundwater, though not enough to irrigate all the land. The groundwater was drawn down so badly by excessive pumping that thousands of acres of irrigated land had to be abandoned because of high pumping costs. Supplemental water from streams was needed, but the streams coming down from the mountains into the San Joaquin Valley were not enough. The principal engineering feature of the Central Valley Project, therefore, is the co-ordinated canal system to bring water from the Sacramento along the mountains to the upper reaches of the San Joaquin, a distance of 500 miles. The other notable engineering feature is the supplying of water in dry weather to the delta near San Francisco Bay, to drive back the salt water that had been seeping into the flat lands.

The difficulties in the Central Valley are not with engineering but with laws and politics. Early mining history and a struggle between the great wheat ranchers fastened inappropriate water laws on the state of California, creating a tangle that interfered with any general plan for developing the water resources. As long ago as 1873 the Army Engineers proposed to bring water from the north to the San Joaquin, but legal tangles made it impossible at that time.

The California constitution of 1878 was designed to limit the amount of land that any one person could hold, but it had no teeth, and the great wheat ranchers in the San Joaquin Valley managed to keep their land. Later the Pacific Gas & Electric Co. supplied them with power for pumping their wells and became their ally in the struggles that were to follow.

When the Reclamation Bureau was set up in 1902 it considered the Central Valley but could not see any legal way to help. The valley lands already had some water and needed only a supplementary supply, but the act was designed only to bring raw desert lands into use. Another point that in the future was to become an issue was that the federal law did not allow the settlers to use water from a Reclamation system to irrigate more than 160 acres, or 320 for a man and wife.

In 1933 the California legislature passed an act setting up

a project for the valley, but the state could not raise the $170 million needed to begin the work. Then the federal public works program overcame that obstacle by offering a loan and grant, which the state accepted.

But Uncle Sam's bounty had strings attached. The federal funds had to be used to supply water under the reclamation law that forbade any one family more than enough to irrigate 320 acres. The big landowners could have water only by agreeing to sell their excess land within three years, at the old value of the land as it was before receiving the new water supply. This legal restriction gained the enmity of the big property holders.

The Reclamation Bureau was legally authorized to build dams with hydroelectric power plants, and the reclamation law required that municipally owned electric systems must have first call on this public power. There were many such systems in California, which competed with the Pacific Gas & Electric Co., and often forced the company to lower its rates. The P.G.&E., therefore, was ready to fight the Central Valley Project.

When the California legislature accepted the project the landowners at first offered no objections. They hoped that by the time the water was ready to flow their representatives could persuade Congress to exempt the Central Valley from the acreage limitation. In March, 1944, Representative Alfred J. Elliott and Senator Sheridan Downey of California tried to have an exemption amendment attached to the Rivers and Harbors Bill. Again in 1947 Senator Downey proposed a bill to exempt from the acreage limitations the Central Valley and two other irrigation districts, one in Colorado and one in Texas.

The effect of Senator Downey's proposed amendments would have been that big landowners who might have been using the land for dry farming or grazing, or speculators who guessed or knew where the government irrigation water would become available, could profit by a large unearned increase in value. But Congress had held from the beginning of the homestead laws that unearned increments caused by public action must be distributed directly to the settlers as part of the inducement to settle and build up the country. This is the same dispute that began with the old land laws and continued in the fight between Pinchot and Ballinger—whether the bonanza values of newly opened lands should be distributed to small owners or handed to big operators.

In this case it was no longer a question of taking up the public lands. Great areas in California had long since come into "strong hands"—the hands of big farmers, railroads, banks, oil companies, distillers, canning companies, and speculators. What they wanted from Senator Downey's bill was the lion's share of the new land values that would be created by federal irrigation.

It was a bitter fight, with no holds barred; at one point the 80th Congress amended the Interior Appropriation Act to the effect that Michael Straus, chief of the Reclamation Bureau, could not be paid out of Reclamation funds. He served without pay for six months before the 81st Congress raised the ban and he got his money.

But not all Californians are great landholders or their employees. There are areas inhabited by farmers with no more than the 320 acres allowed for federally irrigated land. There are country towns serving such areas that stand in marked contrast to many of the towns that serve the big estates. By all the ordinary marks of civilization—stores, schools, churches, libraries, and motion-picture theaters not excepted—the towns surrounded by smaller landholdings are strikingly more civilized than the typical town serving the employees of the big landowners. This observation is often cited as confirming the wisdom of Congress in its insistence for a hundred years on land policies that favored the family-size farm.

The Reclamation Bureau had able men in charge of public relations and in the field negotiating contracts for the new water supplies, and the smaller farmers in California rallied to the bureau's support when they found what the conflict was about. By 1945 the bureau was able to get some important areas under contract to receive water in accordance with the law. In 1947 Senator Downey published a book, called *They Would Rule the Valley*, accusing the government of tyrannizing over the poor Californians. But in 1948 Representative Elliott was defeated and in 1950 Downey decided not to run for reelection.

The Central Valley struggle was complicated in 1940 by the intervention of the Army Engineers, who were persuaded to recommend a "flood-control" dam on the Kings River, a tributary of the San Joaquin. The large landholders saw a chance to get irrigation water from the Army without the acreage limitations of the reclamation law and without paying for the dam, since the Army does not charge the local people for its services. The Pacific Gas & Electric Co. also put in a request for a power license, to preempt the power that would have gone by priority right to the publicly owned systems if supplied by the Reclamation Bureau. Part of the scheme was blocked when Congress found out that water users were about to get a half million dollars' worth of water per year for nothing. Congress passed a law requiring them to make a contract with the Reclamation Bureau for the water.

Nonetheless, the P.G.&E. got licenses from the Federal Power Commission for several power plants. The government brought suit in the federal courts to set aside the licenses, since the Reclamation Bureau needed that power to help pay for its dams and the people needed the power at a fair price. But in November, 1953, Interior Secretary Mc-Kay announced that he was calling off the suit.

The Missouri Valley has been the scene of the greatest conflict between the Reclamation Bureau and the Corps of

Engineers. Like the Tennessee Valley before the TVA, the Missouri Valley is a poor area, with a tendency to lose population. Upstream most of the land needs irrigation, but the river has only a small supply of water—a quarter as much as the Columbia. Downstream the cities need flood control, for the flow is extremely variable. The Army has insisted on promoting navigation, although the river in general flows across the main stream of heavy freight traffic. Except in Nebraska, where all the electric systems are publicly owned, power company propaganda has had a considerable success. The St. Louis *Post-Dispatch* and a few other newspapers have tried to educate the people to want a Missouri Valley Authority like the TVA, but with small effect.

Navigation started on the Missouri more than a century ago. When the West first opened up, traders and settlers traveled up the Missouri, and by 1850 St. Louis was the third American port, after New York and New Orleans. But by 1877 there were easier ways to go west and steamship traffic on the Missouri was abandoned. Yet in 1882 Congress granted the Engineers authority to maintain a 3-foot-deep channel. In 1912 Congress ordered a 6-foot channel. Lieutenant Colonel Herbert Deakyne of the Engineers, however, pointed out in 1915 that river improvements costing $20 million to build and a million a year to maintain were saving shippers only $10,000 a year. Again in 1933 Engineer Colonel George Spalding recommended that the 6-foot channel be abandoned. But by that time the Corps was committed to navigation, and Fort Peck Dam was under way with Public Works Administration money. Since Fort Peck is in Montana, too far upstream for a dam to have much effect on floods in the lower river, the Corps had to justify it as a power and navigation project.

After the 1943 floods Congress told the Engineers to study the flood problem, and Colonel Lewis A. Pick, for the Engineers, made a plan for flood control and navigation, using big upstream dams and downstream levees. Pick took no account of the need for irrigation or hydroelectric power, which he regarded as problems for others to contend with. His critics pointed out that one of his dams, for instance, at Garrison, North Dakota, would flood 21,000 acres that Reclamation had just irrigated at a cost of over a million dollars. In 1943 the President ordered all agencies having public works proposals to submit them to the Bureau of the Budget for coordination into a 6-year plan, which might be used to support employment after the war. The Chief of Engineers disregarded this order and gave the Pick report directly to Congress before the end of 1943.

Then W. G. Sloan of the Billings, Montana, office of the Reclamation Bureau entered the scene. The bureau had long been working on plans for Montana and the Dakotas. Sloan's plan included 90 dams to store two years' flow of the river, irrigate nearly 5 million acres, and produce 758,000 kilowatts of power to help pay the bill. In addition it provided for municipal water supplies, recreation, and flood control in the upper river.

The powerful hunting, fishing, and camping organizations favored Sloan; the farm organizations and labor took the same side. The electric power companies and their business allies favored Pick. President Roosevelt favored a Missouri Valley Authority. But Roosevelt had a war to attend to, so he told Pick and Sloan to agree on something. From that shotgun wedding came the unfortunate Pick-Sloan Plan. What they did was to add practically all their projects together and ask Congress to authorize them all, although many competent people believed that there would not be enough water for all.

The river above Sioux City produces an average of only about 16 million acre-feet of water per year in a dry cycle, which can easily last twelve years. The irrigation plans called for 9,220,000 acre-feet a year, and that might need to be increased in unusually dry weather. The Army's planned navigation channel, 9 feet deep from Sioux City to the Mississippi, would require 14,500,000 acre-feet from the upper river in the 8-month navigating season, plus some to carry off the sewage during the winter. That means that the combined plan called for more than 7 million acre-feet a year to be drawn from storage during dry years. But the storage provided by the dams, allowing for normal evaporation, is not enough, by several years, to last out a 12-year dry cycle. Critics of the plan insist that something will have to be closed down after a few years of drought.

There were also criticisms of parts of the Sloan plan itself, such as the proposal to take water into North Dakota for supplemental irrigation on farms that would need it only about one year in three; such irrigation would be expensive and possibly not worth the cost to the farmer. There was also the disconcerting fact that most of the big dams would be built by the Army, which is not required by law to sell electricity and turn in the proceeds to help subsidize irrigation.

Another criticism is that navigation works on the Missouri, with their levees that narrow the channel, cause bigger floods. Studies made by the Regional Committee for MVA showed that in 1944 at Herman, Missouri, a flow of 577,000 cubic feet per second raised the water only to 30.9 feet on the gauge, but three years later, after the Engineers had improved the river, a flow of only 487,000 c.f.s. raised the river to the 31.2-foot level. Similar results were found at Booneville, Missouri. The committee concluded that the Engineers had been mistaken in thinking that the river could be made to scour out its silt-laden bottom and make a good barge channel by squeezing it together with levees.

Someday, at a cost of a few hundred million dollars, a Missouri Valley Authority may be able to punch through the most ill-considered of the dams, turn more attention to soil-erosion control upstream, confine irrigation to land where it will surely pay, and produce and sell power at fair prices to rural cooperatives, municipal systems, and manufacturing plants.

All these would have been possible under the MVA bill introduced in April, 1947, by Senator Murray of Montana. But most of the people didn't want it and they didn't get it.

Chapter 13

RURAL ELECTRIFICATION

The Country Life Commission of 1908, appointed by Theodore Roosevelt at the suggestion of Gifford Pinchot and Sir Horace Plunkett, reported a standard of living in the farm country of the United States that had made little progress since the eighteenth century. This state of affairs was a challenge to the new conservation doctrine: the use of the natural resources for the greatest good of the greatest number. The greatest number in those days could be found on farms and in rural villages. What could be done to bring them more closely in contact with modern life?

One of the hardest problems was how the modern genii of the lamp, the kilowatt-hours of electricity, could be brought to the farms and villages. On the face of it, the problem seemed impossible to solve. The cost of building power lines along country roads with only three or four farms to the mile appeared to be far more than the average farmer could pay. Individual electric plants, to be driven by a small waterpower or windmill, or later by a gasoline engine, were practical for the most prosperous farms, but the cost of current per kilowatt-hour was high.

There were some farms on well-settled highways near the towns that could be connected to the electric lines at a practicable cost, and there naturally arose the question of how far the service could be extended. In the early years of the century a few technical papers on rural service were published, and one experimental line six miles long was built out from Red Wing, Minnesota. The general conclusion of the power company engineers was that electric lines through the farm country could not pay for their cost.

As everyone knows, electric lines are now in operation along thousands of miles of country roads. Many people also know that these lines are meeting their cost, and at rates that the farmers can well afford to pay. Times have changed since widespread rural electric systems were judged impractical. The technical and political changes of half a century have led to the present state of rural electrification, but only after unremitting pressure by men who were determined to bring the resources of electricity to the farms and the crossroads.

The conservation principle of using publicly owned resources to benefit the people made possible an achievement that was held to be impossible from the narrowly commercial point of view. Good engineering and sound business practices were essential, but they alone were not enough. In addition there had to be low-interest capital, and that could be obtained only from federal government loans. There had to be an organization determined to extend the lines to as many farms as possible, not merely to those that would immediately yield a profit to the electric system. Finally, with the prospect of a rapid country-wide spread of rural electric lines, manufacturers had to be persuaded to develop useful and efficient electric farm equipment. Then, with all the ducks in a row, the farmers could profitably use large quantities of current, and with that heavy electric load the lines could pay their cost. But all the parts had to be supplied before the combination could be successful, and for that there had to be men with faith to commit themselves to building what they could see only in their minds. Foremost among those men who brought about the success of rural electrification were Gifford Pinchot, Morris Llewellyn Cooke, and Franklin D. Roosevelt.

Pinchot became Governor of Pennsylvania on January 1, 1923. He immediately obtained authorization for a "Giant Power Survey," and Cooke worked with him on it. Their plan was to build a state-wide grid of electric lines, fed mainly by power plants at the coal mines, and serving both town and countryside. Their survey indicated that the power companies underestimated the amount of power the farmers would use if they could get it; evidently the costs of rural distribution needed study.

Several years later, in 1931, when Franklin Roosevelt was Governor of New York, he set up a power authority to deal chiefly with power from the St. Lawrence River and called for a study of distribution costs to farms. In this project Roosevelt consulted with Pinchot and Cooke, and appointed Cooke to work on the study. Thus Cooke had the background to bring up the idea of a Rural Electrification Administration when F.D.R. became President.

Early in 1934 Cooke took his REA plan to the President and to various Cabinet members, and the preliminary organization was put together during the rest of that year. The REA was officially created as an independent agency by Executive Order on May 11, 1935, and Cooke was appointed Administrator. A year later Congress authorized the agency by statute.

The REA was given money to lend for the construction of rural electric lines. At first Cooke tried to persuade the private companies to do the work, but they were not convinced that it would pay. At that time none of the municipally owned systems dared venture outside their municipal boundaries. But the Tennessee Valley Authority had already inspired the organization of rural electric cooperatives to build lines and distribute TVA power. Following this example the REA turned its attention to cooperatives, which it fostered with technical advice as well as with financing. Later it extended its work to cover other aspects of rural service, such as financing cooperative power plants and rural telephone systems.

The prospects for success depended on the correctness of Cooke's belief that if farmers could get electricity at a reasonable price they would use far more of it than the electric companies had supposed. The REA engineers had to prove this theory right as quickly as possible in order to avoid early defeats and perhaps the failure of the whole effort.

The REA began with the advantage of an authorization to lend money for line construction at 2 per cent interest, which was about what the government was paying on much of its own borrowing, but considerably less than commercial rates.

Another advantage was that the engineers were able to make important cost savings by reexamining the current practices in line construction. The power companies had based their unfavorable judgments in part on the assumption that rural lines had to be as heavily built as city lines. The REA designed a lighter construction, costing about half as much as the city standard, and this lighter design is now in successful use throughout the United States. On many details of line accessories the REA was also able to save money.

The REA promoted the sale of electric farm machinery, stressing especially the equipment that would increase the farmer's production and earning power, so that as quickly as possible the sale of current would rise to the point of paying for the lines. The REA and the TVA together created such an attractive market for equipment that manufacturers were easily persuaded to come forward with what was needed.

In many parts of the country there was another element that helped the success of the rural cooperatives—low-cost power from federal power plants, supplied under the so-called "preference clause." In 1906 Congress had amended the reclamation law with a clause providing that municipally owned electric systems should have the first right to power from federal irrigation dams. This clause was extended to rural electric cooperatives in the TVA act of 1933 and the REA act of 1936. In the areas where public power was within reach it helped the cooperatives by giving them lower costs for wholesale power than they could ordinarily have obtained from a private company.

Thus by a combination of careful engineering with low-cost government credit and in many areas low-cost wholesale power, and with the unbounded faith and enthusiasm of men who believed in the cause, rural electrification surmounted many obstacles and became a success. Only one farm in ten in the United States had had electricity in 1933. By June 30, 1956, 94.2 per cent of America's 4,507,050 farms had central station electric service. Up to that date REA had made electric loans to 1,078 borrowers, including 979 cooperatives. About 240 of these electric systems were buying current from federal power plants. The rural power systems financed by the REA had an investment of more than $2.7 billion and were operating more than 1.3 million miles of distribution line. They have had a remarkable record of paying off their loans on time, and their sales of power have grown so fast as to call for continual increases of capital investment.

Ever since Cooke had worked with Pinchot on the Giant Power Survey he had dreamed of using electric service to transform farm life. That dream has largely come true. Rural living conditions no longer resemble those of the eighteenth century, and a large part of the change has been caused by electricity. Power on the farm is used not only for lighting and the operation of household equipment but also to pump water, grind feed, refrigerate milk, illuminate chicken houses, and run all kinds of stationary farm machines. Electricity helps soil conservation in various ways; for instance, it encourages dairy farming, one of the best soil-conserving activities. It also provides amenities that tend to persuade intelligent young people to live on farms, and it increases their earning capacity as farmers.

Once the rural systems had developed to the point where they were more than making expenses, some of them could easily have been placed on a commercial basis by selling them to private companies. The private companies could meet the somewhat higher costs they would have to pay in many cases for interest and power by refusing to serve outlying farms that could not return the expense of reaching them. That, however, would have violated a conservation principle that the founders of rural electrification were determined to maintain—the principle called "area coverage."

Area coverage means that as many isolated farms as possible will be served as long as the system as a whole has a fair margin of revenue over expenses. It implies that around the edges of the area the poorer farms will be subsidized to some degree by the richer ones of the system. Sometimes the upland farm, supplied with current, may grow prosperous and become a paying customer. Sometimes it may not pay but still may be saved from becoming a piece of rural slum. Either way, the community is bettered by the practice of serving every possible farm; for the potential resources, material and human, of the outlying farms are best conserved if they have electricity. In recent years the private companies have made strenuous efforts to buy out the cooperatives, with occasional success. People forget the old days when they had no one to look to but the private companies.

One vital reason for insisting on a continuance of the 2 per cent interest rate and of the preference right to buy low-cost federal power is that about 5 per cent of American farms are not yet served, and more of them can be reached if the basic costs are not increased.

From the beginning the private electric companies have generally been hostile to rural electrification. In some places they have tried to prevent the success of a cooperative by building "spite lines" in the most thickly settled parts so as to take the cream of the business, leaving only the uneconomic sections to the cooperative. They have often been reluctant to sell wholesale power at a reasonable price to cooperatives that are out of reach of a federally owned power plant.

It often happens that a private company has a high-voltage line running near a government dam, while a cooperative that wants a share of the power is far away and too small to stand the expense of going after it with a line of its own. This situation brings up the questions of "wheeling" and of "bus-bar sales."

Sometimes the company will transmit the cooperative's share of the power to it for a reasonable carrying charge. This service is called "wheeling." The company transmits the power without buying or selling it.

As an alternative, the government may sell all the current "at the bus bar," that is, at the power plant, to whatever buyer is there to take it, generally a private company. Then the cooperative would receive the same power as before, but it would be buying it from the company instead of merely paying the company for the transmission. Such an arrangement gives the company more control, since it blocks the customer from the chance to draw on the government power by building a transmission line. The companies therefore are disposed to resist the idea of wheeling power for a preference customer and to put pressure on the government to sell them the power at the bus bar.

There is much confusion as to whether wheeling is an obligation on the private companies or an imposition. Over federal lands the government, if it allows a company a right of way, may require it to wheel power for a preference customer at a reasonable charge. But whether the grant of a franchise allowing a company to condemn private land for its right of way should also carry with it an obligation to wheel public power is not clearly established. The government has often forced the issue by threatening to build a parallel line if the company refused the transport business.

In some areas the cooperatives have been able to put together enough customers to justify a cooperative generating plant, with its own transmission lines. A number of these generating and transmission, or "GT," systems have been financed by REA loans. In Texas, for instance, the GT systems have been successful in holding down wholesale power rates. The first one was the Brazos Electric Power Cooperative. Several others were formed but did not have to get into operation because the power companies cut their rates in order to meet the potential competition. In 1954 the cooperatives reported that their average wholesale cost of power was only 5.8 mills per kwh, 2 mills under the national average. GT systems are also operating in at least a dozen other states.

One of the signs of coming bad weather for the cooperatives appeared in 1953 in the Missouri Valley, where the Reclamation Bureau has electricity to sell. The bureau issued a set of "criteria" for the sale of power to municipal systems and cooperatives. They would be allowed to contract, once and for all, for the public power they would take, today and forever, with no allowance for increased demands in later years. The bureau would then sell the rest of the power to private customers at the bus bar on long-term contracts.

This was an unwelcome change, for until 1953 the preference clause had always been interpreted to mean an absolute preference, letting the public and cooperative systems have all the government power they could use, and leaving only the remainder to the private utilities. The preference customers, as a rule, were comparatively small and could not generate their own power as cheaply as the big, interconnected private systems could. Accordingly, when a preference customer grew and needed more power he could not get it cheaply by adding a generator as a private company could do, and if forced to apply to the company for supplementary power he would be in a poor bargaining position. Therefore, the government had always interpreted the law to mean that when a preference customer needed additional power the government plant would supply it, cutting down, if necessary, on its deliveries to private customers. The Missouri "criteria" seemed to indicate a new interpretation less favorable to the municipal and cooperative systems.

When the new rule came out, the officials of cooperatives representing some 2 million voters met and petitioned the President to talk to the Secretary of the Interior. There was an investigation by a Senate subcommittee under Senator William Langer of North Dakota, and the National Farmers Union held a protest meeting in Denver. The rule was somewhat softened, but the cooperatives got the impression that Interior still wanted to undermine the preference clause.

In 1953 a new term came into the discussions of public and private power—what the Interior Department called the "partnership principle." Interior was proposing to build multipurpose dams, for navigation, flood control, irrigation, and waterpower, but without power plants. Private enterprise would be invited to construct the power plants at its own expense, and then would own them for fifty years and would own the power. It was even suggested that the local power company, the nearby municipal systems, and the rural cooperatives, should all take stock in a syndicate to build the plant. Then each one would be entitled to a share of the power in proportion to its investment.

The cooperatives felt that the partnership principle was calculated to cut down most of their traditional preference rights, and they complained vigorously about it to Congress. They incidentally were heard to voice complaints against the word "preference" as applied to their rights, as if the government in the past had been favoring them over others who might have equally just claims, for that seemed to be implied in the proposal to admit private power companies to "partnership." They asserted that public power is part of the public domain, in which the citizens have sovereign rights not shared by any private corporation. Instead of "preference," they have suggested that the proper name should be the "antimonopoly" clause, since its purpose has always been to protect them from private monopoly.

The preference, or antimonopoly, clause was reinforced by a strong interpretative opinion from Attorney General Herbert Brownell in 1955, in connection with the Clark Hill Dam dispute. This multipurpose dam on the Savannah River produces 280,000 kilowatts of power, half of which has been allocated to South Carolina and half to Georgia. The Georgia Power Co., which had already built a transmission line to the dam, wanted a contract to buy the full Georgia share and to continue to supply several municipal and rural systems already dependent on its power. These latter, however, wanted to buy the Clark Hill power from the government, with a wheeling service over the Georgia Power lines at a fair rate.

Before 1953 the situation was deadlocked. Secretary Oscar Chapman of Interior refused to sell the power to the company; the company refused to offer satisfactory terms for wheeling; and the preference customers had not succeeded in organizing a power line of their own.

In September, 1953, Assistant Secretary of the Interior Fred G. Aandahl brought the cooperatives and the company together, and the cooperatives were shocked to find that Aandahl did not immediately decide in their favor. From there on a long argument followed. In October, 1955, it appeared that the Interior Department had drawn up a contract to sell the power to the company under conditions limiting the rates that it could charge to preference customers.

These facts were brought out by a House committee, which accused the department of trying to deceive the cooperatives into accepting an unsatisfactory contract. The department was accused of concealing for about three months the fact that the Attorney General had advised on July 15 that the proposed contract was illegal. In his opinion Brownell had noted that the cooperatives had no transmission lines of their own and no visible means of getting any, but he said:

"To read into the Section 5 grant of a preference to public bodies and cooperatives the requirement of a presently existing ability to take and distribute the power would, in the usual case, constitute its emasculation; and it is well settled that such a construction of a statute should not be taken where a construction is possible which will preserve its vitality and the utility of the language in question."

In 1956 the Georgia Power Co. at last signed contracts for wheeling the power to preference customers without taking title to it.

New policies in the construction of the law on atomic energy have cast a chill over the hopes of municipal and cooperative power users.

In 1954, when Congress passed a bill to allow private companies to build atomic power plants, it included a preference clause covering atomic energy that may be for sale from federally owned plants. But on July 18, 1955, the first federally owned atom power plant was opened for the sale of electricity at West Milton, New York, and AEC Chairman Lewis L. Strauss ceremoniously threw a switch, sending 12,000 kilowatts of power—to the Niagara Mohawk Power Co. Representative Irwin Davidson of New York immediately protested, accusing the AEC of having failed to offer this power first to preference customers in the neighborhood. Two towns and a cooperative had applied for the power, and they felt that under the law the AEC could have helped to negotiate with the company to wheel the power to them. The AEC's seeming preference for a private company aroused widespread concern. Later the AEC yielded on the preference right, but the plant was closed shortly afterward.

The Chairman of the AEC having expressed opposition, both in public speeches and before the Joint Committee on Atomic Energy, to the building of federal atomic power plants, the advocates of public power appealed to Congress. Senator Albert Gore of Tennessee introduced a bill designed to force the pace, first in 1955, and again in 1956 and 1957. The 1956 bill directed the Atomic Power Commission to start at once building full-sized nuclear power plants of the most promising designs so as to begin the job of supplying some of its own vast power requirements. The bill also ordered the AEC to experiment with more advanced designs by building test plants, and to conduct a vigorous program of international cooperation in the design and construction of power reactors. The 1956 bill was narrowly defeated in the House.

Meanwhile the Consolidated Edison Company of New York, the Commonwealth Edison Company of Chicago, and the General Electric Company, are reported to have broken ground for nuclear plants, without government help. The AEC has set up a demonstration program in which it offers technical and financial aid to private utilities, cooperatives, and municipalities. Several cooperatives and municipalities had reached the stage of serious negotiations in June, 1957, the most advanced being a proposal for a small 10,000 kw plant at Chugach, Alaska.

In June, 1955, the cooperatives were somewhat disturbed to learn of the report on public power issued by the Hoover Commission on Reorganization of the Government. The commission recommended abolition of the REA and substitution of a new finance corporation to seek private capital instead of using government money. This would mean a higher interest rate. The report also recommended that the government build no transmission lines if transmission can be provided by nonfederal agencies. That would mean no more pressure for favorable wheeling terms.

The commission recommended various changes that would amount to a repeal of the preference clause and advocated giving private utilities a "fair share" of federal power. The preference customers have always understood that a fair share for private companies was only such power as they themselves could not use, noting, in this connection, that private companies actually get five times as much federal power as is sold to the rural cooperatives. The commission also recommended that when the government builds a multipurpose dam it should invite private capital to provide the electrical component and dispose of the power through a private system. This is the "partnership principle."

It was soon clear that the commission's views would meet with strong opposition. Not only the National Farmers Union but also the Grange and the American Farm Bureau Federation opposed the Hoover recommendations. Attorney General Brownell and Defense Mobilizer Arthur S. Flemming, who represented the Eisenhower Administration on the commission, refused to go along with the controversial parts of the report. Representative Chet Holifield of California called the report a "basic reference work for private utilities."

Holifield criticized the recommendation that the government charge against its customers a tax equivalent of more than a third of its receipts from power. According to his statistics, private companies that, like the federal plants, sell little or no power at retail paid federal and local taxes in 1953 averaging only 13½ per cent.

Holifield noted that the commission's report on lending agencies accused various programs of providing subsidies, but that the commission failed to recommend stopping subsidies in other directions. As he put it: "The ones complained about in this report appear to be, in the main, those which bring widespread benefits to the whole population."

The cooperatives insist that it is the private companies that are getting the heavy subsidies in the form of "accelerated depreciation." When the government wants to encourage a private enterprise to build a new plant sooner than it would ordinarily do, a common method is to allow it to write off the book value of the plant much faster than the plant wears out. This depreciation charge on the books comes out of current taxable income, leaving a correspondingly lower tax liability. Accelerated depreciation, therefore, amounts to a gift from the government by way of reduced taxes.

After the North Korean attack in 1950 the government offered this kind of help to private electric companies for quickly enlarging their plants to handle the increased needs of war. According to the methods used by the utilities in computing the value of these benefits, the total subsidies granted to them between June, 1951, and November, 1955, amounted to a little over $3.6 billion. This was more than the total of REA loans to date, and those were loans, not gifts.

The rural electrification cooperatives in 1956 felt themselves to be under heavy attack, but they were in a strong position. Electric service at reasonable rates is now a well-established feature of farm and village life. The cooperatives, as a rule, are ahead of schedule in their debt payments to the federal government, though they are now often worried for fear they may not be able to get further capital for expansion on favorable terms. They are also uneasy for fear the power companies may succeed in cutting off their supply of low-cost power, forcing them into bankruptcy, and then buying up the remains. But their political influence is considerable and their success has done much to raise the standard of living of their members.

Rural electrification can now be seen to be part of a network of programs that were foreshadowed by Pinchot and T.R. in the first years of the conservation movement. Three lines of action in particular were destined to be closely linked by their concern with a complex of resources, especially farm and forest lands and hydroelectric power.

First there was reclamation of desert lands by irrigation. Irrigation called for dams and the dams produced electric power. The acreage limitations and the power preference clause registered the determination of the founders of conservation to protect the people against monopoly controls over the land irrigated and the waterpower developed by the federal government.

There was also the determined and finally successful effort of the conservation leaders to bring electricity to the farmers as the main instrument for shifting their living standards from the eighteenth to the twentieth century. Here, too, there was the necessity of fighting monopoly influences connected with the supply of power.

Finally, the leaders of conservation, even as early as the Inland Waterways Commission in 1907, launched the grand conception of unified river basin development. They insisted that all the resources of each river basin ought to be used according to a consistent set of principles for the benefit of the people. This conception, representing the full picture of the plans and hopes of Pinchot, Theodore Roosevelt, Morris Llewellyn Cooke, George Norris, and their many allies, took form, after many years of slow development, in the Tennessee Valley in 1933.

Chapter 14

RIVER BASIN DEVELOPMENT

~~~~~~

By 1933 all the separate branches of conservation were well defined. Specialists were working in forestry, in soil conservation, in range management, and in the protection of minerals, water resources, and wildlife on the national domain. Even rural electrification was ready to be born. The time had come to embody the original idea that Gifford Pinchot had grasped in 1907—the idea of combining the management of all these resources in one unified program. The natural area for such a program would be a river basin.

Some elements of general river basin management have appeared at various times in a number of the great river valleys, such as the Central Valley of California, the Colorado, and the Columbia. But only the Tennessee Valley has so far shown a full-scale example of unified development as it was conceived by the original conservationists.

The Tennessee basin came to be chosen for a development program for the principal reason that the federal government had already built a dam at Muscle Shoals on the Tennessee. This dam and its accompanying power plant were started during World War I to produce nitrates for munitions, but they were not finished until after the war. From then on there was a battle over whether the govern-

ment should operate the plant or sell it. Senator George
Norris, who, as a member of the House in 1910 had fought
on Pinchot's side in the controversy with Ballinger, made
it his special task to push for federal ownership and operation not only of the Muscle Shoals installation but of a
series of coordinated dams on the Tennessee. He twice got
Congress to pass bills for that purpose, but they were vetoed
by Presidents Coolidge and Hoover.

When Franklin D. Roosevelt came to the White House
the idea of using the Tennessee as a great example of unified development had already taken definite form, and the
TVA act was passed in May, 1933. The act chartered a corporation, the Tennessee Valley Authority, and gave it a mandate to plan and build dams and to operate them "primarily
for the purposes of promoting navigation and controlling
floods" and, "so far as may be consistent with such purposes," to make and sell electricity.

The act also directed the Authority to promote reforestation and soil conservation, to encourage the agricultural and
industrial development of the valley, to aid in national defense, and to cooperate with state and local authorities. It
said in so many words: "This Act shall be liberally con-
strued to carry out the purposes of the Congress." These
purposes embraced the use of all the resources of the valley for the greatest good of the greatest number for the
longest time. That is, they embraced conservation in general.

In the next twenty years almost all the possible dams on
the Tennessee and its tributaries were built, and it is now
possible to see their effects on the primary purposes of flood
control and navigation. The reservoirs are managed so as to
be at low-water level on January 1, the beginning of the
flood season, and they are kept low between floods until
March 15; then they are allowed to fill gradually with the

spring rains to store water for navigation and power needs during the summer.

The effects of the TVA flood control are most clearly felt along the main stream of the Tennessee, and to a lesser degree on the lower Ohio and the Mississippi. On April 17, 1956, for instance, a "moderate" flood was reduced at Chattanooga 16 feet below what it would have been without the dams. During that season three flood crests at Cairo at the junction of the Ohio and the Mississippi were reduced 0.9 to 2.1 feet by TVA action, with savings in damage estimated at $696,000. The total direct damage prevented by TVA flood control from 1936 to 1956 is estimated at about $61 million at an expense of about $32 million, including depreciation of structures.

In February, 1957, came the biggest flood since the famous one of 1867. Except for the TVA dams this one would have caused damage at Chattanooga alone variously estimated at $50 million to $65 million. The actual damage was negligible. In managing the reservoirs to control this flood the TVA engineers threw away for the time being some 700,000 kilowatts of power, putting a severe strain on the power system that in itself required a fast basin-wide manipulation of capacity and loads to prevent a breakdown.

As for navigation, in 1954 the Corps of Engineers reported about 1¼ billion ton-miles of commercial traffic on the Tennessee system, with a saving of about $12 million to the shippers and at an expense of $3.7 million to the TVA. Traffic in 1955 increased to 1.6 billion ton-miles, so the waterway is evidently regarded by shippers as a money saver. The largest single barge tow up to 1955 was composed of 12 barges, loaded with coal, coke, grain, steel, and fuel oil, a total cargo of 21,500 tons, or enough to load a couple of large merchant ships. The Tennessee channel is maintained at not less than 9 feet in depth, but most of the distance traveled by the barges is in open lakes with plenty of room to run at full speed.

When the TVA was created it found itself in possession of the nitrate fertilizer plant at Muscle Shoals, built in the early 1920s and by 1933 entirely obsolete. Considering the soil conservation problems of the valley, the Authority decided that phosphate fertilizers would be the most useful to begin manufacturing. Commercial mixed fertilizers at that time usually contained only about 18 to 20 per cent of plant food. The rest was inert material that made them expensive to transport and too expensive for many farmers to use freely. The TVA set out to develop more concentrated phosphates that could be manufactured cheaply enough to encourage their widespread use. In 1955 the latest material announced was a nitrogen and phosphorus combination called diammonium phosphate, having 74 per cent of plant food in it.

The introduction of these new fertilizers called for two lines of action—one to make the farmers want the materials and the other to convince the fertilizer industry that it could supply them at a profit. Accordingly, the TVA has made contracts with about 30,000 farmers to run 5-year demonstrations using TVA fertilizers. In return for getting the fertilizer at about half price the farmer plants soil-conserving grass and trees on land liable to erosion, keeps records, and allows other farmers to come and observe his results.

The immediate purpose of the fertilizer program is to help the farmers practice soil conservation and reduce the amount of silt flowing into the reservoirs. Conservation also increases the farmers' incomes. The TVA has not confined its fertilizer demonstrations to the valley but has spread them over most of the United States, for one of its purposes was to create a nation-wide market so that private industry would take up the manufacture of high-grade fertilizers on a commercial scale. As a matter of fact, the manufacturers have flocked to Muscle Shoals to find out about the TVA techniques of production and there has been a general upgrading of the commercial product. Undoubtedly the freight saving on the new fertilizers has been one cause of the vast increase in the demand since 1935.

In addition to promoting the use of grass and other cover crops to hold the soil the TVA encourages forestry and tree planting, as a means of soil and water conservation and also as a source of income for the farmers. The worn-out corn or cotton land will grow a profitable crop of pulpwood and timber—so profitable, in fact, that those who try it are not likely to put the land back into any of the soil-eroding crops. Experimental plantings of pine after about twenty years have shown cumulative profits on the investment ranging from 7 to 9 per cent per year. The main reason for these unusual growth rates is the climate with its 51-inch average annual rainfall and long growing season. The TVA, not content with the normally rapid growth of trees in the valley, has begun working to improve the planting stock. It has selected the biggest seedlings from some 40 million grown in its nurseries and has found several dozen specimens that show nearly double the usual rate of growth.

To encourage tree planting the TVA by 1955 had produced 280 million seedlings. The total area reforested came to 240,000 acres, about one-sixth of the land in the valley that needs to be planted. An important newsprint mill has been established in the valley, indicating the probability of a future increase in the planting of trees for pulp.

Construing its mandate liberally, as directed by the act, the Authority has taken up many lines of research that seemed likely to lead to improvements in the local agriculture and industry.

The TVA introduced walk-in refrigerators in crossroads stores where several farmers, clubbing together, could store a whole beef animal. In the first installations the farmers bought the refrigerating unit and built the cold room by TVA blueprints, giving the storekeeper a part of the space in lieu of rent. This new system, which has now become common, allowed the farmers to eat their own beef at a far lower cost than by selling the animals and buying packing-house meat. The main purpose was to promote the raising of cattle instead of hogs, since on sloping land the soil is better protected under pasture with cattle on it than if the people raise corn and feed it to pigs. The TVA developed a high-powered small quick-freeze machine to handle small fruits, which are also better for the land than corn or cotton. TVA engineers designed an inexpensive system for drying alfalfa hay in the barn, so that the farmers in the wet climate of eastern Tennessee can profitably use the soil-conserving alfalfa. They improved the process of extracting cottonseed oil so that local oil mills could survive and the residue from the press, containing all the minerals in the cotton, could be conveniently returned to the farms for cattle feed or fertilizer. The introduction of these improvements was aided by the availability of cheap TVA electric power to farms and factories.

The TVA surveys mineral, forest, and water resources and places its information at the disposal of businessmen who are looking for investment opportunities. The businessmen of the valley know that the TVA is engaged in promoting prosperity and they do not hesitate to go to it for technical assistance. In the course of years the TVA has also developed various specialties of its own, such as a particularly efficient system of office management that has been studied and copied in private industry. It has gathered detailed records of its notably low-cost methods of building dams and power plants, both hydroelectric and steam.

The TVA reservoirs are much used for recreation, although they suffer from the disadvantage of falling water levels during the summer. In 1955 the value of recreational facilities along the lakes was estimated at more than $53 million. These are private, state, or local government concessions; the TVA does not operate them. People made about 28 million "person-day" visits to the lakes for recreation purposes in 1955.

Commercial fishing in four TVA reservoirs in Alabama yielded more than $400,000 in the year ending June 30, 1956, and more than half a million dollars' worth of mussel shells were taken in the Tennessee River—about three-fourths of the fresh-water mussel shells used by the United States button industry. Another feature of the lakes is that since the TVA came in malaria, which had been common in the area, has been entirely wiped out, the five cases discovered there in 1955 having all originated in Korea. In the main the malaria control has been accomplished by raising and lowering the lake levels about a foot at frequent intervals so as to strand the mosquito larvae along the shore.

The TVA, as the first example of comprehensive river basin development, including stream control, soil conservation, cheap power, and many kinds of encouragement to private enterprise, soon became world famous. Many foreign governments sent representatives to study it, and all sorts of large river projects abroad have been called "TVAs."

There are, however, several features peculiar to the TVA which may be vital to the success of any attempt to imitate it.

The TVA is a corporation, chartered by Congress and governed by a board appointed by the President and confirmed by the Senate. The states of the valley have no members on the TVA board, which therefore is answerable only to the President and Congress. It can decide where to build a dam, for instance, on engineering grounds rather than by political bargaining. The TVA makes contracts freely with business concerns, local governments, states, and federal agencies, for cooperative activities regarded as beneficial to all concerned.

Finally, and most important, the TVA has a successful arrangement of powers among large and small agencies and interests, public and private. The Authority manages the flow of the river for flood control and navigation, produces and sells wholesale power to the independent retail electric systems, and carries on various research jobs that no one else seems ready to undertake. Each state, county, and municipality does its own planning and management on its own level, with full information and cooperation from the TVA. The industrial company and the businessman, large or small, can look to the TVA for whatever information and cooperation it is able to supply, knowing that the TVA depends, for its success and for political support against its enemies, on its record of promoting the prosperity of the region. The farmer can get advice and help from the TVA if he wants to practice good farming that will make him prosperous and will help to keep his land from washing into the reservoirs. No orders come down from on high, only information and appropriate kinds of service. On each level of action those on that level make their own decisions. That is so close to the theoretically ideal relation of large and small free operations that it leads to results of great interest to students of developmental techniques.

The controversial aspect of the TVA is its power program, since that competes directly with the private power industry. Any private electric company located near a publicly owned system feels the pressure of its customers demanding low rates to correspond with those of the public system nearby. The TVA has encouraged municipally owned and rural cooperative distributors in its area and sells power to them under contracts binding them to offer rates much lower than those generally charged by private systems. The distributors accept these contracts because they make a profit and also please their customers.

In 1956 the TVA was selling wholesale current to 98 municipalities, 51 cooperatives, and 2 small private systems. In

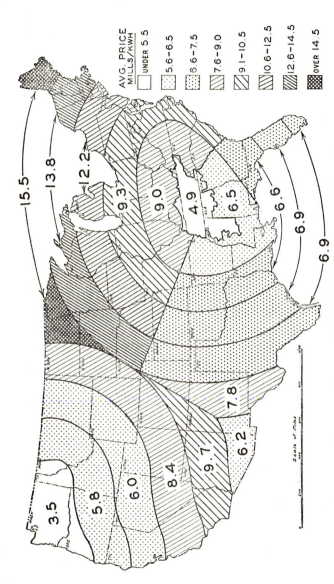

AVERAGE PRICE OF POWER TO REA BORROWERS FISCAL YEAR 1952

The influence of TVA's and Bonneville's low wholesale rates to rural electric cooperatives is indicated by the average price per kwh which grows higher as the distance from
TVA and Bonneville increases. (*Courtesy of Tennessee Valley Authority*)

that year the average household in the TVA area used 5,812 kilowatt-hours a year, compared with an average of 2,879 kwh in the United States as a whole. The TVA consumer paid an average price of 1.16 cents per kwh; the national average for household electricity was 2.62 cents.

In the fiscal year ending June 30, 1956, the TVA generated 57.5 billion kwh of electric power, and obtained 2.1 billion more from the surrounding power companies by purchase or exchange, a total of 59.6 billion. Hydroelectric plants were able to supply only 14.4 billion kwh in fiscal 1956 because of dry weather, about 2 billion below the expected yearly average. More than 43 billion kwh came from the TVA steam plants. These steam plants are efficient, producing on the average one kilowatt-hour of current from 9,780 British thermal units of heat, compared with an average for the nation in 1955 of 11,700 Btu per kwh. Generating costs in the six principal TVA coal plants ranged from 1.67 to 1.92 mills per kwh.

Of the 59.6 billion kwh at its disposal in fiscal 1956 the TVA sold 30.5 billion to the Atomic Energy Commission and other federal defense agencies, 15.5 billion to municipalities and cooperatives, and 7 billion to a small number of industries that buy large blocks of power directly from the Authority. (It does not sell directly to small consumers.) The fertilizer operations used 500 million kwh, transmission losses consumed 2.5 billion, and most of the remainder went to the Aluminum Company of America under an agreement to coordinate the management of several company-owned dams in the valley with the TVA system for greater efficiency. It is evident that the main problem of supply is caused by the requirements of the AEC.

The extent to which it is fair to compare TVA operating results with those of private companies has been much disputed. This is the famous "yardstick" controversy, which began in 1933 when the TVA officials stated that their power program was intended to serve as a yardstick to measure what private power ought to cost the consumer. This assertion was taking in too much territory, and the power companies leaped to seize the opportunity to point out the many differences between the TVA's privileged position and their own.

The TVA's hydroelectric power costs and wholesale rates could not be defended as a yardstick by which any private company's results could be fairly judged. But in recent years the Authority has begun once more to speak of the yardstick, this time in more realistic terms. Its steam plant construction costs, for example, are properly a measure of what a private company ought to be able to do, since the engineering should not depend on who owns the property. In this field TVA costs per kilowatt of capacity are below the average. Again, the contracts that the TVA makes with its preference customers might be used for comparison with those offered by other federal power systems. Dam-building costs per cubic yard of concrete and a few other items may fairly be compared with results in private practice. But most important, the TVA is a world famous yardstick of unified river development, an example of how it can be done, what results it produces on the prosperity of the region, and what enemies it has.

The reason that hydroelectric power production cannot be included in the yardstick is that the hydroelectric plants are operated as part of a unified system of dams that serve primarily for flood control and navigation, both of which services carry part of the cost of the dams. It is known that combining all the uses of the river works is less costly than it would be to build and operate all three systems separately, if that were possible; but the exact proportion of the cost that ought to be attributed to power has been much debated.

The TVA has made an allocation of costs to the purposes of flood control, navigation, and power by a calculation based on the estimated cost of a separate system of dams for each purpose if they had been built for that alone. The allocation for flood control is said to be conservative because it is less than the actual saving in flood damage; and the transportation allocation also is more than covered by freight savings. The remaining cost of the dams, together with the whole cost of power plants and power lines, must be carried by revenue from power sales. The disputes are caused by varying assumptions about how much of the cost of the dams should rightly be charged against power.

The cost of the power installations as computed by the TVA has been more than covered by receipts from wholesale electric sales. From 1933 to 1955 the total power revenues added up to $1,017 million. Operation, maintenance, depreciation, and payments in place of local taxes amount to $705 million, leaving a net income for the government of $312 million, or more than 4 per cent on the average power investment. Over the same period the average cost to the government for borrowed money was about 2 per cent. Haskin & Sells, New York certified public accountants, reported to the Hoover Commission in 1949 that: "The Authority is presently earning more than sufficient power revenues to repay the investment in power facilities with interest."

The Tennessee Valley is one of several regions, mainly in the Southeast and Northwest, where in the past twenty years federal public works and war expenditures have stimulated economic development at a more rapid pace than the national average. It happens, also, that the state of Tennessee is a relatively simple example, with available statistics that can be cited to indicate something of what the government received in return for its outlays.

The costs of flood-control and navigation works are normally borne by the federal government as a subsidy, on the theory that, while it is impossible to collect the costs directly from those who benefit from these river works, they yield an indirect return by increasing the taxpaying ability of the population. The TVA has tax figures for the state of Tennessee that tend to indicate that the U.S. Treasury obtains a substantial return on the over-all investment in the TVA.

In 1933, for example, the taxpayers of Tennessee were contributing only 0.56 per cent of the total federal income tax revenue. If they had continued the same 0.56 per cent in 1952, their tax payments to the federal government would have been only $185 million. Actually, however, their income taxes came to 0.95 per cent of the total, or $310 million, a difference of $127 million. While the average taxpaying ability of the American people was going up, something caused that of the Tennesseans to rise even faster. During that period the most important differences between Tennessee and the rest of the country were the TVA and the atomic plants that were placed in the valley to get the advantage of plentiful and cheap TVA power.

According to these figures, the government was getting from Tennessee alone an extra tax revenue in 1952 of more than $100 million a year that seemed to be largely attributable to its investment in the TVA program, the total cost of which at that time had amounted to about $1,500 million. The TVA takes the position that the increased tax return tells more about the success of the enterprise even than the fact that it is paying off its power costs.

The element of truth in the original belief of the TVA that it was a power yardstick for the United States was the fact that the municipal systems taking power from the TVA were from the beginning so managed as to be fairly comparable with any city distribution system whether publicly or privately owned. This point was clarified in 1939 by a Joint Committee that had been set up by Congress to investigate the workings of the Authority. In its report the committee stated:

"The yardstick is not in the Authority's wholesale rates, but in the retail rates of the various municipalities and other local organizations that have purchased Authority power and distributed it at unusually low rates. If their operations are shown to be of a kind that may be substantially duplicated in other parts of the country, their rates may be considered a Nationwide yardstick, or measure of results to be expected."

In order to meet this condition of comparability, the TVA persuaded the municipal systems taking its power to bind themselves by the contract to keep their accounts in such a way that it would be easy to compare their costs and rates with those of privately owned systems of similar sizes. For instance, they pay the city the equivalent of the usual taxes levied on private companies. The purpose of these rules was to make each item of expense correspond with what a private company would have to pay if it owned the same system. The cost of wholesale power varies in different cities according to the source of the power, but that difference is easily discovered and taken into account. Distribution and management expenses, on the other hand, have always been controversial, and so also was the question whether low rates would increase the sales and reduce the unit costs enough to yield a fair profit. The TVA has found that its municipal customers are making good profits at the low rates that they have to charge under their contracts. By 1956, in fact, 53 of the 152 TVA power distributors had voluntarily reduced their rates below the original TVA schedule.

When the TVA was established it was immediately attacked by the neighboring Commonwealth & Southern and other power companies on the ground that it was unconstitutional. The utilities accused the TVA of being essentially a power project camouflaged by the constitutional federal interest in navigation. After several years of litigation, the Supreme Court finally decided the suits brought by the companies in favor of the TVA.

The fact that the U.S. Treasury, and thereby the general U.S. taxpayer, is getting the benefit of a substantial profit from the whole sum invested in the Tennessee Valley Authority's operations is not, of course, known to most of the voters. On the other hand, what is well known is that the people of this formerly depressed area have benefited by a federal program and to that extent have enjoyed a competitive advantage over more prosperous areas that had no such program. The power companies have laid out large sums of money in advertising to persuade the public that it is not only meeting increased competition from the Tennessee Valley, but is also having to pay for subsidizing electricity there to be sold at less than cost. These arguments have had a considerable effect in undermining congressional support for the TVA.

In addition, the TVA has, of course, made some bureaucratic errors, such as its long exclusion of the Soil Conservation Service, that made it some enemies and embarrassed its friends, but such errors have been comparatively few, considering the size of the operation.

There have been many sporadic attempts in Congress to dismember the TVA or starve it of funds for growth, but they were unsuccessful. In 1953, however, signs of hostility began to multiply in Congress and in the Administration, and the people of the valley became alarmed. They formed an association, "Citizens for TVA, Inc.," and raised a campaign fund to fight any attack that might come. Such an attack was not long in materializing.

The TVA was in a vulnerable position because it needed capital for the rapid expansion of its electric plants. The demand for domestic and industrial power in the valley had risen steadily since the low TVA rates were introduced. On top of that came the Atomic Energy Commission, which required vast amounts of power to manufacture atomic fuel and had not reached the point of building atomic power plants to supply its own needs. The TVA had used up its available waterpower and had built several large steam plants to supplement its hydroelectric power. Near Paducah, Kentucky, the AEC had had experience with a power plant built by a large private concern, where the costs had greatly exceeded those of a comparable TVA steam plant. Nevertheless, there was growing opposition in Washington to allowing the TVA to build any more plants.

At the same time the city of Memphis was asking the TVA for more electricity. President Truman's final Budget in January, 1953, called for money for the TVA to build another steam plant near Memphis, but the new Congress was not inclined either to supply the money or to authorize the TVA to borrow it in the open market.

Joseph M. Dodge, first Director of the Budget under the Eisenhower Administration, brought forward a plan to supply power for Memphis without further expanding the TVA plants. He arranged with Edgar H. Dixon, President of Middle South Utilities, and Eugene A. Yates, Chairman of the Board of the Southern Co., to form the Mississippi Valley Generating Co., and to build a 650,000-kilowatt plant at West Memphis, Arkansas, across the Mississippi from Memphis. This plant would sell power to the AEC, which, to be sure, had no need for it at that location but would trade it to the TVA in return for an equivalent supply elsewhere. The net effect would be that Memphis would receive Dixon-Yates power from the TVA, and it would cost the TVA considerably more than the power it could have produced in a plant of its own.

The TVA board was less than enthusiastic for the Dixon-Yates plan and so, apparently, were the members of the AEC, except for the chairman. The AEC was ordered to sign the contract, which it did.

The people of the valley rose in wrath, with their senators, representatives, governors, and mayors, and with the Citizens for TVA, Inc., marching in the van. They charged that the intention was to eat into TVA territory by forbidding the

TVA to build new capacity to meet its own increasing load and then letting private companies come in and get the business at higher costs. They were aroused by reports that the originators of the Dixon-Yates proposal were opposed to letting the TVA stay in business at all and were planning to sell the TVA power system to private operators.

As in the case of the Pinchot-Ballinger affair, the battle lines were drawn, but the issue of the moment was decided neither on its merits nor by political influence, but by accident.

The most awkward blow was the disclosure by a Senate investigation that Adolphe Wenzell, a vice-president of the First Boston Corp., had been an adviser to the Budget Bureau while the Dixon-Yates project was being organized. The First Boston Corp., it appeared, was the financial agent of the new Mississippi Valley Generating Co. There seemed to be a conflict of interest between Wenzell of First Boston and Wenzell of the Budget Bureau. The government also seemed to be concealing evidence until driven into a corner and forced to admit what was at first denied.

While the Administration was in this awkward position, the city of Memphis announced that it proposed to borrow $100 million and build its own plant. With the obvious advantage of friendly relations with the TVA and the opportunity of a tie-in to smooth the variations in its power load, Memphis expected to get its electricity at much less than Dixon-Yates prices.

The government canceled the Dixon-Yates contract and expressed satisfaction at the local initiative shown by the people of Memphis. The feeling in the valley was that for the moment a dangerous attack on the TVA had been warded off, but the people there were disposed to remain on guard.

As for the AEC, Eugene M. Zuckert, one of its former Commissioners, says:

"The effect of the Dixon-Yates contract upon the Commission and its relationship with Congress can hardly be overstated. If ever an agency of government needlessly became involved in a deep and bitter ideological battle, the AEC did when a few powerful shortsighted men, presumably high in Administration fiscal circles, cast it in the role of cat's-paw in the Bureau of the Budget's attempt to discipline severely—if not destroy—the Tennessee Valley Authority. . . .

"Once lost, the AEC's 'above politics' stature, which before the Dixon-Yates fiasco was undisputed, was replaced by a deep distrust of almost all actions of the Commission, particularly by the Democratic members of Congress who opposed the Dixon-Yates arrangement.

"Even to the hardy Republicans who had supported the Dixon-Yates contract in a sincere belief that it was a perfectly proper deal, the rude awakening that followed the Presidentially directed termination of the contract has been a source of irritation, embarrassment, and concomitantly disquieting suspicion that 1901 Constitution Avenue [the AEC] didn't quite play it straight with them." (Reprinted by permission from *Atomic Energy for Your Business,* by Arnold Kramish and Eugene M. Zuckert, David McKay Co., New York, 1956, p. 130.)

The other most spectacular attack on river development in recent years has been the battle of Hells Canyon.

Hells Canyon on the Snake River, a tributary of the Columbia, is deep and well suited to a high dam. In 1908, at Pinchot's suggestion, Theodore Roosevelt reserved the Hells Canyon waterpower site, and the Interior Department has long had a plan for a high dam there, to be an important link in the comprehensive development of the Columbia River basin. Some of the world's largest phosphate deposits are nearby, and they will need great quantities of cheap power for their manufacture into fertilizers by processes that have been worked out by the TVA. The storage back of the high dam would add to the power capacity of all the dams downstream as far as Bonneville, near Portland.

But the Idaho Power Co. wanted to build three low dams in the same stretch of river. If those three dams were to be built, the high dam would be blocked, since it then would cost too much to buy and submerge the power company's property.

The decision whether to give a license to the company was in the hands of the Federal Power Commission. When the matter first came up in President Truman's Administration, Oscar Chapman was Secretary of the Interior, and he registered an objection with the commission. In 1953, Secretary Douglas McKay withdrew the objection. Then the fight began.

Citizens of the Northwest organized the National Hells Canyon Association and raised money for lawyers and engineers to testify before the commission. When the power company's lawyers argued the advantages of letting local enterprise develop the resources instead of depending on the federal government, the association replied that the Idaho Power Co., being a Maine corporation owned largely in the East, was not a local enterprise.

The company argued that its project would save the government money, since the company would supply the capital. This is an appealing argument, since in our Congressional appropriations a capital investment is treated as if it were a simple annual operational expense. Hells Canyon is not the only place where the government has shown signs of wanting to avoid investing money by getting a private concern to do the investing, even at a higher ultimate cost to the taxpayers.

The company argued that the government would get about $10 million a year in taxes if the company were to build and own the dams. The association replied that if the high dam were built the greater amount of electric power that it would produce would support about half a billion dollars' worth of additional production in the Northwest, and that in turn would pay added tax revenues of at least $45 million a year.

After many months of listening to arguments and studying the twenty thousand pages of testimony, the Power Commission's examiner reported that the high dam would produce 1,200,000 kilowatts of power at a cost of 2.7 mills per kilowatt-hour, whereas Idaho Power's dams would yield only 505,000 kw at a cost of 6.69 mills per kwh. The high dam would also provide superior flood storage. Yet he recommended the power company license because, as he said, of the "prevailing political climate." The commission decided to grant the license.

The Hells Canyon Association announced that it would take the case to the courts and also would seek action in Congress to force the building of the high dam. The American Public Power Association printed a letter saying that at least three other projected high dams on the Columbia system, with important quantities of possible storage, were under similar attacks by private companies wanting to build less adequate dams.

After the decision in its favor, the Idaho Power Co. was reported to have applied for accelerated depreciation privileges amounting to a federal subsidy of over $300 million —about as much as the total estimated cost to the government of the high dam. Late in 1956 another project on the Snake River threatened to develop into "another Hells Canyon." This was a proposal by the Pacific Northwest Power Co. to build two dams yielding a total of 1,000,000 kw, blocking the construction of the Nez Perce high dam which would produce 1,650,000 kw.

The Columbia River developments, including the Bonneville and Grand Coulee dams, have been the nearest thing to a second TVA so far attempted in the United States, but the Columbia River basin is the scene of a network of conflicts. The federal power plants compete with a strong group of private companies that also produce hydroelectric power. Canada is at odds with the United States on several points, including the diversion of water from the upper Columbia to the Frazer River. There are conflicts between Canadian and American aluminum companies. The irrigation interests upstream conflict with flood control downstream. Upstream power companies are at odds with downstream ones, the salmon industry with the Corps of Engineers, and the Engineers with Reclamation. In the midst of all these problems the Bonneville Power Administration, which manages the federally owned dams, is not equipped to provide an adequate unified resource development program.

The chief weakness of Bonneville is that it is controlled by the faraway Interior Department. It is not, like the TVA, a self-contained corporation directly responsible only to the President and Congress and backed by an effective body of local sentiment to fight for it against political meddling. In 1941 there was an attempt to correct this weakness. A group of old hands in the conservation movement, including Senator Norris, Judson King, David Lilienthal, Harry Slattery, and Leland Olds, drafted a bill for a Columbia Valley Authority, to be a corporation similar to the TVA. Secretary Ickes, however, heard of the plan and succeeded in mustering sufficient opposition in Congress to block it.

New England has long resisted the idea of river control, with its accompanying threat of public competition against the local power companies. In 1955, however, after the great hurricane floods of August and October, there were signs of a demand for some kind of flood control. Moreover, the opposition to cheap power was by no means unanimous. For example, former Governor Paul A. Dever of Massachusetts, testifying before a House subcommittee after the 1955 floods, pointed out that a Boston factory paying $1,380 a month for 60,000 kwh of electricity could get the same amount for $820 if it were in Birmingham, Alabama, a difference of

$6,720 a year. (And Birmingham does not even have TVA current. It is only near the TVA.) Governor Dever said that a difference of that amount must be a factor in the location of industry. Most New Englanders, however, do not appear to agree with Dever. In 1956 the signs appeared to point toward some increase in river works for flood control, but any electric power they might produce would be sold to private companies at the bus bar so as to avoid disturbing the rate structure.

While the TVA and other attempts at river development were struggling with legal and political obstacles, an important constitutional point was settled in the New River case, decided by the Supreme Court in 1940. The Court in its decision recognized a federal right to "the protection of navigable waters in capacity as well as in use." In other words, even if a mountain tributary is too steep for boats, a power dam there may hold back water that is needed in a dry spell for navigation lower down, and the dam must therefore be subject to federal control.

The case arose because a power company wanted to build a dam at Radford, Virginia, on the New River, a tributary of the Kanawha. The Kanawha flows through West Virginia and carries barge traffic. The Federal Power Commission notified the company in 1927 that under the Federal Power Act of 1920 it must get a license from the commission before building the dam, since the dam would affect interstate commerce. President Hoover was advised by Attorney General William D. Mitchell that the river was not navigable and that the power law did not stand in the way of a license. The company appealed the commission's ruling to the courts. But before the case could be settled, Hoover was no longer in office and there was a new Attorney General, Homer S. Cummings. He appointed Huston Thompson, who had been Assistant Attorney General under Woodrow Wilson, as Special Assistant to handle the case for the government. Thompson was not content to prove that the New River had in fact been used for navigation at various times—such, for instance, as the floating of logs. He tackled the fundamental issue of the control of tributaries. He made it clear to the Court that unified engineering treatment of the streams, the ideal already embodied in the TVA, would be forever impossible if the Constitution were interpreted to allow isolated and uncontrolled water projects on the tributaries of navigable rivers.

And that was what the Court settled by its decision in 1940. The power companies still hope to build small dams that will break up a river basin plan, such as the project at Hells Canyon. But the constitutional right of the government to block such dams is no longer in question. That is what came of the New River decision.

The principle of river basin planning has therefore been well established in constitutional law, and one example of it, the TVA, has been established in practical form. Further examples in the United States are obstructed at present largely by the opposition of the electric companies to the public power features of river development. But in foreign countries the effect of the TVA experience has been widespread and profound.

Difficult as the organization of the TVA is to reproduce, the TVA success has inspired many river basin projects abroad, from India to Brazil to the Highlands of Scotland. These examples of conservation in its most comprehensive form may be expected to multiply as further experience leads to improvements in river basin management technique.

Chapter 15

CONSERVATION OF FUELS

Most modern nations are committed to the hope of raising the standard of living of their people, and that in turn calls for an increase in their energy requirements year by year. Political necessity demands a rising production per capita, and the growth of population adds to the pressure. In the United States, for example, President Truman's Materials Policy Commission in 1952 estimated that the demand for energy would be 3 per cent more each year from 1950 to 1975, and in Western Europe various authorities expect increases of 1½ to 2½ per cent a year. But that is only a small part of the coming world demand.

The rapidly developing countries, such as the Soviet Union and many in Latin America, are increasing their use of energy much faster than the United States. The average growth of energy use in Latin America since World War II has been more than 5 per cent a year, and the percentage in the Soviet Union has been even higher.

Finally there are the "underdeveloped" countries, where most of the people now work on the land with human and animal muscle, and with practically no mechanical help.

At the present time the use of energy varies widely. Canada and the United States use about thirty times as much energy per person as Paraguay and Haiti. Part of the difference is related to the climate, which requires house heating in the more northerly latitudes, but most of it comes from the relative degree of industrialization and the amount of transportation. The world political situation, if we have no shooting war, will stimulate efforts to help develop the low-income countries, and that will mean industrialization and a great increase in their demand for energy.

Altogether, if the Materials Policy Commission's estimate of 3 per cent increase per year is projected to the year 2000 it would mean a world energy requirement about four times that of 1950. United Nations sources have estimated that it might be more than five times that of 1952. Whatever it turns out to be, it will be a big increase. The question is, where can we get that much coal and oil and other sources of energy? But even more important, where do our children go from there?

Harrison S. Brown, of the California Institute of Technology, has pointed out that if our complicated world civilization should collapse, it is not certain that the survivors could rebuild it. The system might collapse in several ways —by an atomic war that killed almost all animal life on earth; by political failure to establish a reasonable degree of conservation; or by technological failure to adjust its demands to the depletion of minerals that are necessary to its established methods of production. If there were any survivors, they would probably be starved down into low-grade agricultural communities, lacking machinery, insecticides, fertilizers, and diversified markets. They could not easily give their children much education. Finally, the previous depletion of the easily mined fuels and metals that were the mainstay of man's early development might leave them with nothing but low-grade deposits that could be used only by a vast going concern of technology, commerce, and political economics—exactly what they had lost.

This is a sad picture, but it does emphasize the value of keeping some high-grade reserves of ordinary fuels and metals, such as those in wildlife refuges and national parks, as a sort of backstop in case of a not-quite-universal catastrophe. We do not know, even now, whether Western Europe could have survived as a land of free and civilized peoples after World War II if the United States had not had plenty of resources to offer during the early stages of recovery.

Accordingly, even though there seems to be a prospect of enough atomic energy to meet the world's power needs for a long time to come, the conservation of the other fuels and their economical use is not entirely futile.

In August, 1955, the United Nations held a conference in Geneva on the Peaceful Uses of Atomic Energy, at which the reports from atomic scientists of many nations were optimistic. To be sure, a leading expert on the biological effects of radiation, who was prepared to warn the conference on the dangers to human heredity, was excluded, by request of the United States Atomic Energy Commission. The arguments over this bit of suppression gave world-wide publicity to the fact that the atom may still be more a threat than a friend to man. But, for good or ill, man is going to develop the power of the atom and will hunt for ways to dispose of the wastes so that they will not gradually poison earth, sea, and atmosphere.

By 1957 the British, who had gone ahead of this country in the development of nuclear power, were reporting a cost of about 8 mills per kwh, not counting any credit for bomb material produced as a by-product. The same plant in the United States, privately built, would cost about twice as much. The average cost in Britain in new large plants burning coal or oil is 7 mills, and it is expected that by 1970 nuclear power will be well below the cost of that from conventional fuels.

A series of studies of the economics of nuclear power made by the National Planning Association indicates that it is likely to begin competing with coal and oil-burning plants by 1965 in Europe, in many parts of Asia and South America, and in New England, Florida, Minnesota, and Alaska. By 1975, according to these forecasts, most of the new plants of large size constructed in the United States will be built for atomic power.

Uranium is found almost universally in rocks, in low concentration, and the supply of ore sufficiently concentrated to be worth mining by present methods seems to be fairly large. At Geneva, Sir John Cockroft reported a million tons in sight in the world, and he expected that in time a million tons of uranium would give the energy of 100,000 million tons of coal. The United States has about 2,000,000 million tons of coal still in the ground, though most of it is of low grade. One-twentieth as much in equivalent uranium is not to be despised, and the surface of the uranium reserve has hardly been scratched. Moreover, before the next few decades or generations have gone by, the scientists hope to have solved the problem of combining hydrogen atoms into helium without having to use the inside of an atomic bomb explosion as the cooking pot. If that problem can be solved on earth, there will be enough power, for the deuterium form of hydrogen that will presumably be used for power is plentiful in the ocean.

But shall we therefore bid goodbye to other sources of energy? For a long time to come the answer seems to be no.

For one thing, so far we do not see any good way to use atomic energy to drive automobiles or locomotives because of the weight and cost of shielding materials and the problem of disposal of the poisonous ashes. Oil and gas supply about two-thirds of the total energy used in this country, and much of it is for purposes, such as house heating, that cannot so far be met by direct application of atomic heat and cannot be met cheaply by electricity produced by atomic plants or otherwise.

At some price electricity drawn from an atomic power station can be used for heating, and even, with better storage batteries, for driving motor vehicles. But at present it seems more convenient, as well as cheaper, to have portable fuels. Waterpower in the best locations, such as Grand Coulee, is still far cheaper than atomic or even coal power, and it may remain so for a long time. On the other hand, the idea that waterpower is "renewable" because the sun puts the water back on the mountain every year is only partially true. The Hoover Dam in the Colorado River is fast filling up with silt, and nearly every other power dam in the country is gradually losing its storage capacity. Waterpower, therefore, is renewable only so far as it comes from the run of the river, not counting storage, and in many rivers the low-water flow is negligible. In most dams the storage capacity will be used up in fifty or a hundred years unless the erosion of the watershed can be stopped. Only vigorous soil conservation can hope to put off the loss of the bulk of our waterpower. An invention that is much needed is a practical process for washing the silt out of reservoirs.

In any case, if all the waterpower in the world were fully used it would meet less than 40 per cent of the world's demand for energy, even today.

Another source of power is the sun acting directly on the instruments of man or indirectly through winds and through the growth of plants. These, together with run-of-the-river and tidal waterpowers, are the only important power resources that are being currently renewed from outside the earth. None of them shows prospects of being a major contribution to the massive total of the energy requirements of civilized man. There are some isolated places, however, where these renewable resources can be used with profit. Artificial photosynthesis, by which the scientists hope to make carbohydrates out of sunlight and air in tanks, and a remarkable battery developed by Bell Telephone Laboratories to produce electric current directly from sunlight will no doubt be useful, but they show no signs of being serious competitors of the atom or of the conventional fuels, coal and petroleum.

So we come back to the great fossil fuels, coal, oil, and gas. At best, we can expect them to last us as fuels for only a few centuries. After they are far gone, the remainder will be saved for chemical uses, largely as materials for synthetics and special lubricants. In view of the uncertainties of the atom and the need of reserves for unforeseen technical developments, it seems fair to say that the fossil fuels are still worth treating with some economy.

The United States has about a third of the known coal in the world, but it varies greatly in quality. The anthracite which around 1900 was universally employed in the Northeast for house heating has been gradually going out of use, through increasing depletion of the easily mined veins and through competition of the more convenient oil and gas. Some of the best veins of bituminous coal have been seriously depleted, but there are still plenty of workable veins. The improvements in technology have helped save coal during this century. For one thing, it took about seven pounds of coal to generate one kilowatt-hour of electricity in 1900; now it takes less than one pound. For another, the railroads, by changing from coal to diesel locomotives, have not only cut their raw energy requirements per ton-mile by four-fifths but have cut off one of the greatest markets for coal. These coal-saving developments and the growing use of oil and gas long kept the demand for coal from rising in proportion with the national income, and actually no more bituminous coal was used in 1950 than in 1914.

The number of man-hours required to mine a ton of coal often increases with the depletion of the easiest seams, as it did in Great Britain after about 1880. This increase has so far been counteracted in the United States by the invention of new mining and loading machinery and the cooperation of union labor in its use. At the same time, thanks to John

L. Lewis's effective leadership, union labor has greatly increased its earnings per ton. As a result coal prices have risen since about 1914, and consumers have reacted by developing more efficient boilers and turbines. Mr. Lewis himself, on being reminded that his wage demands might tend to price coal out of the market, has said that coal mining was not a fit life for human beings and its gradual disappearance would be desirable.

On the other hand, the growth of demand for electric power and industrial heat may well create a growing demand for coal, which in most parts of the United States is the cheapest boiler fuel, at least until perhaps 1970 or 1980, when nuclear energy may begin to compete in the largest plants. Thereafter, if the technology of producing gasoline from coal should develop sufficiently, that alone might create a big new demand.

The net effect of Mr. Lewis's policies so far has been that coal miners get much higher wages than other skilled workers; so that, although their number is gradually diminishing, enough remain to turn out more and more coal with the high-powered modern machinery, and at moderate costs.

Altogether there seems to be little sign of coal becoming obsolete even as common boiler fuel. And the limited supplies of coking coal need to be carefully conserved lest we be forced by scarcity to resort to more costly processes for making iron.

In some places strip mining has created a conservation problem. The overlying land is dug off and piled to one side, and then the horizontal coal seams are mined with the steam shovel. The overlying material is turned into a rock heap, but at some extra cost it can be smoothed off and planted with trees, which can reach down and collect the scattered nourishment in the mass of broken stones. Difficulties arise when the restoration is said to cost too much or if the restored land is worth less than before. Then it may seem reasonable for the government to prohibit strip mining or to require the mining company to restore a useful land surface.

In 1955, for instance, the Stearns Coal and Lumber Co. in Kentucky, which had sold some lands to the Cumberland National Forest, but had reserved the mining rights, proposed to mine the coal by strip mining instead of going underground. Secretary Benson appointed a special board, with Charles P. Taft as chairman, to examine the proposal. On the board's advice Benson refused to permit strip mining, since it would cause water pollution, disrupt the forestry program, and hurt the recreational value of the reserve.

Petroleum has been a concern of the conservation movement since Theodore Roosevelt's time. T.R. began the withdrawal of oil lands in the public domain, but the process of creating oil reserves was not completed before he went out of office. Under Taft, Secretary Ballinger held that the President did not have legal power to make such withdrawals. Pinchot protested and aroused public opinion. The Geological Survey recommended that the lands be withdrawn, stressing the future needs of the Navy, and in September, 1909, President Taft withdrew all oil lands in the public domain subject to further Congressional action. Congress gave him the desired authorization in the Act of June 25, 1910. Taft then reaffirmed the withdrawals and specifically set up two naval oil reserves in California and one, the Teapot Dome, in Wyoming.

Enforcement, however, was spotty, and oil companies poached some of the reserved oil.

Under Woodrow Wilson a bill was introduced by conservationists to permit leasing oil lands in the reserves, but not including the naval reserves. Senator James D. Phelan of California moved amendments to give amnesty to trespassers and to allow leases in the naval reserves. Pinchot opposed these amendments and so did Josephus Daniels, Sec-retary of the Navy. But Secretary Lane of the Interior—and of California—was for them, and President Wilson, who was in Paris, cabled instructions taking Lane's side. At Pinchot's urging Senator Robert La Follette the elder filibustered the bill to death in the 65th Congress, but the 66th Congress passed it.

Then came the Elk Hills case. The Southern Pacific Railroad had been given as a subsidy some 170,000 acres of public land, later enclosed in the boundaries of the California naval reserves. The grant was conditioned on the land having no mineral values, but, although there seemed to be oil there, the railroad claimed title to 6,000 acres in the Elk Hills district. At first the railroad won its case, but later lost it in the Supreme Court. Meanwhile, in a second case, the Southern Pacific claim to 165,000 acres was allowed by the Circuit Court of Appeals on the basis of the earlier decision in the Elk Hills case before the Supreme Court reversed it. Normally, Attorney General A. Mitchell Palmer should have appealed the second case after the Supreme Court had reversed the earlier one, but he neglected to do so. Thus the government not only lost half a billion dollars' worth of oil lands, but as the lost lands were in alternate sections, there was danger that all the oil might be drained out of its own reserved land in the area.

But the great scandal in connection with the Navy's oil lands developed around Teapot Dome. The Naval Appropriation Act of 1920 gave the Secretary of the Navy authority to protect the reserved oil from being drained by taking it out, if necessary, and, if necessary, even by leasing the land to private oil companies. President Harding, although he had promised Gifford Pinchot that he would keep this power in the Navy, transferred it to Secretary Albert B. Fall of the Interior, who had no great interest in conservation. Fall then granted important leases to Harry Sinclair and E. L. Doheny in Teapot Dome and Elk Hills. In late 1923

a Senate committee investigated these leases and found brib-
ery. Doheny confessed that he had made a $100,000 "loan"
to Secretary Fall. Fall took refuge in the Fifth Amendment,
but he afterwards went to jail for taking the $100,000 bribe.
For a short time the Democrats gloated, until it came out
that some of their leading party members were implicated.
For, after the Democrats had gone out of office in 1921,
Doheny had put four ex-members of Wilson's Cabinet on
his payroll. Ex-Secretary Lane got $50,000 a year and Wil-
liam G. McAdoo, Wilson's son-in-law and the front-runner
for the Democratic presidential nomination in 1924, also got
a retainer of $50,000 a year. Doheny himself was a well-
known Democrat and contributor to party funds.

Amos Pinchot, Gifford's brother, called it sarcastically "a
pleasant mixup in Washington." He and five million other
disgusted citizens voted for Robert La Follette, but Calvin
Coolidge, whose personal skirts were not oil-stained, was
elected President in 1924.

This was not all that was to happen to oil down to the
day, twenty-eight years later, when Texas voted Republican
after a Republican promise to support a bill to give the
states the federal offshore oil.

Oil has been much involved in monopoly since John D.
Rockefeller got control of the kerosene business by obtain-
ing a stranglehold on oil transportation. To this day ownership of pipelines and tanker fleets is an important means
of controlling the prices of petroleum products.

According to the common law, oil belongs to the man who
brings it up out of his well, even though it flowed in from
under his neighbor's land. When a field comes into production, any landowner who wants to get his share has to drill.
Then, if the state decides to limit output, the custom has
been to give each well an equal quota. The whole situation
has encouraged the drilling of unnecessary wells, with a waste
of oil-well materials if not of oil.

In 1924 President Coolidge established a board to consider the problem of overproduction of oil. The board recommended that the states work together with the help of the Interior Department to conserve oil. Then at the time of the depression the new East Texas and California fields came in and flooded the depressed markets. State prorating laws, aimed at controlling the flow, were at first invalidated by federal courts, but in 1932 the Supreme Court approved prorating and in 1933 the NRA was encouraging restrictive practices in general. The Interior Department made official findings of "demand," to be used for prorating purposes, and federal law prohibited interstate shipment of "hot oil," obtained by violating the quota.

These restrictive state laws were named "conservation" laws, but their main purpose was to limit production to what could be sold at a price satisfactory to the oil men. As Professor Eugene V. Rostow of the Yale Law School says in his book, *A National Policy for the Oil Industry:* "The contribution which the prorating states make to the cause of conservation is incidental and secondary."

Rostow questions whether inflicting monopoly prices on the public may not be too high a price to pay for the small amount of conservation that prorating may be said to carry with it. Another kind of conservation, more worth trying, would be to limit the number of oil wells to be drilled. An oil field could be allowed a well system planned by engineers to get out the oil with the least possible waste, giving all the property owners their share according to their property. But there seems little probability that the industry, with its vast political influence, would care to submit to scientific control of well drilling by the government. On the other hand, in recent years there has been a definite tendency for newly discovered oil fields to be smaller and for more of them to be operated under unified management with economical spacing of the wells.

In the meantime there is believed to be a good chance

President and Prophet. Theodore Roosevelt and Gifford Pinchot
on the Mississippi, 1907.

U.S. Forest Service

Devastation strikes (Oregon).

After logging, there was no fire protection (Washington).

High stumps show wasteful logging, but Douglas fir is coming in (Oregon).

On this cut-over land, new pine is coming in under fire protection (Alabama).

Clearcut areas are planned for fire protection and seeding (Oregon).

U.S. Forest Service

The forest works to hold the land on the 'watershed (Colorado).

A flood plain in Wisconsin shows eight feet of silt deposited in about 10,000 years since the glaciers retreated and five feet deposited in 75 years of man-made erosion. M. L. Cooke gave this picture to F.D.R., who kept it on his desk for several years before his death.

U.S. Soil Conservation Service

On this blown-out farm, even the trees are dead (Texas).

A red pine plantation will hold the sand (Michigan).

Thirty-eight years ago, this was a worn-out cotton field (Mississippi).

In 1948 this was overgrazed pasture (Mississippi)

In 1953 the same land showed the effects of five years of protection.

Gulley treatment combats erosion (South Carolina).

Contouring and a farm pond offer an example of good planning (Pennsylvania).

A flood rises after a 4-inch rain (Oklahoma).

Watershed conservation proves effective the morning after a 4-inch rain (Nebraska).

Kolana Rock, Hetch Hetchy, is shown as it was in 1910.

Kolana Rock is the background for a low-water scene in 1955.

Gifford Pinchot in 1933.

of finding new oil fields in the United States, which reduces the urgency of the problem of future scarcity, though the cost of finding new oil supplies has skyrocketed. There are also vast quantities of oil shale from which oil can be distilled at little or no more than the cost of oil from wells. At a somewhat higher price oil can be made from low-grade coal.

There may be more chance of attacking monopoly in oil than of imposing any effective conservation in its production and use. If there ever should be a political climate favorable to antimonopoly action in the petroleum business, what would it be desirable to do? Rostow suggests that a free market in oil would lead to only small increases in production, but enough to give the country definitely lower prices.

The essential monopoly power is the ownership by oil companies of pipelines, refineries, and filling stations. Rostow would separate the companies not merely into smaller integrated concerns but into independent oil producers, common carriers, refining companies, and service stations. Then perhaps a few of the larger separate units might also need to be cut in two.

The common belief that efficiency requires mammoth corporations is justified in a few industries, but not in oil. An efficient refinery, for instance, need not be what in the oil business would be called large.

With smaller concerns that did not control either their suppliers or their distributors price competition would be more effective. This, Rostow suggests, would be more important for the American people than the small bit of resource protection they can hope to get from the oil industry. Also, if the companies could be cut to some reasonable rate of profit, it might be politically easier, for instance, to admit more imports and otherwise economize on the American reserves.

Natural gas is closely associated with oil, and in the past a large amount of gas has been wasted because it came up out of the oil wells and there was no market for it. In recent years pipelines to the industrial North and East have brought gas to market from the South. This is about the only actual conservation undertaken by the petroleum industry.

As in oil, the gas pipeline is a bottleneck, and in the absence of regulation the gas from many separate producers can be brought to a particular market and sold under monopoly conditions. The efforts of the industry to get the interstate gas business out from under the regulation of the Federal Power Commission indicate that the producers expect to make a great deal more money if released from federal control. Their proposals have led to controversies in Congress, mainly between the representatives of the producing and those of the consuming states.

Conservation has little to do with the issues in these controversies except for the general prejudice of conservationists against monopoly. Nor can either political party make an issue of gas and oil monopoly, since both Democrats and Republicans are found working for the petroleum interests and there are signs of petroleum money in both parties and in states far from any gas or oil wells. There may be hope of bringing the petroleum industry into some rational relation with conservation and with the public interest in free competition and fair prices only if and when something arouses the public to take a consuming interest in the price of gas and gasoline.

For a time during the Suez crisis of 1956–57 that interest seemed to be rising, but hardly high enough to overcome the influence of oil in the government.

An interesting result of the embarrassing farm surplus problem is a special inquiry that may lead to scientific progress of some use in conserving minerals, especially fuels. The Soil Bank Act of 1956 set up a Commission on Increased Industrial Use of Agricultural Products and directed it to recommend legislation that would encourage new uses for farm products "not needed for human or animal consumption."

A large number of suggestions were brought in by fifteen "task groups" that the commission appointed. Much thought was given to a long-standing proposal to use grain alcohol as a motor fuel, to be mixed with gasoline. The main objection has been the cost. It would, to be sure, dispose of surplus stores of corn and wheat and it would save corresponding amounts of gasoline; but the commission estimated that the proposed substitution would cost the country at least $2 billion a year. The commission took into account the fact that, as things are now, the government is buying and selling, or even giving away, great quantities of grain at considerable loss in its efforts to support farm prices; and the question had to be considered whether turning the surplus into motor fuel would cost the taxpayers any more than the present methods of handling it.—In Congress, of course, if this question is seriously debated, the decision is likely to hinge rather on the relative political strength of the corn and wheat growers, as against the oil companies.

The commission was inclined more definitely to recommend the use of increased quantities of grain alcohol as raw material for synthetic rubber and plastics.

Another proposal that came up was that Congress provide the funds for a widespread examination of wild plants with a view to finding species suitable for cultivation. "In this Age of the Atom," said Wheeler McMillen, Executive Director of the commission, "we devote most of our effort to growing and using a few Stone Age plants." Only about 150 species of plants in the world are cultivated as commercial crops, and practically all of these, except for rubber and sugar beets, were chosen by primitive man before the dawn of history. Science might find half a dozen other plants that would supply food, fiber, medicine, or plastics on such a scale as to take over a noticeable fraction of the land now used for corn and wheat. If so, the immediate surplus problem might be somewhat eased and new industries might be created that would be in the crop-processing class rather than depending on mineral raw materials. There would seem to be advantages in pursuing this kind of inquiry in the years to come.

Chapter 16

CONSERVATION OF
MINERALS AND METALS

The peculiarity of mineral resources, including fuels, stone, and metals, is that when taken for human use they do not grow back like a well-managed forest. Metals that have been put to use can, to be sure, often be salvaged as scrap and used again, but metals are often dissipated into forms that cannot be salvaged. The lead in high-test gasoline, for instance, is scattered in use and can never be recovered.

At first sight conservation of minerals looks like a hopeless struggle to save enough of the nonrenewable resources so that posterity can maintain a high standard of living. But the picture is not all hopeless, and the day when the earth will be a burnt-out and worn-out rabbit warren of dilapidated mine workings is still a long way off.

There is time for improvement in political intelligence applied to the prudent use of mineral resources, and in the use of technology. Political intelligence might include a better understanding of what kinds of mining should, in the public interest, be subsidized, what controls should be set up in the public domain, and how much material should be imported and stockpiled.

As for technology, the time of spectacular changes is probably not over. For instance, if we ever get unlimited hydrogen power, some extremely low-grade ores, such as common granite, might be treated for the minute quantities of metals they contain, as we now get magnesium from seawater. Such a basic process would come close to providing an infinite reserve of ore for an increasing number of metals. Aluminum will be plentiful as long as abundant power is available, for when the bauxite is gone aluminum can be made, at a slightly greater cost, from certain extremely plentiful clays.

But until such power and processes are available for other resources, we had better try to conserve the ores and fuels that we know how to use at a reasonable cost.

Considering the minerals that can be used by our present methods, the United States has plentiful supplies of some and little or none of others. The rich iron ore of Minnesota, for instance, is now so far gone that American steel companies have staked out large new supplies in Labrador and Venezuela. At the same time the technology of taconite, a more difficult iron ore of which we have great quantities, is being developed.

But manganese and chromium, and several other metals used in making special steels and for other purposes, have to be imported from distant parts of the world. Technical progress would be hampered if supplies of these supplementary metals were cut off or depleted.

The United States is fortunate in having rather large supplies of sulphur and phosphates. Sulphur is the lifeblood of industry, for it makes sulphuric acid, the master chemical. Phosphates are the life of man and all the animals, for our bones are made of phosphate, and there can be no substitute for it. In many parts of the world the cattle have a wasting disease from not getting enough phosphate in the grass they eat, as was pointed out in 1929 by Sir John Boyd

Orr later the head of the UN Food and Agriculture Organization. For in the course of trade the cattle grown on the pastures have been shipped away with their bones inside them, and the bones were not sent back, so the pastures have been depleted of phosphates.

It is not only the cattle that suffer when the land is short of phosphates. People who eat vegetable food grown on depleted land also suffer from shortage of phosphate in their bodies. And the land itself suffers, for the plants that grow on it are puny and do not protect the soil from erosion. One of the first requirements in a soil conservation program is to get the sloping land covered with strong vegetation, and that often calls for adding phosphate.

While the phosphate mines last—and that will be a long while—new phosphate can be put on the land to help save the soil and to grow food for animals and man. Thousands of years hence, when the phosphate of the land has practically all gone into the sea, a much less numerous human race can still get it from seawater, by way of fish that pasture in the sea or by some technical process. But for now conservation calls for mining more phosphate and putting it on the land. In the United States, to be exact, it calls for mining more phosphate from the great deposits in the neighborhood of Hells Canyon.

Some materials are not so precious as phosphate, either because they are not necessary for human life or because they are plentiful. Copper, for instance, is scarce in the United States; the mines do not seem to be good for another century. But there is copper in Peru and Chile, and those countries need dollars that they can get by selling copper to this country. Besides, aluminum will substitute for many of the uses of copper. Copper in minute quantities is essential in the human body, but that can be had from seafood.

Lead and zinc are found in the United States, but not

in quantities that will last many years. Lead has certain uses where nothing else will do as well, and in the future it may be scarce throughout the world. Two of the most wasteful uses of lead are in paint and in high-octane gasoline. Conservation would suggest government pressure toward using the more common titanium for paint and a technology for gasoline that does not require lead. Zinc is dissipated in most of its uses, such as galvanizing, paint, and even dry-cell batteries, most of which are never salvaged; zinc is going to need substitutes in uses where it is not essential.

Some of the metals are used in forms that can be recovered and melted over—such as the steel in the frames of buildings, and in machinery and railroad rails, the lead plates in storage batteries, or the copper in heavy electric equipment. How much scrap will be saved and reused is mainly a matter of prices and of labor costs for sorting and handling. When any metals become scarce and costly, more of them will be salvaged. Governments can promote conservation by offering subsidies to encourage the salvaging of metals that are not yet scarce but will become so later.

Although substitutes are often available, such as aluminum for copper in electric wires or plastics for tin in cans, that is not a sufficient reason for wasting minerals in the happy confidence that science will always provide. Technology is developing not only substitutes but also new uses for old and new materials. Many of the little-known metals have peculiar qualities for alloying or for electrical work that no other material can duplicate. Any one of them may be of vital importance to a whole industry, if only for making a hard tip on a fountain pen or an almost microscopic electric valve to replace the familiar radio tube. It is therefore to be expected that as technology progresses there will be more and more tendency to find unique needs for each mineral, whether plentiful or scarce.

The fact that every country lacks some of the materials needed by high technology raises the question of "strategic materials." The United States had a painful experience during World War II when the Japanese advance in Asia cut off supplies of rubber and tin. The effect has been to encourage the stockpiling of metals and other materials that do not spoil in storage and to seek for domestic supplies such as synthetic and guayule rubber. In the mining business one of the strongest arguments for a tariff on metals is that it will encourage the opening of more mines, rendering the country less dependent on foreign supplies.

The idea of strategic materials has to be constantly revised to make it fit new international conditions. For even without a shooting war a scarcity problem might arise from the establishment of governments in Southeast Asia or in Africa that refused to trade on acceptable terms. A blockade of that sort might last for many years and might make it necessary to adapt our technology to the lack of certain materials that could no longer be had. Such a condition would, of course, stimulate exploration throughout the remaining free world. In the meantime a good stockpile would be a comfort during the painful readjustment that might be required. The uncertainty of world conditions also adds to the value of technical progress in the salvaging and substitution of materials.

The mining industry is naturally in favor of constant prospecting to discover new mineral deposits for it to work on when it uses up the old ones. Mining men believe that the government ought to give them every encouragement, especially by various forms of tax relief. At the Ford Foundation's Conference on Resources for the Future held in Washington in December, 1953, the mine operators were strongly in favor of tax exemption for a mine until it had paid back all its exploration expenses. Most of them also wanted to keep the provision that allows a high percentage of their net income to be tax-free to make up for the depletion of the resource.

William S. Paley, who had been chairman of President Truman's Materials Policy Commission, pointed out that the theory of the depletion allowance—to supply money for the exploration of new deposits—would be undermined by also getting full tax exemption on exploration costs; but the mining men were inclined to want all possible tax exemptions. Their main argument was that by encouraging exploration the government would get a bigger revenue because of faster growth of the mining industry—the usual, and often sound, argument for subsidies.

The mining industry would like to be protected from low prices, but is not agreed as to tariffs, price supports, or subsidies other than tax exemption, largely because of the government controls that might be attached to such benefits. There is some sentiment in favor of direct government help to the old-fashioned individual prospector, who, until he finds something, has no taxes to pay and therefore gets no benefit from tax exemption. And the Bureau of Mines and Geological Survey might be allowed to do a little exploration at public expense, in directions where the industry does not see a good chance of profit.

The mining industry is deeply interested in the ownership of minerals discovered on the public lands. The miners are naturally in favor of letting the discoverer file a claim and obtain full ownership rather than having to take a lease, with royalties to pay and some government control. They recognize that their position has been weakened by timber locators and dude ranchers who staked mining claims to get land with no intention of mining anything.

Mining has from the first been given the top rating among all possible uses of the public land, regardless of the value of the minerals in relation to other uses of the land such as forestry, watershed protection, and recreation. This policy has tied up large areas of the national forests in more or less dormant mining claims that have hindered forestry and grazing.

In July, 1955, a new law came into effect, promoted by the American Forestry Association, with the cooperation of government officials and mining interests. The new law stops the granting of land for sand, gravel, pumice, and cinder deposits; these may only be sold or leased at the discretion of the administering bureau without granting landownership. For other minerals, the claim will give no rights to other uses of the land, such as cutting the timber or building a hotel, until the mine is actually proved and the title transferred. Time will show whether the new law will bring the improvements expected of it.

Conservationists are inclined to believe that the government ought to have more latitude in reserving lands for forests, watershed protection, recreation, and grazing, and allowing only so much mining as would not interfere with these other uses. In other words, they feel that it may be almost time to deprive mining of its absolute priority and to make it take a place among possible uses, leaving the government a free choice to give priority according to the local circumstances.

In discussing what policies the government ought to adopt, it is useful to keep in mind that strong political obstacles stand in the way of any theoretically perfect conservation program, if such could be invented. All that can be hoped from a wider public understanding would be a tilting of the balance in Congress when there happens to be a close balance. There is no use in proposing, for instance, that the government purchases of gold and silver might be reexamined to see whether additional supplies of these metals are of any foreseeable use. If the country has all the gold and silver it needs for the near future, questions might arise not only about the subsidy that pays men to go on hunting for these metals but also about the policy of sacrificing other uses of the land to make room for new gold and silver mines.

Another question that is perhaps a little more practical is whether the taxpayers want to give more encouragement than is now given to the opening of new mines in the United States. Two different questions are raised here. The first is, do we want to explore as fast as possible and see what we have as a reserve in case of trouble with foreign supplies? Most people would say yes. The other one is, do we want the mining industry to dig out these resources as fast as possible, as they will be inclined to do if they are the ones who do the exploring? Here the answer is not so simple.

Whatever the government finds it politically possible to do, the mining companies are going to go on locating more deposits and working them as long as prices are attractive. The real question is whether the government services ought not to be authorized to do more prospecting on the public lands, with a view to discovering resources that they can put in reserve, since the government need not hurry to get the money back for the cost of exploration. Such public exploration would, of course, narrow the hunting ground for the mining companies, and any bonanzas would be public property to be leased on royalty instead of being given to a private discoverer. The mining companies do not like the idea, for the same reasons that the pioneers have always disliked government reservation of bonanza resources.

As time goes on, the underdeveloped three-quarters of the world will begin to need more minerals to feed growing industry and rising standards of living. If nearly every family in the world, for instance, could afford a small radio every ten years, in time the strain on some materials might become noticeable. Eventually, therefore, we must expect increasing trouble in locating raw materials abroad that the owners are willing to sell to us.

In the near future, however, as the underdeveloped parts of the world build up their agriculture and industry, they will want to buy tools and machines from the older industrial countries, especially the United States and Western Europe. Those developing countries that have good supplies of minerals can well afford to trade some of them for machinery that will increase their capital wealth. While this situation continues, the United States may do well to import minerals freely and go a bit slow on domestic mining, while not neglecting exploration and technical progress.

Technical progress can do much to economize the mineral resources of the nation. Some of it may be applied by private enterprise and some by government. Waste in mining is generally caused by taking the cheapest way to get out the ore and extract the metal. In the mine, when prices are low, it pays to take only the best ores and leave the poorer grades where they may be lost forever if the working should be abandoned. Aboveground, crude smelting methods let much of the value get away in the refuse, where it may or may not be possible to salvage the metal later with new techniques. Improvement in mining and smelting may allow a bigger proportion of the ore to be mined and a bigger proportion of the metal to be recovered from the ore.

Other technical improvements, such as the treatment of taconite iron ore or the TVA electric treatment of phosphate rock, allow the use of lower grades of ore, thus in effect increasing the available resource. Still other techniques, such as the Cottrell process for precipitating factory smoke, make possible the salvaging of valuable chemicals that otherwise would be wasted in polluting the air or the rivers.

Private industry can use all these technical improvements if the values saved are enough to pay the cost of the extra trouble and equipment. The government can profitably contribute research and patents that are useful but not quite able to pay their cost commercially, since the value to the nation of an increase in its resources may be worth paying for out of public funds. On the same principle the government can offer subsidies for mining methods that recover more of the valuable minerals than a strictly profit-making enterprise could afford to glean.

The use of subsidy to prevent picking the eyes of the mine and to assure getting out as much as possible of the metal before abandoning the working requires some unequal treatment of mines to avoid offending the public by giving excessive windfall profits to the rich ones. It would seem on general principles that either a mine should not be running at all in the present state of technology and prices or else it should be cleaning out the vein once and for all while the props are sound and the water is pumped out. But a private business cannot start and stop on any such self-denying principles while its overhead expenses go on. To apply conservation the government has to stand by with money to pay for any deviations from normal business practices that it may require. This means regimentation, and the industry is afraid of it, but it may in time seem to be worth the price in some of the less plentiful metals, such as copper, lead, and zinc.

In regard to fuels, metals, and other minerals, conservation is not one simple, clear-cut doctrine that can readily be applied to every problem. The ideal of the best or wisest use of the resource for the greatest good to the most people now and in the future can be more easily applied to forests, soil, water supplies, and codfish than to the "wasting" resources found in mines. But it is possible to indicate some guiding principles that may be helpful in forming an opinion on the political disputes over mineral resources:

1. Any concentration of mineral values that can be profitably mined, or that may become profitable with a foreseeable advance of technology, is a resource worth treating with respect.

2. Any waste that can be avoided with profit is worth avoiding at the expense of the person who gets the profit,

and the avoidance of such waste is a fit subject for legal compulsion if the resource has any public interest.

3. Any waste that can be avoided at some net cost may be worth avoiding for national reasons, as a longer-range matter of building or preserving national economic strength. That means subsidy. Whether the saving is worth the cost to the taxpayers is theoretically a complicated problem in future values. The line is really drawn not by mathematical computation but by political pressures between conservationists and others.

It is plain that some of the minerals, especially silver, oil, and gas, are tangled in politics in ways that make any effective conservation policy only a remote possibility.

Technical progress, if it brings no more basic inventions as dangerous as atomic fission, will probably do more good than harm. It is possible to hope that the worst things that were hidden in Pandora's box are out or will soon be out. Our mere survival is, to be sure, no longer guaranteed by universal ignorance of the means of universal destruction; but there is still hope, to be sought in moral and political adjustments. So far as the use and conservation of minerals are concerned, the most important elements will evidently be, on the one hand, the attainment of world peace and, on the other, the development of technology. Politically, the main result of that fact is that conservationists, along with other intelligent citizens, need to press for good schools, for the right of scientists to think and discuss, and for more generous appropriations to government research. With sufficient technical knowledge, and the possible increase of political intelligence in future centuries, the world supply of minerals would seem likely to be sufficient for some reasonable size of world population to have what it will consider a good standard of living for a long time.

Chapter 17

WILDLIFE CONSERVATION

"The kings of England formerly had their forests 'to hold the king's game,' for sport or food . . . and I think that they were impelled by a true instinct. Why should not we, who have renounced the king's authority, have our national preserves . . . in which the bear and panther, and some even of the hunter race, may still exist, and not be 'civilized off the face of the earth'—our forests, not to hold the king's game merely, but to hold and preserve the king himself also, the lord of creation—not for idle sport or food, but for inspiration and our own true recreation? or shall we, like villains, grub them all up, poaching on our own national domains?"—Henry David Thoreau, "Chesuncook," *Atlantic Monthly*, 1858.

Many people think that baseball is the chief outdoor sport in the United States. But measured by number of paying customers baseball does not rank at the top. In 1953 only 18 million people are reported to have bought tickets to baseball games, while 32 million bought hunting or fishing licenses; there were also about 4 million salt-water sports fishermen who were not required to have licenses. As a source of business, wildlife ranks high. A report from Wisconsin in 1955 shows that, while the population had increased 25 per cent since 1947, small-game hunters had increased 125 per cent, and out-of-state fishermen 600 per cent. As a sports writer in *Scottish Field* has put it, "Although a female trout may lay 4000 eggs at a spawning, anglers seem to be multiplying even faster."

Hunting and fishing are two kinds of outdoor recreation that we happen to have handy statistics about, but countless millions who do not fish or hunt go into the open for camping or picnicking, or simply to look, for the good of their souls.

In the early years of the century, while Pinchot and T.R. were emphasizing the hard "practical" necessity of securing the "wise use" of forests and minerals, the last survivor of the sky-darkening multitudes of the passenger pigeons was living out the final years of its species in the Cincinnati zoo. In those years a strong emotional drive was added to the conservation movement by the great bird lover T. Gilbert Pearson, head and builder of the Audubon Society. Pearson aroused sympathy and indignation over the slaughter of birds for use in millinery, besides preaching the economic value of birds, and was the main driving force in bringing about protective legislation. Ever since Pearson's time the interest in wildlife has been a vital component of the conservation movement in the United States.

The conservation of wildlife becomes more urgent and attracts more millions of voters to its support as a direct result of the population explosion that now threatens the United States and the form that the explosion is taking. At a meeting of the National Planning Association in December, 1956, Dr. Luther Gulick pointed out in an address on future city planning that the population of the United States is likely to pass 300 million within two generations and that most of the increase will appear in the suburban developments around the metropolitan centers. In the next fifty years these areas will probably have to make room for 120 million more people than they have today, more than doubling their present population. These people will need not only houses and yards but water and sewers, schools, churches, trading centers, hospitals, parks, and divided highways with cloverleaf access roads. "At the rate we are now going not less than one million acres of land a year is being added to the metropolitan 'developed' landscape." The open country where city people used to take the children for a walk on a Sunday afternoon is already half covered with housing, and the housing is full of people who want to get into the open country too. They have cars and some money to spare, and suburban living does not satisfy the outdoor urge enough to keep millions of families from starting out on weekends for the mountains or the shore, or from taking their vacations away from home. Most of the controversy about the use of wild land is subject to confusion by failure to recognize that getting outdoors and away from home is part of a high standard of living, and becoming increasingly so as the country becomes more crowded.

In all the political struggles over competing uses of the public lands, the commercial, "tangible," practical values are contrasted with the "intangible," sentimental values cherished by the nature lovers, and the fact that the population is increasing is cited to emphasize the necessity of keeping our eye fixed on the practical needs of these oncoming millions. But it may be worth remarking, on the other side, that so long as the standard of living actually continues to rise, it is a general principle that the importance of tangible values will necessarily diminish and that of the intangible, or sentimental, values will increase.

When a population is at a bare subsistence level the basic necessities of course take priority. The hungry citizen naturally cares far more about eating than about birdwatching. In the United States, if the time should ever come when it would really be of first importance to invade the wildlife sanctuaries in search of food or minerals for want of supplies elsewhere, that would be scraping the barrel indeed, presumably in the last stages of the Malthusian disaster, with hordes of starving people crawling all over the planet. But that is another story, and one that may never happen if the population explosion is stopped within a century or so. Meanwhile, the contestants in Congress are not thinking of Malthusian man *in extremis*. They all assume a rising level of living, which must mean the opposite of scraping any barrel of basic necessities. When people are affluent they can, by definition, take the necessities for granted and can focus their attention on wanting the amenities. Even in the markets the economic values also focus on the amenities, as anyone can observe by looking at magazine advertisements. And an amenity is merely something that is wanted for intangible, emotional, or aesthetic reasons rather than to relieve hunger or cold. Accordingly, it is fair to say that so long as in all the arguments a rising standard of living is taken for granted, the nature lovers are going to have increasing success in their demands for more reserved outdoor space.

In addition to space for human beings to camp and picnic there must also be refuge areas for wild creatures to live and breed, or they will die off, leaving only those that like crowds of people, such as the starlings and the rats.

The preservation of wild areas for land animals, birds, fish, and vacationing people is almost entirely a job for government, federal, state, and local. It costs public money and it competes with other uses of the land; but an increase in such areas is insistently demanded by millions of people who love the outdoors. The present indications are that the use of land for outdoor life will grow at the expense of more tangibly productive purposes. Grazing of cattle, for instance, may have to give way to the grazing of deer and other game animals on some of the "scenic" western ranges. Campers are likely to bring more wealth to the states that have good scenery than those states can get by wasting their natural beauties on cows, however contented. Cattle can be fed and fattened on land that will produce beef but not recreation. Lovers of the outdoors emphasize such monetary considerations whenever they find any, because the spiritual need for a sight of open country and the values of outdoor recreation for physical and mental health are all weak arguments before an appropriations committee. In Congress money is apt to talk, and what it is saying louder and louder is that the outdoors has profit in it.

Another practical reason for reserving space for wildlife is that without organized protection, largely governmental, too many forms are going to become extinct, crowded out by civilization. Many kinds of plants and animals are particular about where they live. Any work of man, whether it is cutting down the forest, draining the marsh, plowing the ground, or letting mud run into the brook, will kill some of the creatures that lived there. Flying over in noisy airplanes is bad enough; it is worse to tramp through the bushes with heavy bulldozers. The human race has cared little about killing off whole races of living things, until some spectacular food resource like the passenger pigeon ceased to exist and left a noticeable void. The American bison was barely saved, almost as narrowly as the European variety, a few moth-eaten specimens of which are still preserved in a park in northern Germany.

We can never tell what practical use our technology may find for some animal or plant, provided it still exists. Who would have thought, for instance, that the humble mold penicillium would suddenly spring into prominence as the source of a lifesaving antibiotic? Or that thousands of monkeys would be needed for the production of Salk vaccine? Who knows what kind of animal may provide an important medical or industrial material nowhere else to be found? We may have use for only one kind of creature in a million, but which one?

If the human race is going to preserve any considerable number of wild creatures it cannot preserve them in zoos.

They must live in sanctuaries where all the elements of a natural habitat are present, as they came down from past ages, when plant and animal, worm and bacterium, were being developed to live together in that place and climate.

The national parks, the national forests, and the national wildlife refuges have reserved some areas that are protected from hunters and kept as nearly as possible in their natural conditions. Some private tracts of forest or marshland are still preserved by the present owners—but who knows what their heirs will do? There is a growing demand for a general policy, under scientific direction, to find and reserve permanently many different areas of undisturbed nature. A bill for this purpose came before the 84th Congress but too late for action, going over into the next Congress to be resubmitted in 1957.

Even for the seemingly less complicated job of propagating game birds, animals, and fish, the experts are coming to be more and more aware of the importance of a proper habitat. Louisiana, for instance, tried breeding and putting out quail during four years from 1949 to 1952, and then gave it up. The Wildlife and Fisheries Commission released more than 144,000 pen-reared quail, all with leg bands; and got back from hunters only one band for every 200 birds released. The commission came to the conclusion that if the food and cover had been better the birds would have increased naturally, but with scanty food and cover those that they added simply died off. The birds cost about $2 each, so every bird shot and accounted for cost the taxpayers about $400. Similar results have often been found when hatchery trout are put in a stream where the forest has been cut off, letting in the sun to warm the water, or where silt has got in from eroding fields. What wild creatures need first of all is a good home like the one their ancestors were used to.

Under an act passed in 1937 the national excise taxes on sporting arms and ammunition were earmarked to be given to the states to aid wildlife refuge management, the states being required to match the federal grants. For several years before 1955 Congress failed to appropriate the full amount due, but in 1955 it released $13½ million of accumulated tax money. There were complaints, however, that the Budget Bureau was cutting down on funds for buying additional refuge land.

In 1953 the Secretary of the Interior appointed a survey committee to look into wildlife refuges, which recommended in 1954 that a number of the reservations held by the Fish and Wildlife Service should be reduced in size. There were strong pressures for turning over some 4½ million acres of big-game ranges to the states or to grazing districts. Most of this land had originally been made into wildlife refuges because it was so eroded and overgrazed that it had no value for cattle. But the Fish and Wildlife Service then took care of it for twenty years or more and it came back into good condition. Naturally there were interested persons who wanted the Interior Department to let them use it. The conservation editor of *Field and Stream* magazine reported in May, 1955, that he was concerned to find the Fish and Wildlife Service evading his questions.

Later in the year conservationists were disturbed to learn that the Secretary had ordered practically all the refuges opened to oil and gas drilling. The law permitting this use had been passed in 1920, but previous secretaries had been reluctant to issue leases except in rare cases where private land could be obtained for wildlife use only by allowing the owner to reserve drilling rights. In 1956 the House Merchant Marine and Fisheries Committee unanimously censured the Interior Department's leasing policies and obtained an agreement that in future the department would submit leases to it for consideration before acting.

In 1955 conservationists were alarmed too at indications that the Fish and Wildlife Service might be easing the controls on duck shooting at certain influential hunting clubs in California, Ohio, and Maryland. The point at issue was "baiting"—putting out corn at a convenient distance from the blinds to attract the ducks within range. Baiting had been made a federal offense in 1935 after an alarming decline in the number of wild ducks in the United States.

In California in the 1950s the ducks created a problem by settling on irrigated fields and eating up all the lettuce or alfalfa at one meal. For $5 a farmer could get a permit to shoot them on his land even in closed seasons. But the damage to crops made a good excuse for influential hunting clubs to offer an "experimental feeding program," to keep the ducks happy away from the farms and lure them to haunt the shooting ranges instead. The feeding program was permitted, starting in 1953. It has not provided enough feed to be a noticeable fraction of all that the ducks eat, but it did give ½ of 1 per cent of the 193,000 licensed duck hunters in California an advantage over the rest.

In Maryland the antibaiting law was resisted from the first by various prominent hunters who wanted more than average luck. Dr. Ira N. Gabrielson, who was Chief of the Bureau of Biological Survey in the late thirties, recalls how an ex-governor of Maryland pounded on his desk and shouted that he didn't care whether there were any waterfowl left after he was dead; he wanted to shoot ducks while he was alive. In December, 1954, the sentiment was much the same. Federal agents arrested 141 baiters on the Eastern Shore of Maryland. One club owner complained that he and his fellow members had killed only ten ducks apiece in the season. If this average were equaled by the unprivileged hunters it would wipe out every duck in the country.

In 1953 Albert M. Day, who had been Director of the Fish and Wildlife Service, was demoted to be an assistant to the Director. In June, 1955, he left the service and went into private employment. Some months before Day resigned Ralph A. Tudor, who had been Under Secretary of the Interior for a short time, said in a magazine article that before he left San Francisco to take up the job in Washington he was besieged by "friends in the banking business" who wanted him to "do something about the Fish and Wildlife Service." So, Mr. Tudor reported, he asked for suggestions about a satisfactory man to head the Service, and was advised to get John L. Farley, which he did. Mr. Farley, in an interview, denied having heard anything from California about shooting regulations, but the conservationists plainly showed distrust and fear of strong pressures from influential hunters. In December, 1955, the Wildlife Management Institute criticized Farley for transferring the Lenore Lake National Wildlife Refuge to the Washington State Department of Game, saying that he had ignored a promise to notify the House Merchant Marine and Fisheries Committee of any such proposed action in time for protests to be heard.

The Wichita National Forest in Oklahoma, containing 59,099 acres, was made a game reserve by Theodore Roosevelt in 1905. It was stocked with buffalo from the New York Zoological Park in 1907 and with Rocky Mountain elk from the Yellowstone in 1912. Deer, antelope, and wild turkeys have long flourished in the reserve. Commercial cattle were excluded after 1937 because of overgrazing, but Texas longhorns, now regarded as historic relics, are preserved along with the buffalo.

The Wichita Refuge is used by hundreds of thousands of people each year for camping, fishing, swimming, and observing the wild animals. Girl and Boy Scouts have summer camps there. In the 10,700 acres on the southern side of the refuge, which came to be the center of controversy, are the finest of the mountains in the area, six good recreation lakes, several important picnic and camping sites, and the winter pasture of the buffalo and longhorns. This land was wanted by the Army to add to the shooting range of the Fort Sill Artillery and Guided Missile School.

In July, 1955, the Army told Congress that, although there

were half a dozen other places in the country where it could fire the "Honest John" 762-millimeter rocket, the expense of taking the students to another location for practice would be prohibitive. The Army also stated that the area it wanted to take over was inaccessible and that four-fifths of it had already been fenced off and closed to the public. The Army's statement led to some dispute in Congress, for C. R. Gutermuth, of the Wildlife Management Institute, had been on the ground the month before and contradicted the Army's description. Writing on July 18, he pointed out that the land was not closed to the public—far from it—and that at that moment a large camp of Girl Scouts could be seen operating at a campsite in the disputed tract.

But Congress appropriated $1,000 for the Army to use for administrative costs of the transfer. The Army asked for this appropriation as a sanction from Congress to impress the Secretary of the Interior, whose consent in the end would be required. Late in July, however, the Interior Department announced that its policy was not to give up "major units of our wildlife refuge lands" but rather to get more land as soon as Congress would put up the money. In August it announced that more than 5 million persons had visited national wildlife refuges in 1954, an increase of 11 per cent over 1953. The two most popular places were the Crab Orchard Refuge in Illinois and the Wichita Refuge, each with over 850,000 visitors. In the meantime a flood of protesting letters poured into the White House and the Interior Department. On October 27 Secretary McKay announced his rejection of the Army's request. The Army, however, continued to press for Congressional action to override the rejection but was beaten for the time being when a bill for that purpose was pigeonholed in the House in the summer of 1956.

Finally, in February, 1957, a settlement was agreed upon at a meeting between Interior and the Army, together with representatives of the private conservation organizations.

The Army agreed to take a narrow strip along the border of the refuge and to pay for relocating the two campsites in this area. It also agreed to shoot only out of the area into its main reservation, and not the other way, and also to preserve the area as a wildlife sanctuary and assist in protecting it against hunting by military or civilian personnel. The Wildlife Management Institute expressed satisfaction with the settlement.

Meanwhile there was strong support in both Senate and House for a bill to forbid all withdrawals of public land for military use in excess of 5,000 acres, except with the approval of Congress, and to apply the fish and game laws specifically to military reservations. Early in March, 1957, when the National Wildlife Federation convened in Washington, the counsel of the House Interior Committee reported to the convention on this bill, and told the members that lands held by the armed forces "in excess of military needs now could form a strip 2½ miles wide from New York to San Francisco."

A particularly distressing conflict was precipitated by the U.S. Air Force when it proposed to set up a bombing range a mile south of the Aransas Wildlife Refuge on the Gulf coast of Texas. This refuge is the winter home of the almost extinct whooping cranes, which breed in Canada. There was a long controversy, and the Canadian government joined in the protests against this project. It was called off in October, 1955.

Alaska, being far away and not a state, has been the scene of some unrestrained acquisition by the armed services. In 1955 sportsmen were aroused by a sudden demand for a chemical warfare test area, covering some of the finest ranges of the mountain sheep, moose, caribou, and grizzly bear, and containing some of the few unspoiled grayling fishing streams. The sportsmen thought the military could look for land with less valuable game on it. In the places where wild species are threatened with extinction or irreparable damage, conservationists feel that the Services ought to be required to prove that no other location is possible before demanding the right to devastate refuge lands.

Salt-water fish are mainly commercial resources whose value is easily measured in dollars, and therefore even the most economy-minded legislators can accept them as fit subjects for conservation. No type of sea fish is likely to become extinct merely from overfishing, though a sea animal that breeds ashore such as the Alaska seal could have been utterly destroyed if the interested nations had not agreed in time to limit the catch on the Pribilof Islands. The sea fisheries can be overfished, however, and their profit can be greatly reduced by the resulting increase in the gear and labor required to catch a ton of fish. Only governments can correct an overfished condition, and then only if all the governments with interests in a particular area will act together.

If the crop of mackerel or lobsters is going to be about so many thousand pounds a year, then the most profitable fishery would be one that would harvest the crop with the fewest men and the least gear. The essence of an overfished condition is that the number of boats and men increases without a corresponding permanent increase in the catch, so that everyone makes less profit and the breeding stock of fish may be more or less diminished as well.

The cure for an overfished condition is to limit the number of boats, nets, and men allowed to go fishing or to limit the annual catch. Of course that cure will fail if there is any invasion from another state or nation that has not agreed to abide by the regulation.

One of the best examples of sea-fish conservation is the rebuilding of the Pacific halibut fishery by the United States and Canada acting together.

The halibut are caught with a trawl about 1,900 feet long, called a "skate." The difficulty of the fishery is measured in the number of skates hauled per million pounds of halibut.

In 1907, for instance, about 50 million pounds were caught with 178,571 skates, but by 1913 only 56.2 million pounds came from 436,273 skates. Yield per unit of work was down more than 50 per cent.

By 1923 an international treaty had been signed and a commission set up to make an exhaustive study of the habits of the halibut and its life history. In 1930 a new treaty gave the commission authority to set a total catch for each fishing ground. The fishermen made their own agreement for dividing up the quota. Each vessel, after bringing in a load, is required to keep away from the halibut fishing ground for a specified time, which is regulated according to the state of the market and the rate at which the quota is being used up. During the lay-up period the vessels and crews can take a rest or go for albacore, salmon, or herring.

The effect has been that the fishermen get much larger catches per skate; the trips are shorter; and it happens that the fish come in the medium size that will fetch the best prices. Naturally there can be no competition in the form of trying to catch the most fish per year, since each vessel has its own limit and must be laid up longer if it catches more. The crews can compete in skill to catch their allowed quota as quickly and cheaply as possible and get home. This is an example of a conservation problem that had to be solved by establishing a heavily regulated monopoly, with free enterprise only in the respects where it cannot hurt the basic resource.

The regulation has in fact been so successful that in 1955 it could be slightly relaxed. The commission found that it could allow an unregulated season of about two weeks, in certain areas, to harvest the surplus fish left over from the regular season's fishing.

The national parks are used by so many people that they have become seriously overcrowded. They have long suffered from Congressional economy, for most of their visitors are tourists who are not so effectively organized as the sportsmen to put pressure on legislators. In 1953 Bernard De Voto, that intrepid fighter for conservation, solemnly proposed that the government close the national parks because of their dangerously crowded facilities, unsafe bridges, and generally run-down condition. His purpose in making this proposal was to focus the indignation of park visitors and others on the failure of Congress to provide enough money. Something over 50 million people visit the national parks every year, and millions more are turned away.

What ought to be done is in some dispute. There is a question whether the number of tourist accommodations and of tourists admitted to the present park areas may not already be too large. There seems to be a growing demand for a combined program of adding more acreage and putting the existing parks in good order. One sign that the tourist vote was beginning to show an effect was the attempt of politicians of both parties to throw the blame for park conditions on the other party during the 1955 session of Congress. By 1956 there was a strong movement toward more generous appropriations in support of "Project 66," an Interior Department program of park improvement.

Similar pressures have been felt in the national forests, which had over 45 million visitors in 1955 and were expected to get as many as 66 million by 1962. In January, 1957, the Forest Service announced a 5-year plan to provide new camping and picnicking places for 40,500 families, nearly doubling the existing facilities.

In the political conflicts over conservation the organizations that are particularly concerned with wildlife and with the outdoors are generally found on the same side as the other conservationists. They want the forests to be saved from fire, and after cutting to be quickly returned to new growth.

They want all watersheds covered with vegetation that will hold the soil and keep it out of the streams. They want all sewage and industrial poisons kept out of the rivers, so that the salmon and shad can run as they used to do when our ancestors first came and so that people can sail and swim without fearing disease or poison.

The principal disagreement between the outdoor and wildlife organizations and other conservationists is about the big dams that drown out swamps and running streams and sometimes block the salmon and the shad from going up the river to spawn. The wildlife experts point out that homes for wild creatures are "uses" too, and should not be destroyed without first weighing their value against rival uses. They say that marshlands have values to be considered before a decision is taken to drain them for farming. They are concerned about the growing number of hydroelectric dams on the Columbia, fearing that the up-running fish may find the long series of fish ladders too much for their strength, and that too many of the seaward-bound fingerlings may get crushed in the turbines. For example, they were worried about the Bruces Eddy Dam in Idaho, which would block the salmon run in the Clearwater River. This dam was slipped into the Public Works Projects Bill in 1956 and failed only because the President vetoed the bill.

Since all wild creatures are legally the property of the state until someone catches them, the state would have a constitutional right to insist that when a power dam or a drainage project destroys a wildlife habitat some equally good land nearby must be reserved as a home for the creatures displaced. Some such requirement would lead to a full consideration of the wildlife cost of the project in dollar terms, just as the cost of buying out the human owners of the property is fully considered because they must be paid. Such a suggestion is not fantastic, especially where the people who cherish the wild denizens of the area in question are numerous enough to be a political force in the state.

The wildlife experts have many suggestions for accommodation between rival uses of land that will allow the wild things to survive even in territory used for other purposes. In forests, for instance, they like to see the woods cut in small units so as to produce many areas of new growth among the older sections, since this arrangement makes the best home for certain kinds of game animals. In farming country the amount of winter cover and of food can be adjusted to support more game animals and birds if anyone cares to attend to it. Birds to eat the local insects can be attracted by merely letting the fencerows grow up to bushes in the old-fashioned way. At least three states—Michigan, Ohio, and Virginia—have experts to make wildlife plans for farmers and to supply seeds and planting stock to use in planting cover thickets and wildlife food crops.

In late years there has been a noticeable tendency for the hunting, camping, and fishing fraternity to preempt the name "conservationist" as applying exclusively to themselves, somewhat to the distress of those who have devoted their energies to the older causes of forestry and soil conservation and to defending the nation's waterpower. The conservationists are concerned mostly with the means of health and enjoyment, and have only a comparatively slight interest measurable in commercial profits. Most of their real values are "intangible," but the wildlife fraternity is no less enthusiastic in its arguments on that account.

Despite the conflicts of values that are bound to occur here and there between one kind of conservation and another, the central doctrine is not divided. There are only differing viewpoints about what constitutes the greatest good of the greatest number. In one sense, those who study and defend the wild creatures have a right to call themselves peculiarly the conservationists, since they more than any others are fighting to conserve some part of the ancestral heritage in which the body, mind, and spirit of the human race were formed. These conservationists are close to the central truth that Gifford Pinchot and Theodore Roosevelt taught the people half a century ago—that all resources are parts of the web of human interests and life, to be used together with as little mutual injury as possible.

Part Four

THE WORLD

Chapter 18

CONSERVATION OF
WORLD RESOURCES

~~~~~~

The World Conference on Conservation, which Pinchot and Theodore Roosevelt planned for 1909 and Taft killed, is now in full and continuous operation in the United Nations and its Specialized Agencies. For the UN, despite its deep and persistent conflicts, is more than merely an awkward "League to Enforce Peace." The UN has, to be sure, helped to prevent some wars and to contain other conflicts. But, while the UN political committees struggle heavily with the immediate problems of international conflict, down in the grassroots other agencies of the world organization are building international cooperation.

The UN Food and Agriculture Organization, for instance, studies the world resources of land, forests, and fisheries, and helps the nations to use these resources more efficiently. The UN World Health Organization and the UN Children's Fund fight the great debilitating diseases, including malaria, tuberculosis, and dysentery, that cripple the productive capacity of whole populations. Other UN agencies, such as UNESCO and the International Labor Organization, work in many ways to improve the living conditions of people in far parts of the world, and conservation is a part of all their plans.

While the United Nations organizations are well launched on the beginnings of world conservation, the United States is still called upon to play a leading part in the conservation movement, abroad and at home.

The United States is called upon to set an example to the world in the prudent management of its inheritance, because it is the richest nation and has plenty of means to pay the costs of prudent management. It also can pay for research in the techniques of conservation at home and abroad. Other countries may be hard pressed merely to feed their people, without spending labor and material to protect their land or to find out how to protect it, unless they get help from abroad, but there is no such desperation in the United States.

The people of the United States now have the advantage of fifty years' discussion of the conservation of resources, speaking well of the idea in principle and fighting about its application in practice. We have made progress toward sound forestry and soil conservation—enough to escape some of the dire consequences that the early leaders of conservation were predicting with good cause fifty years ago. We have not escaped high prices and poor quality in lumber, however, and in 1955 there were new duststorms on the high plains.

The temptation of a rich and somewhat immature nation is to be extravagant—to prefer the bird in the hand, a rise in the immediate standard of living, to paying taxes for technical research or the control of soil erosion. The American people, however, show many signs of resisting that temptation. Many special interests, of course, oppose appropriations for conservation work, but experience has proved that those special interests can often be overcome by the pressure of public opinion acting on the legislators. The United States shows indications of a widespread public opinion in favor of paying what is necessary for building a sound economic system.

A "sound" economic system is one that is operated in such a way that it can be expected to go on being productive in future years, or even future thousands of years. That is the technical core of the doctrine of conservation. That doctrine has undoubtedly been accepted by large numbers of people in the United States, though not by all. Despite the widespread acceptance of the principles of conservation, however, the national housekeeping of the United States shows a good many deficiencies and the campaign for a more prudent management of national resources will no doubt continue a long time.

The evidences of depletion, erosion, and deterioration in the United States are sufficiently widespread to raise questions about the country's fabled riches. How much of the high income of the American people is real income? And how much is just the effect of spending money that grandfather left hidden in the family Bible? Some of it is real. A workingman with modern training, management, and technology can produce more in a day than his grandfather, and so is entitled to get more. But much of his increased production is merely the effect of using more mechanical power, and that power comes mostly from coal mines and oil wells. The worker is entitled to his share while it is being distributed, but it would not be realistic to think that all he and his employer are getting has been created by current use of muscle and brainpower. In addition to the inevitable depletion of mineral resources we are still using up forests, topsoil, and water supplies that ought to be renewed every year.

And what is coming to be more and more important, we are wasting our human resources. People are handicapped by disease or crippling that we know how to prevent. Children pass through the school years without being given as good schooling as we know how to give. We are losing potential scientists and many other kinds of potential experts that we shall sorely need in the future. Many workers are inefficient because their management is not modern. All these shortcomings in human conservation have an unfavorable effect on physical resource conservation as well. They interfere with the basic change from gadgets to services that will evidently be one of the main features of our future development, as the supply of raw materials gradually lags behind the rising standard of living. They also interfere with the growth of political knowledge and wisdom that will be necessary if we are to shift our policies to meet the problems of the twentieth century before the twenty-first is upon us.

There are indications that the United States may run short of some important minerals in the present century. According to the report of the Mid-Century Conference on Resources for the Future, the amount of petroleum, lead, copper, and zinc taken out of the ground in this country during the first half of the twentieth century has been considerably greater than the known reserves we have left.

American industry is demanding more of nearly all the important minerals than American mining can supply. In 1919, for instance, we produced 24 per cent of the lead in the world outside the Soviet orbit and used 25 per cent; but in 1950 we produced 25 per cent and used 64 per cent of the supply. In other minerals the picture is similar. This would seem to indicate that the higher the national income rises the more the United States becomes a have-not nation in terms of mineral resources. The need of conservation, therefore, would seem to grow more urgent as the nation appears to grow richer. And all the economic forecasters look for a continuing increase in American production, at least for such time as they are willing to forecast.

If the United States should fail badly in maintaining its necessary resources, we might find ourselves unable to give adequate help in the development of the poorer countries, and with hope deferred they might fall into disorder of disastrous proportions. Even in 1956, at the height of American material prosperity, the year began with chilly signs that important sections of American public opinion had become tired of standing up to our international responsibilities. The Administration's proposal to adopt a long-range program of foreign aid met with serious opposition in Congress, based on opposition among the voters. The popular revulsion against facing the facts was even more pronounced in 1957. Such waverings of the spirit are to be expected from time to time, but if they should find a basis in actual physical depletion of essential materials the prospect would be ominous.

The United States, however, with all its shortcomings, has made notable contributions to world conservation and will probably make more. In the first place, while it is possible that some kind of world cooperation for the wise management of resources would in any case have grown up in the League of Nations and the United Nations, the fact is that the first proposal for a world conservation movement came from Theodore Roosevelt, stimulated by Gifford Pinchot, in 1909. These men may fairly be given substantial credit for the fact that when the time began to be ripe the idea was already widely known and ready to take practical form in international enterprises.

In the meantime the United States has contributed its share to the techniques of conservation. It has helped in the development of the modern science of forestry. It has contributed a large part of what is known about soil conservation, including improvements in the ancient art of terracing. More important, perhaps, has been the demonstration, under modern conditions of trade and markets, that many kinds of conservation will pay for themselves in a short enough time to rank as commercially profitable.

A country, then, does not have to be rich before it can indulge in the luxury of conserving its resources. It may be poor, and yet, if it can get some technical advice and borrow some capital to invest in conservation, the benefits will generally pay back the capital, and sometimes at a high rate of profit. The amount of outright grants required, therefore, does not seem to be more than the richer nations can supply. At the present time the United States is able to carry a good share of the burden, and other Western nations have recovered from World War II to the point where they also are able to help.

The United States can also contribute its two most notable recent inventions in the technique of organization—the industrial management technique known as "human relations engineering" and the unified resource management technique of the TVA.

Human relations engineering is a method of eliminating conflict and creating harmony in large-scale industrial organization. Its essential feature is that the management convinces the wage earners of its respect for them and for their ideas of how best to do the work. When this relationship is successfully established it greatly increases production and the monetary rewards of both employer and workers. In the United States human relations engineering is reported to be operating with some success in companies employing possibly 10 per cent of our industrial workers. There is growing interest in the method among Western European industrialists. This technique is in its infancy, but it shows signs of being the infant Hercules that in time will overcome class conflicts in organized economic activity.

The TVA also is a potent force, as many foreigners have recognized more quickly than the majority of Americans outside the Tennessee Valley. A TVA type of organization is a hard thing to start, but once under way it may become a force not only for prosperity but also for peace between nations having interests in the same river basin. There is no more practical way for people to learn to get along together than to find themselves pressed by necessity to cooperate on some simple, easily understood enterprise, such as developing a river that they can use only in cooperation.

The world has many sore spots, sore with ill-feeling, ignorance, and poverty. New and practical ways of curing some of the principal troubles of mankind have been invented, and more are being invented. The United States is in a position to help cure some of these troubles, either working directly with another country or cooperating through international organizations, and fortunately most of the time it shows a disposition to do either or both as may seem most effective.

All those who are concerned about the future of the United States are obliged to give thought to the future of this country as a part of a more and more closely related world. The conservation movement, which even in 1909 clearly pointed toward world-wide cooperation, now takes on fresh meaning for the United States as a part of the world-wide movement seeking peaceful progress. The United States, as a leading free nation, of course has to contribute to world conservation for many reasons, first among which is its own peace and security.

Giving technical assistance, especially to Latin America, was an established American custom long before President Truman made it a leading national policy as the fourth point in a list of policies in his inaugural address in 1949. The United Nations also had the beginnings of technical assistance in many of its specialized agencies before 1949; Point 4 stimulated the UN to set up an enlarged program, in which the United States also plays a leading part. The assistance does not always go from the Western industrial nations to the ancient agricultural countries of Asia and Africa. It also takes the form of mutual aid among the less industrial countries, and some of it comes from them to the industrially developed West. The anti-high-blood-pressure drug reserpine, for example, has come to America from

India. If peace is maintained, the opening up of new resources, both of raw materials and of techniques, especially through the UN systems of technical exchange, may well transform the world to the advantage of the human race.

The people of the United States are well fitted to understand from their own experience many of the nationalist attitudes that now create awkward situations in various parts of the world. The desire of "underdeveloped" countries to have industries of their own and to depend less for their income on the export of raw materials may well strike a sympathetic chord among our people, for two hundred years ago this country too was underdeveloped. We depended on selling timber and tobacco to England, and our hopeful efforts to start our own iron manufacturing were frowned upon by our royal master across the Atlantic.

Accordingly, in our Point 4 program and in our cooperation with the UN agencies we can understand the desire of other countries to have better-balanced economic systems and to offer their citizens a wider variety of ways to make a living. We can also understand how desirable free institutions are and how hard they are to establish and keep in operation. We know that the world needs not only raw materials, energy sources, and technology; it needs still more the advantages of a free search for truth and of workable organization that will allow human beings to bring out and utilize their best qualities.

As Barrow Lyons well says in *Tomorrow's Birthright,* the solutions from here on are more in statesmanship than in technology. The world has some technology, and more is on the way. There have also been some good examples of statesmanship. In our efforts to develop a strong and prosperous free world the kind of statesmanship that seems most likely to succeed will include the vision of wise use of the world's resources for the good of man, now and in the future.

The world's resources are only imperfectly known, but enough has been discovered about them to serve for some intelligent planning of world conservation policies.

The total land area of the world is 36,000 million acres, but no more than 10 per cent of that is under cultivation. The rest includes a great amount of land that is unfit for human use within our present technical means. Vast land areas are deeply covered with ice; others are steep mountains or desolate tundra. More than a quarter of all the land area is desert, some of it caused by human abuse of the land.

Around the edges of the deserts are grasslands that hold the dry soil in place. Men with cattle can live along these frontiers if the cattle do not become too numerous. But if they raise too many cattle, or if they plow up the grass, the desert will march in. The world has many old scars where the deserts have long since taken over, and there may be new deserts developing, on the borders of the Sudan, for instance, and in the new-plowed lands of the Soviet Union.

The UN experts say that the present cultivated area of the world might possibly be increased about a third by clearing, draining, or irrigating. Much of that extension would amount to the abandonment of other important values, including forests and outdoor recreation, in the desperate search for food. In the meantime soil erosion is doing serious harm to cultivated lands not only in the United States but also in Mexico, South America, Africa, China, and Russia. If you fly along the China coast or the east coast of Africa you will see the yellow stain of mud where the rivers come out into the sea—a sign of too many people and too many cattle, grinding the land to death under their feet.

The UN Food and Agriculture Organization is making a world-wide survey of farm, forest, and fishery resources to serve as a basis for conservation and land-use planning. Although the information now on hand is sketchy, it seems that there are considerable areas where production could be quickly increased by means that the inhabitants are capable of learning to use.

Fisheries are believed to supply about 1 per cent of the total food eaten by man, and about 10 per cent of his animal protein. The FAO estimates that world fish production could probably be doubled without hurting the resource base and points out that other sea products, such as plankton and seaweed, can be made into food for man and animals. Experiments are under way with fresh-water algae— one-celled fast-growing plants that produce edible protein when fed with water, sunlight, and carbon dioxide.

An international Conference on the Conservation of the Living Resources of the Sea was held in April, 1955, at the invitation of the UN General Assembly. The Assembly noted that the international law of offshore waters and of the high seas was being studied by its International Law Commission. The conservation of fish, fur seals, whales, and other kinds of sea life calls for enforceable controls that are closely related to other forms of international sea law. Representatives of forty-five nations attended the conference, which adopted a report explaining the technical requirements for successful regulation of open-sea fisheries. It is notable that these nations, from both sides of the Iron Curtain, recognized the value of conservation and the fact that the price of a successful program is cooperation and discipline, based on scientific knowledge.

The mineral resources of the world are even less well known than the resources of farmland, forest, and sea. Large tracts of land are buried in almost impenetrable jungle, where the mineral deposits are likely to be safe from human exploitation for some time to come. Admiral Byrd believed that the Antarctic Continent has mineral wealth in great quantities hidden under the icecap. But even in civilized and fully accessible countries little is known of mineral deposits that show no signs on the surface. New methods of detecting ore bodies far below the surface will probably add considerably to the known resources of even the most highly developed countries.

In 1955 the UN began a survey of the world's known iron ore deposits. This survey proposes uniform definitions of reserves (suitable for use under present conditions), potential ores (usable at higher prices), and resources, the sum of the reserves and the potential ores. The experts estimated in a preliminary way that the world's known reserves of iron ore are about 85,000 million tons. Not only are there additional masses of potential ore that can be used if the better ore should be depleted, but also there are probably good ores still hidden by the jungles.

Other plentiful metals are aluminum, magnesium, titanium, and boron, all comparatively new in technical use because they were hard to smelt until the coming of plentiful electric power. Among materials that seem to be scarce in the world are copper, lead, zinc, nickel, cobalt, columbium, tantalum, tungsten, molybdenum, and vanadium. If these should become seriously depleted in the future, some of our high technology may have to be scaled down. But there is certainly time for much progress in conservation to take place before the world supply of any important metal will be desperately short.

At the present time most of the people of the world are ill-fed, and more than half the human race cannot read or write. Hundreds of millions of people have one or more of the poverty-making diseases, such as tuberculosis or malaria —slow killers that leave the victim unable to work but still alive and demanding food. All in all, throughout the world the human resources are in a bad state of repair.

Human beings regarded as "resources" are of course both positive and negative. On the plus side they produce food and on the minus side they and their children eat it up. If there are too many people on the land, considering its fertility and the available farming techniques, the surplus people are a minus resource. On the other hand, in a "new" country in the process of rapid development of previously unused resources there may not be enough workers to farm all the land and run all the industries and services that make up a civilized community. In that case all able-bodied new arrivals are plus resources, and their arrival causes property values to go up. They can produce more than they consume, because the land and other resources are there waiting to be put to use.

For several centuries Western Europeans were colonizing and settling other lands, some of them almost empty, such as the Americas, Australia, New Zealand, and parts of Africa. People were especially valuable in these new settlements, where a shortage of labor and plenty of raw materials set the stage for economic and political development. To save labor and to be lavish with raw materials seemed the sensible way of opening up a rich country. Those pioneering days are past, not only in the United States but almost everywhere. Most of the new frontiers are not in empty lands but in new science and invention, and in a new realization of human interdependence. Under these new conditions any unskillful worker is likely to have a poor market for his services. The conservation of human resources, therefore, is more and more taking the form of seeking to make every person as healthy, skillful, and well organized as possible, not only for his own sake but to meet the needs of the community.

Where the people are badly crowded and desperately poor, they are also liable to be the victims of oppressive landlords. The "underdeveloped" country more often than not suffers from the extravagance of the landed gentry, who feel no duty to conserve land and people. They often demand half or more of the farmer's crops as rent and waste it on luxuries instead of using a good share of it to improve the land

and build up the people. In a well-governed country, on the other hand, a substantial part of the national income is invested in useful enterprises; and as the economic system grows more mature the people turn their attention to the conservation of their basic resources.

In the less-developed parts of the world the process of introducing conservation practices will be somewhat different from the struggle that has gone on in the United States. Here, by 1900, our resources were in full process of development. We had a widespread educational system; we had many capitalists starting new enterprises; and we had a government strong enough to take control of its own vast landholdings and to collect taxes for any program approved by the people. There was money for conservation as soon as the people wanted it, and there was some knowledge of how to go about it. In an underdeveloped country it is not so easy to find the money for any new program of this kind or to get the people to support it.

In a poor and crowded country the people could no doubt grow much bigger crops and perhaps have enough to eat if only they had a good education in an agricultural college, as so many of our highly productive farmers have in the United States. But who is going to provide the agricultural colleges, and the fertilizer, the insecticides, the farm machinery, the hybrid seed, and all the other expensive materials and equipment for a rich farm? Who is going to teach the peasant to read and supply him with reading matter from which he can learn what he needs to know? Who will cure him of his malaria so that he may feel energetic enough to learn to read? There are answers to these questions, but they cannot all be supplied from as far away as United Nations, New York. Most of the answers have to come from inside the country.

The key to progress in any underdeveloped country is the governing minority—the politicians, the landlords, the traders, and the moneylenders. If they are wasters, the resources of the country will be wasted. But if they are builders they can get technical advice and some financial help from abroad, as the people of the United States did from England and Holland and other countries in the early part of the nineteenth century. In any country, if those who have the wealth and the power want to build they can start building; and if they have foresight and understanding they can begin to provide for the conservation of their resources.

In India, for instance, the ruling political party has constructive ideas for raising the living standards of the people. The tradition of landlordism and of unbridled luxury for the few is under heavy fire. A voluntary land-reform movement is under way that has persuaded many big landowners to donate land for small farms. The government is promoting reclamation projects to open more land, and is also promoting education, modern agriculture, and industry. When India became independent it was fortunate in finding leadership that could direct the development of the country toward a more effective use of its resources and a more prosperous way of life. India competes with Communist China, where strenuous building is going on also, to show the peoples of Asia which type of political system gives what the Asians will regard as the best results.

There have been some elements of a soil conservation policy in China since 2700 B.C., but in many parts of the country even this policy was not enforced. The trees were cut off the mountains, the land washed down, and the valleys were filled with sand and gravel. Most of the people were crowded into the great alluvial plains of the main river valleys. There, on some of the richest soil in the world, live some of the poorest people. They are poor because there are too many of them, and they cannot spread out into the lost lands that their ancestors devastated centuries ago.

The waste of resources is usually a disease of civilization. Primitive tribes do not often have the tools or the numbers to do much harm to the forest or the prairie where they live. But if they come under the influence of civilization, as many African tribes have begun to do in the past century, their native diseases are reduced and their numbers increase. They have to pay taxes to support civilized services, and so they put new demands on their resources. They begin to cut down the forests, plow the grasslands, increase their flocks and herds, and, unless their government is strong and intelligent, fail in conservation. Then their land washes or blows away and is lost.

A heroic effort to restore wasted land has been made in Israel, under the expert advice of Walter Lowdermilk. He writes in a letter, for example: "I have taken a keen interest in their problems of farming stony steep slopes, especially to tobaccos, fruits, and grapes. It is a continuation of my attempt to get 'Hill culture' studied and demonstrated by our Soil Conservation Service, which failed because Directors of our State Experiment Stations were not interested."

The UN has a strong part to play in the countries that are trying to escape from grinding poverty. The UN grassroots campaigns to wipe out malaria, yaws, or tuberculosis, to teach people to read, and to teach the first elements of an improved agriculture are all high-powered stimulants to progress. The grassroots programs often yield extremely large returns on the money invested, thanks to recent products of modern science, such as cheap antibiotics, DDT, and methods of producing high-yield hybrid seed. As an example, at an average cost of about 15 cents per child for penicillin, some 3 million children had been cured of yaws by the year 1955. Yaws is a deforming and crippling disease that if allowed to go on does not usually kill the child but leaves him helpless, a sorrowful and lifelong burden on his family and the nation. To avoid such a burden 15 cents and some administrative costs are a small price to pay. Again, for a small amount of DDT, a whole village can be freed of malaria, with a marked increase in the people's ability to work.

After the first, or grassroots, improvements, progress from then on is harder and the profits from investment are less spectacular. But if the people who have power are intelligent, energetic, and willing to accept the conditions necessary to progress, their country can come up from a condition of extreme poverty to one of visible improvement and hope of a better future. A country that can meet these conditions can find many sources of help, such as the UN Technical Assistance Program, the United States Point 4, the Colombo Plan set up by the British Commonwealth nations of Asia, or the agencies of the Association of American States.

In the long run (if we escape World War III and there is a long run) the foundations of world peace can be laid if there is an effective alliance of men and women of all races, religions, and cultures in the war against poverty, disease, and ignorance. At present we know hardly anything of the physical resources of the planet, or of the human resources that can be called into play by international cooperation, but we have the beginnings of knowledge and of world-wide organization and the ideal of conservation and of wise use of resources is accepted in one form or another by all nations. As Franklin Roosevelt wrote the day before he died: "The only limit to our realization of tomorrow will be our doubts of today."

The world needs conservation as it needs technical progress and free institutions. For the resources of the world, as far as they have been discovered and are now available for use, seem to be wasting away at an alarming rate, although some conservation work is already being done in some countries. Fortunately the UN technical agencies, though hampered by limited funds, are beginning to be well organized, and they are committed unreservedly to the doctrine of a wise use of world resources, now and in the future.

The world has a long way to go before its economic life

can be said to be on a sound basis. But there is some margin of undiscovered raw materials and undiscovered technology; no universal crisis of material resource scarcities is immediately upon us. Less than half a century after Pinchot and Roosevelt set out to arouse the world to the need for conservation the world is aroused, organized, and already working hard on the long task of putting its affairs in order.

Chapter 19

FIFTY YEARS OF CONSERVATION

Although the word "conservation" was first widely used in its present meaning in 1907, and the idea began only in that year to take hold of the imagination of the American people, the principles of conservation have a long ancestry both in this country and abroad. Here were brought together lines of historic development derived in part from the feudal system of medieval Europe and in part from the democratic political system that grew up with expanding industry and trade in Europe and North America.

The idea of conserving resources, including even the lowliest of the workers, was an integral part of the feudal order of society in the Middle Ages. The best of the lords and landed gentry took care of their estates as well as they knew how, so as to hand them down in sound condition to their heirs. In protecting their own family interests they also defended their own farmers and woodmen from enemy attack, and incidentally gave them the economic security of a humble but permanent place in the system. The prime purpose of feudalism was not the greatest good of the greatest number, but the welfare of the lord and his family. And yet it did offer a kind of security in the present and it did impose a duty of thinking prudently about the future. In a sense, conservation is one expression of the fact that in modern times the privileges and duties of the feudal lord have been transferred with little change to the sovereign people.

After the Middle Ages the feudal system was displaced by the growth of the mercantile system and of industry. The industrialist brought in new techniques for combining raw materials, capital, and labor to produce goods for sale. But in the drive for progress much of the traditional protection of resources, including people, vanished. Industry and trade ravaged the forests and the land where they were the controlling influence. Industry reduced thousands of workers to factory hands living in slums, with no one to care what happened to them.

The purpose of industry and trade was not to benefit the wage earners but to provide the greatest good to the owners of the business. The early economists did suggest that whatever was good for the owners was good for everyone, but in practice this theory did not lead to the protection of either material or human resources.

On the other hand, the struggle of the businessmen to free themselves from feudal controls was an important element in the growth of political freedom and democracy, of which the United States has become one of the principal heirs. In their turn the philosophers of democracy emphasized the ideal of the greatest good for the greatest number, a doctrine that was destined to become one of the foundation stones of modern conservation.

The conservation movement started as a revolt against the destructive practices of industry and trade, both in the United States and in Western Europe. In the United States the revolt was led by men whose inheritance and temperament were derived from the most constructive elements of the European landed gentry. Their tradition, coming down in part by way of Washington and Jefferson, imposed the duty of conserving both material resources and human beings, not merely for the benefit of the upper classes but for the general welfare of all the people, and not only for today but for the long future.

The conflicts over conservation, down to the present time, are generally aroused by the resistance of segments of industry and trade, where real or fancied interests are opposed to the prudent use of resources. But the conservation movement has been able to resist such opposition largely because it has kept the areas of conflict as limited as possible. Gifford Pinchot, when he was studying in Europe in 1890, found the key that would open the way to widespread cooperation from industry and trade, in the admonition of his teachers that he must show the lumbermen that good forestry would pay. Thus at the very beginning modern conservation escaped from what had threatened to be a frustrating doctrine, that forests and mines must not be used but locked up for the use of future generations.

Instead of locking up resources, the positive effect of the new doctrine in opening up larger opportunities is plain to see. It can be seen in the permanent yield of well-managed forests, in heavier crops on the farms, and perhaps best of all in the rise of general prosperity in the Tennessee Valley where conservation has been adopted in the most comprehensive form.

Although Pinchot himself began with a specialized concern for the forests, which were being visibly depleted in the latter part of the nineteenth century, he soon recognized the kinship of all the material resources that might need prudent management—including land, water, and minerals. And he was always clear that the prudent management of these resources as a national policy must be for the benefit of all the people, and not only of the few who would monopolize the benefits for themselves. When he ran into opposition he found monopolies standing in the way of conservation. During his fight with Ballinger, Pinchot knew he was fighting to prevent an undue concentration of power.

He won that fight, but it has to be fought again in every generation.

As the conservation movement approached its fiftieth anniversary, it was still engaged in controversy, but it had branched out in many directions, and many of its gains were strongly entrenched and generally regarded as permanent.

Forestry had been adopted as a policy by most of the big lumber operators, and the danger of a catastrophic loss of American timber resources appeared to have been warded off for the time being. Soil conservation was well developed and protected by powerful organizations of farmers against political raids. Rural electrification had reached more than nine out of every ten American farms and was defended by a strong organization of cooperative distributing agencies. Wildlife protection and provision for outdoor recreation also were highly developed despite continuing attacks from land grabbers inside and outside the government.

Human resources had come to occupy a growing share of the conservation movement. Social security protection under national auspices was established in the middle thirties. Public health services expanded to correspond with growing technical knowledge of disease prevention. Education was extended to a larger and larger share of the population, putting violent strains on the school and college system. There were disputes about details, but these lines of progress and others of the same general kind were well established and accepted in principle by both the major political parties.

By 1953, when a new Administration came into office, most of the conservation policies that had originated under both Republican and Democratic auspices since the beginning of the century were assured of continuance with little modification. There were differences in Congress about how much money could be profitably spent on one program or another and there could be bureaucratic conflicts over who should control a particular program, such as that which flared up in 1953 over soil conservation. The perennial efforts of private and public agencies to invade the public domain continued, of course, with occasional help from the agencies responsible for its protection.

But on one front there was a particularly violent outburst of fighting. The private electric utilities saw a chance to go on the warpath, with the aid of a new Secretary of the Interior, a Chairman of the Atomic Energy Commission, and a Director of the Budget, all favorable to their side.

So there soon developed an attempt to kill off the TVA by throttling its appropriations for expanding capacity, and most dangerous of all by the Dixon-Yates proposal to inject private high-cost power into the TVA power system. Partly by luck and carelessness, this plan fell through, leaving the TVA stronger than ever. Since the TVA is the most conspicuous example to the free world of what the Americans mean by conservation, this outcome may be regarded as a notable piece of good fortune for the American position in the world, even though it did not result from a definite action by the electorate.

Almost as crucial was the conflict over the high dam proposed for Hells Canyon in Idaho. The new Secretary of the Interior refused to continue his predecessor's fight for the dam against the Idaho Power Co. When the friends of the dam tried to get action in Congress the utility lobby went into action, and with help from the Administration enough votes were mustered to defeat the high dam. In the Idaho delegation, Senator Welker took a conspicuous part on the side of the power company and Representative Gracie Pfost led the fight in the House for the dam. Both were due to face the voters in November, 1956.

On another front the Interior Department, controlling the sale of most of the federally owned power, set out to strangle some of the rural electric cooperatives by restricting their preference right to buy cheap public power, which had been established under Theodore Roosevelt in 1906 for municipal systems and extended to the cooperatives as soon as they were created. The department also proclaimed a so-called "partnership principle," designed to give control of public power to private companies. The partnership was one in which the government would supply the waterpower site and usually most of the capital, but would leave to the private companies the control of the sale of power, thus excluding the cooperatives and municipal systems from their preference rights. So here it was again as in Ballinger's time—a Secretary of the Interior from the far Northwest sitting in Washington and planning to transfer the power resources of the public domain to private interests regarded by many citizens as hostile.

With the coming of the 1956 election the battle lines were drawn where the voters could take a hand, with power as the central issue. The principal battlefront was in Oregon, where Senator Wayne Morse, previously elected as a Republican, was now running for reelection as a Democrat. Senator Morse was already known as one of the leading champions of conservation in general and of public power in particular. The Secretary of the Interior, who had previously been Governor of Oregon, was drafted to enter the lists as champion of his own power policies. This contest immediately took on national importance second only to the presidential race. Nearly half the fund set aside for helping Republicans get elected to the Senate was assigned to Secretary McKay; and there was a nation-wide drive by Elmer Davis and other liberal leaders to collect contributions for Senator Morse. The issues were well aired, and in the end the people, while voting for Eisenhower for President, emphatically chose Morse as Senator. To underline the verdict, they also transferred two Republican House seats in Oregon and the governorship to the Democrats.

Similarly, in the neighboring state of Washington, Senator Magnuson, who had voted for the high Hells Canyon dam, was reelected with ease. In Idaho, Senator Welker was defeated by a young newcomer, Frank Church, who ran on the Hells Canyon issue, and Gracie Pfost was triumphantly reelected. In Montana there were no senatorial races, but there was a Republican congressman, and he was unseated.

Thus in the Northwest, where the public power aspect of conservation was the main issue, the people gave a plain mandate to which both parties were bound to pay attention. The people of that area made it clear that when conservation is attacked by their representatives in Washington they will change their representatives.

The battle in the Northwest was a good test to finish off the first fifty years; there will be more such tests in the next fifty. For example, there are already signs of renewed efforts to dismember the national forests and the federal grazing lands and turn them over to private operators or to the states, where they can be more easily raided. And, while the need of the public for recreation areas grows, powerful attacks against these areas are being mounted, not only by the armed services but also by developers who want to drain swamps, build dams and causeways, and open the country to settlement. There will be plenty of hard fighting for conservationists to do at home while our foreign services are endeavoring to use conservation as an instrument of peace abroad.

Meanwhile, the victory for conservation in the election of 1956 was a fortunate circumstance for the American position in the world. Conservation is a vital part of what we have to offer to a distracted world that is in need of a better way of life and a better hope of peace. The path to peace is rough and obscure, but surely one of the possible paths lies in the direction of cooperation among the nations for some constructive purpose. The doctrine of conservation, developed in this country through fifty years of experience and struggle, offers a guide to forms of constructive cooperation that people of good will all over the world can accept. It has stood the test of time and storm. It seems to be good for the long pull, as the world struggles to adjust itself to the changes that are under way.

It was the Western world that started the three lines of constructive change that in modern times have been working together to transform human life—the scientific revolution, the anticolonial revolution, and the modern revolution against political and economic tyranny. The American people themselves began the modern anticolonial revolution nearly two hundred years ago, and they now view with strong sympathies the wave of that movement for independence sweeping along the borders of Asia and Africa and into the satellite empire of the Soviet Union. The American people have also had a role in the development of Western science and in the struggle for individual rights. The conservation movement in the United States and in the world is vitally related to all these revolutionary changes that must work themselves out before the world can have a secure peace.

Western civilization is much to blame for present-day world conditions, but it also has much to offer. It can play a successful part in meeting the new conditions only by enlisting the combined forces of science, freedom, and devotion to the welfare of all people, as our experience at its best has taught us how to do. The conflicts over conservation throughout its successful growth in the past fifty years have been parts of the necessary struggle to bring our civilization into its best array so that it may effectively offer the world prosperity and peace.

INDEX